Literacy for the New Millennium

I dedicate this series of books to all those who center their professional lives on fostering the development and practice of literacy.

LITERACY FOR THE NEW MILLENNIUM

Volume 4

Adult Literacy

Edited by Barbara J. Guzzetti

Praeger Perspectives

Westport, Connecticut
London

Library of Congress Cataloging-in-Publication Data

Literacy for the new millennium / edited by Barbara J. Guzzetti.
  v. cm.
  Includes bibliographical references and indexes.
  Contents: v. 1. Early literacy — v. 2 Childhood literacy — v. 3 Adolescent
literacy — v. 4 Adult literacy.
  ISBN-13: 978–0–275–98969–9 (set : alk. paper)
  ISBN-10: 0–275–98969–0 (set : alk. paper)
  ISBN-13: 978–0–275–98992–7 (v.1 : alk. paper)
  ISBN-10: 0–275–98992–5 (v.1 : alk. paper)
  [etc.]
  1. Literacy. 2. Language arts. I. Guzzetti, Barbara J.
  LC149.L4987   2007
  302.2'244—dc22   2007018116

British Library Cataloguing in Publication Data is available.

Library of Congress Catalog Card Number: 2007018116
ISBN-13: 978–0–275–98969–9 (set)   ISBN-10: 0–275–98969–0
ISBN-13: 978–0–275–98992–7 (vol. 1)   ISBN-10: 0–275–98992–5
ISBN-13: 978–0–275–98993–4 (vol. 2)   ISBN-10: 0–275–98993–3
ISBN-13: 978–0–275–98994–1 (vol. 3)   ISBN-10: 0–275–98994–1
ISBN-13: 978–0–275–98995–8 (vol. 4)   ISBN-10: 0–275–98995–X

First published in 2007

Praeger Publishers, 88 Post Road West, Westport, CT 06881
An imprint of Greenwood Publishing Group, Inc.
www.praeger.com

Printed in the United States of America

The paper used in this book complies with the
Permanent Paper Standard issued by the National
Information Standards Organization (Z39.48–1984).

10 9 8 7 6 5 4 3 2 1

CONTENTS

PART III: ADULT LITERACY BEYOND THE CLASSROOM

SET PREFACE

This set of four volumes—*Literacy for the New Millennium: Early Literacy; Literacy for the New Millennium: Childhood Literacy; Literacy for the New Millennium: Adolescent Literacy;* and *Literacy for the New Millennium: Adult Literacy* presents a current and comprehensive overview of literacy assessment, instruction, practice, and issues across the life span. Each volume presents contemporary issues and trends, as well as classic topics associated with the ages and stages of literacy development and practice represented in that text. The chapters in each volume provide the reader with insights into policies and issues that influence literacy development and practice. Together, these volumes represent an informative and timely discussion of the broad field of literacy.

The definition of literacy on which each of these volumes is grounded is a current and expanded one. Literacy is defined in this set in a broad way by encompassing both traditional notions of literacy, such as reading, writing, listening, and speaking, as well as the consumption and production of nonprint texts, such as media and computer texts. Chapters on technology and popular culture in particular reflect this expanded definition of literacy to literacies that represents current trends in the field. This emphasis sets this set apart from other more traditional texts on literacy.

The authors who contributed to this set represent a combination of well-known researchers and educators in literacy, as well as those relatively new to the profession of literacy education and scholarship. Contributors to the set represent university professors, senior scientists at research institutions, practitioners, or consultants in the field, teacher educators, and researchers in literacy. Although the authors are experts in the field of literacy, they have written their chapters to be reader friendly, by defining and explaining any professional jargon and by writing in an unpretentious and comprehensible style.

Each of the four volumes shaped by these authors has common features. Each of the texts is divided into three parts with the first part devoted to recent trends and issues affecting the field of literacy for that age range. The second part addresses issues in assessment and instruction. The final part presents issues beyond the classroom that affect literacy development and practice at that level. Each of the texts concludes with a chapter on literacy resources appropriate for the age group that the volume addresses. These include resources and materials from professional organizations, and a brief bibliography for further reading.

Each of the volumes has common topics, as well as a common structure. All the volumes address issues of federal legislation, funding, and policies that affect literacy assessment instruction and practice. Each volume addresses assessment issues in literacy for each age range represented in that text. As a result of the growing importance of technology for instruction, recreation, information acquisition, communication, and participation in a global economy, each book addresses some aspect of literacy in the digital age. Because of the importance of motivating students in literacy and bridging the gap between students' in-school literacy instruction and their out-of-school literacy practices, each text that addresses literacy for school-age children discusses the influence and incorporation of youth and popular culture in literacy instruction.

In short, these volumes are crafted to address the salient issues, polices, practices, and procedures in literacy that affect literacy development and practice. These texts provide a succinct yet inclusive overview of the field of literacy in a way that is easily accessible to readers with little or no prior knowledge of the field. Preservice teachers, educators, teacher trainers, librarians, policy makers, researchers, and the public will find a useful resource and reference guide in this set.

In conclusion, I would like to acknowledge the many people who have contributed to the creation of this set. First, I recognize the outstanding contributions of the contributors. Their writings not only reflect the most informative current trends and classic topics in the field but also present their subjects in ways that take bold stances. In doing so, they provide exciting future directions for the field.

Second, I acknowledge the contributions to the production of this set by staff at Arizona State University in the College of Education. My appreciation goes to Don Hutchins, director of computer support, for his organizational skills and assistance in the electronic production of this set. In addition, I extend my appreciation to my research assistant, Thomas Leyba, for his help in organizing the clerical aspects of the project.

Finally, I would like to thank the staff and editors at Praeger Publishers, who have provided guidance and support throughout the process of producing this set. In particular, I would like to thank Marie Ellen Larcada, who has since left the project but shared the conception of the set with me and supported me through the initial stages of production. My appreciation also goes to Elizabeth Potenza, who has guided this set into its final production, and without whose support this set would not have been possible. My kudos extend to you all.

Barbara J. Guzzetti

PREFACE

LITERACY FOR THE NEW MILLENNIUM: ADULT LITERACY

Adult literacy is an adult's ability to read, write, listen, and speak to accomplish daily activities in the community, in the family, and on the job. The Adult Performance Level Program popularized the idea of functional literacy, which the Adult Performance Level Program defined as reading and writing at a minimal level in day-to-day living. These functional literacies include everyday literacy practices, such as reading a newspaper or writing a check. This definition of adult literacy is based on economic growth.

A social view of adult literacy extends this definition by emphasizing the critical thinking and reading, writing, speaking, and listening skills needed to participate in a democratic society. This view of literacy stresses social power, action, and change. This perspective sees literacy as not merely an autonomous set of skills and practices predetermined by others. Rather, this view is one of literacy as embedded in culture, and socially and politically constructed.

This book is based on a blend of these two views of adult literacy. Chapters in this text address both the cognitive and social perspectives on and aspects of adult literacy. The text encompasses traditional topics of adult literacy, such as assessment and adult education programs, while also examining topics related to literacy in the new millennium, such as the incorporation of technology, the changing demands of workplace literacy, and family literacy.

The text is divided into three parts. Each part consists of two to five chapters that provide a broad overview of issues, trends, programs, assessment, and instruction related to adult literacy in everyday life. Together, these chapters address adult literacy in family and workplace settings across the stages of adulthood.

Part I, "Issues and Trends in Adult Literacy," provides an overview of recent topics and concerns in the field, beginning with a chapter by Laurie Elish-Piper in which she examines changing definitions of and historical influences on adult literacy. Elish-Piper then discusses the current expectations for adult literacy, including prose literacy, document literacy, quantitative literacy, and health literacy, while presenting characteristics of adult learners and their difficulties with reading. The chapter concludes with a brief overview of literacy instruction for adults.

In the second chapter, Alisa Belzer and Ralf St. Clair explore the ways in which powerful political, social, and economic factors influence adult literacy education. They have coined a term—"anthropolicy"—that allows them to argue for the importance of analyzing the ways in which polices are influenced by these forces and, in doing so, provide the perspectives of practitioners. Their interviews with two teachers and a program administrator working in adult literacy illustrate the ways in which the field has changed. These narratives highlight three policy themes that have had a critical effect on practice, including literacy as a workforce development strategy, assessment, accountability and standards, and increased and more specialized funding.

Part II, "Adult Literacy Instruction and Assessment," addresses topics related to the nature of adult learning and development and appropriate instructional methods and programs for adult literacy learners. This part begins with a chapter by M. Cecil Smith, who describes teaching and learning in adult literacy education. Smith notes that the system of adult education is different from that of pre-kindergarten through 12th-grade education, and therefore, the preparation and qualifications of adult literacy teachers are distinct from those of teachers in elementary and secondary schools. The author provides information about the preparation of adult basic education teachers and the roles and responsibilities of volunteer tutors and discusses instruction in reading, writing, and mathematics, particularly through computer-assisted instruction. Smith also describes the benefits that adults derive from their participation in basic literacy skills programs.

Chapter 4 complements the preceding chapter by describing the structure of adult literacy programs and how they operate. Hal Beder discusses adult literacy programs as well as the inherent problems in their structure. According to Beder, these programs are generally grant funded and typically sponsored by organizations that primarily serve children and youths with high drop-out rates and part-time teachers who make them structurally marginal in comparison to K–12 schools and institutions of higher education.

In the third chapter of part II, John Strucker offers a picture of the adult basic education and English-as-a-second-language population and describes the economic and social importance of acquiring English skills. He identifies problems associated with wide ranges of funding levels, funding sources and providers, and personnel. He summarizes best practices in adult literacy education and discusses challenges to the system in providing those practices. He concludes with a discussion of important reforms for the future.

In the final chapter of this section, chapter, Irwin Kirsh, Marylou Lennon, and Claudia Tamassia argue that adult education programs have been recognized as increasingly important in a changing United States where rewards for education and skills are increasing. This recognition led to the development of the Adult Education Program Survey, which gathered information about the skills and characteristics of participants in federally funded adult education programs. The authors present data that together with economic and social trends call into question the resources allocated to adult learners that are needed to meet current and future challenges.

Part II, "Adult Literacy beyond the Classroom," addresses adults' literacy needs and practices in settings outside adult education programs and examines the needs and practices of adults as they enter their senior years. This part begins with a chapter on family literacy by Victoria Purcell-Gates, who explores the notion of family literacy by defining it and relating it to children's success in school. She provides a background on the interest in family literacy and describes the ways in which policy makers have appropriated the term and created a call for family literacy programs. Purcell-Gates describes family literacy programs and provides evidence of the effectiveness of these programs. She concludes her chapter by discussing implications from research for school and parents and offering suggestions for teachers and parents for literacy activities to encourage children in becoming independent readers and writers.

In the next chapter, Larry Mikulecky defines workplace literacy and describes how workplace literacy programs emerged due to concerns about literacy skills in the military. Mikulecky describes the influence of immigration, the need for new certification programs in industry, and the necessity of retraining workers to meet the demands of a changing digital world. He provides examples of workplace literacy and concludes with a discussion of issues associated with the field and the future of workplace literacy.

In the next chapter, Anne DiPardo argues that while older adults' literacy practices are shaped by society's conceptions of aging, these practices can also serve to challenge and revise popular notions of later life. DiPardo makes the case that an increasingly powerful contingent of older adults is engaging in a range of literacy activities for multiple purposes. These include both traditional pursuits, such as life reviews and memoir writing, and innovative programs that foster intergenerational connections and social activism. DiPardo concludes by making the point that changing technologies are also facilitating new literacy practices for older adults as they join their younger counterparts in using new forms of texts and textual practices to sustain relationships and influence the world.

In the following chapter, David J. Rosen writes about how technology can be integrated into adult literacy classes and computer labs and how technology can supplement distance learning at home. Rosen writes about computer-assisted instruction but also makes a case for using technology as tools and for project-based approaches to learning that can take advantage of technology. He concludes the chapter by describing new uses of technology, such as podcasts, wikis, and mobile leaning, in adult literacy education and reminds readers of the usefulness of developing a state plan for incorporating technology into adult literacy education.

The book concludes with a chapter by Jackie Taylor in which she outlines the availability of adult literacy resources. In doing so, Taylor describes instructional resources, program resources, and advocacy tools for leveraging resources. She includes resources for locating research and professional advice for the lay public, as well as those involved in adult literacy education and research.

Part One

ISSUES AND TRENDS IN ADULT LITERACY

Chapter One

DEFINING ADULT LITERACY

Laurie Elish-Piper

Some adults struggle with reading, writing, and mathematics in their daily lives. These struggles may limit their employment opportunities and community involvement and negatively affect their health. For example, if adults do not read and write well enough to obtain either a high school diploma or a GED, they may be relegated to low-wage jobs that do not offer long-term security, health insurance, or other benefits. There are four main reasons that some adults do not learn to read well (Chisman, 2002). First, some of these adults may have been the products of ineffective schools in inner-city and rural areas where quality education was not available. Second, some of these adults entered school behind their peers and never caught up, which led them to drop out of school. Third, some adults speak a native language other than English and have limited English literacy skills. Finally, some adults may have learning disabilities, chronic illnesses, and other conditions that impede their literacy development.

According to the National Assessment of Adult Literacy (NAAL), 44 percent of adults in the United States have limited abilities to use literacy to perform tasks in their daily lives (National Center for Education Statistics, 2006). Since so many adults in the United States have limited literacy skills, it is important to understand the many dimensions and components of adult literacy.

WHAT IS ADULT LITERACY?

Adult literacy is a broad concept that encompasses many components; therefore, its definition is complex and multifaceted. A traditional definition of adult literacy focuses on a functional set of specific reading and writing skills that adults need to acquire to function in the world. Typically, these skills are emphasized through school-type activities such as reading a text and answering comprehension questions or completing workbook exercises on grammar. This traditional definition persists in the media and in some programs serving adult literacy students. For example, radio commercials advertising adult literacy programs often use phrases such as "Improve your reading skills" or "Build your basic skills," which emphasize the functional aspects of adult literacy rather than contextual issues such as applying literacy in the workplace, in the home, or in the community.

The most common contemporary definition of adult literacy centers on an adult's ability to read and write in relation to daily activities at home, at work, and in the community. Other definitions of adult literacy broaden the notion of literacy to include technology skills and the ability to solve problems, view, and visually represent. Still other definitions take a more progressive stance and view adult literacy as a political and transformative process that occurs in social, cultural, and power contexts.

CHANGING DEFINITIONS OF ADULT LITERACY

Definitions of adult literacy have changed significantly over the past century (Newman & Beverstock, 1990). During the early 1900s, literacy was simply defined as the ability to sign one's name. In 1910 the U.S. Census Bureau categorized literacy as the ability to write in any language. In 1930 the U.S. Census Bureau made the ability to read in any language part of the definition of literacy. By 1940, the U.S. Census Bureau defined adult literacy in terms of the completion of at least five years of school and the ability to pass a written examination at the 4th-grade level. In 1958, the United Nations Educational, Scientific, and Cultural Organization defined adults as literate if they could read and write a simple statement about daily life. By the mid-1960s the standard level of performance for adult literacy had risen to the 8th-grade reading level. In 1978, the United Nations Educational, Scientific, and Cultural Organization defined literacy as the ability to use reading, writing, and mathematics in activities required for meaningful participation in an adult's group and community.

The 1991 National Literacy Act defined literacy as an adult's ability to read, write, and speak English; compute; and solve problems at the level needed to accomplish goals, function at work, and develop to one's potential. Building on this definition, the 1992 National Adult Literacy Survey (NALS) described literacy from a task-based perspective as a skill consisting of three components: prose literacy, or the ability to find and use information from connected texts such as newspapers, stories, and poems; document literacy, or the ability to understand and use information from charts, tables, graphs, and maps; and quantitative literacy, or the ability to use information in prose and document texts to complete mathematical operations (Kirsch, Jungeblut, Jenkins, & Kolstad, 1993). Each of these types of literacy is described in more detail in Table 1.1.

The Workforce Investment Act of 1998 defined adult literacy as "an individual's ability to read, write, speak in English, compute and solve problems at levels of proficiency necessary to function on the job, in the family of the individual and in society."

An analysis of definitions of adult literacy indicates that until the mid-1980s, definitions focused on functional literacy and the attainment of skills and competencies linked to specific daily tasks (Demetrion, 2005). A concern with this view of functional literacy is how to identify a set of literacy skills and competencies for all adults regardless of their goals, situations, and lives. In response to this concern, some adult literacy educators and researchers began to define literacy as the "possession of skills perceived as necessary by particular persons and groups to fulfill their own self-determined objectives as family and community members, citizens, consumers, job-holders, and members of social, religious, or other associations of their choosing" (Hunter & Harman, 1985, p. 7). This shift from a rigid set of literacy skills and competencies to a more complex view that incorporated individual goals, needs, and strengths put the emphasis on the individual adult learner and his or her social and cultural context.

What, then, constitutes adult literacy within this broader framework? Barton (1994) defines literacy in terms of literacy practices, literacy events, and domains. Literacy practices are the "general cultural ways of utilizing literacy" that arise out of adults' communities and daily lives (Barton, 1994, p. 5). Literacy events are the specific activities that incorporate literacy and

Table 1.1
Types of Literacy Assessed on the National Adult Literacy Survey (1992) and the National Assessment of Adult Literacy (2003)

Type of literacy	Description
Prose literacy	The ability and skills needed to search, comprehend, and use information from continuous texts such as newspapers, editorials, brochures, and instructional materials
Document literacy	The ability and skills needed to search, comprehend, and use information from noncontinuous texts such as job applications, maps, tables, and schedules
Quantitative literacy	The ability and skills needed to identify and perform computations using numbers from printed materials, such as balancing a checkbook, completing an order form, or figuring out interest on a loan

Source: National Center for Education Statistics (2005); Kirsch, Jungeblut, Jenkins, & Kolstad (1993).

are observable, such as reading a newspaper or writing a note. Domains are the contexts that adults function within, such as the family, the community, a house of worship, and the workplace. Looking at literacy through these three overlapping components makes it clear that adult literacy is a social and cultural practice that is defined and shaped by the contexts in which an adult lives, works, and interacts. This view of adult literacy, therefore, makes it difficult to identify a specific set of literacy skills and competencies that all adults must master due to the varied contexts in which adults live, work, and interact.

One attempt to merge these different definitions (i.e., functional literacy and literacy as social and cultural practice) is the 2003 NAAL definition. This definition states that adult literacy is "using printed and written information to function in society, to achieve one's goals, and to develop one's knowledge and potential" (National Center for Education Statistics, 2006, p. 2). The remainder of the 2003 NAAL definition describes adult literacy in terms of the specific skills needed to perform tasks (e.g., word recognition and making inferences). This is the most widely used definition in adult literacy programming at the present time.

EXPECTATIONS FOR ADULT LITERACY

The expectations for literacy in society and in the workplace have increased steadily over the past century. Presently, most jobs require a high school diploma or certificate of General Educational Development, and many jobs require even higher levels of literacy and schooling. Jobs that previously were available to adults with limited schooling and low levels of literacy (e.g., service jobs, construction work, and factory jobs) now often require a high school diploma or GED. The demands of the modern workplace have been a significant contributor to the need for increased literacy skills.

To match the demands of the workplace, greater emphasis has been placed on school completion over the past century. It is interesting to note that in the early 1900s, only 6 percent of students graduated from high school. By the 1940s, the number had risen to slightly more than 50 percent; presently almost 85 percent of students either graduate from high school or possess a GED. Clearly, the increasing demands for literacy have contributed to higher school completion rates, but a diploma does not fully ensure that an adult possesses the skills, strategies, and abilities to succeed in the workplace and in life. According to the NAAL, 52 percent of the adults tested who had graduated from high school still scored at the two lowest levels on prose literacy, 42 percent scored at the two lowest levels on document literacy, and 66 percent scored at the two lowest levels for quantitative literacy. This means that even high school graduates may struggle with reading and interpreting a newspaper article, reading and using information from a chart or graph, and completing a mathematical task embedded in print. As the demands for literacy evolve and increase, schools, workplaces, community agencies, and colleges and universities have tried to revise their programs and services to meet today's needs. This challenge, however, is not new.

HISTORICAL INFLUENCES ON ADULT LITERACY

The roots of adult literacy reach back several hundred years (Newman & Beverstock, 1990). After the Civil War, recently freed slaves flocked to schools to learn to read and write. These schools were supported by the American Missionary Association, the Society of Friends, and the African Methodist Episcopal Church (Foner, 1988).

In 1911, Cora Stewart, a school superintendent in Kentucky, started so-called moonlight schools for adults. Classes met in the evening after work, and instruction was provided by volunteers. Because materials for instruction of adults were not readily available, Stewart wrote special instructional materials that focused on basic language, history, civics, agriculture, rural life, and hygiene. Stewart contributed to the war effort by helping American men become literate enough to join the military. Her materials and book were given to over 50,000 U.S. soldiers during World War I. A lasting contribution made by Stewart was the establishment of a literacy commission that served as a model for other states.

During World War I, the U.S. Army found that thousands of soldiers could not read printed directions needed for their jobs. The army raised awareness of adult literacy problems and established functional literacy training programs to teach job-oriented literacy skills to military personnel. While the army has been involved in adult literacy education for many years, its work has not been extended to the civilian population. The Army Continuing Education System offers educational services to enlisted members and to their adult family members. The High School Completion Program is an off-duty program that leads to a high school diploma or GED. The U.S. Army also offers a basic skills program that provides soldiers with instruction to improve reading, writing, speaking, math, and science skills, for reenlistment or reclassification and for lifelong learning. The army also provides Internet courses for military members who are unable to attend traditional classroom programs. The army currently allows individuals without a high school diploma or GED to enroll in the Army Education Plus Program, which provides an all-expense paid opportunity to earn the GED. Once the GED is completed, the individual is able to complete basic training. To be eligible for the program, individuals must have been out of high school for at least six months, pass a physical examination, and complete the Armed Services Vocational Aptitude Battery (U.S. Army Education Division, 2006).

Another major contributor to adult literacy education was Frank Laubach. Laubach was an educator, sociologist, and minister who is best known for the worldwide initiative Each One Teach One. Laubach's approach to adult literacy was based on his belief that literate adults have the ability and responsibility to help other adults improve their literacy skills. His reading instruction program emphasized phonics, using keywords for vowel and consonant sounds. He developed literacy programs in more than 60 countries and produced literacy charts and primers in over 150 different languages. His approach led to the development of the *Laubach Way to Reading* series. In 1969, Laubach Literacy Action was organized in the United States and Canada, and in the 1990s, more than 80,000 volunteers and 100,000 learners were involved in Laubach Literacy Action programs (ProLiteracy, 2006b).

Ruth Colvin founded Literacy Volunteers of America in 1962 in Syracuse, New York, after she realized that thousands of adults in the Syracuse area could not read or write. She realized that traditional classroom methods would not work well with the adults she wanted to help; therefore, she developed community networks of volunteers to work as tutors. Since its inception, Literacy Volunteers of America has served more than 400,000 adults through 460 programs based in 40 states in the United States (ProLiteracy, 2006b).

In 2002, Laubach Literacy Action and Literacy Volunteers of America merged to form ProLiteracy Worldwide and ProLiteracy America. ProLiteracy Worldwide is now the largest nongovernmental literacy organization in the world. In 2004–2005, ProLiteracy had 1,200 programs in the United States that served 202,834 adults through the efforts of 113,802 volunteer tutors (ProLiteracy, 2006a).

Myles Horton was a community organizer and activist who believed that by working collaboratively, people could solve problems in their communities and lives. Horton opened the Highlander Folk School in Tennessee in 1932 to focus on teaching adults what they needed in order to become active members of the political community. Classes focused on election laws, the benefits of unionization, and human rights. Horton's program expanded through the use of volunteer teachers offering classes in community locations. It is estimated that Horton's program taught 100,000 African American adults to read and write enough to be able to vote (Newman & Beverstock, 1990).

Paulo Freire viewed adult literacy as the way to transform political, economic, and legal systems, which he saw as oppressive. Freire worked with Brazilian peasants to help them move out of a "culture of silence" to take on actives roles in their lives, communities, and institutions. He espoused a liberatory approach to literacy education in *Pedagogy of the Oppressed* (1970). This contrasted with the traditional model of education, which Freire described as the banking concept, wherein the teacher is the dispenser of knowledge and the learner is the passive recipient. Freire's work brought attention to the political nature of literacy and to how low-income adults often lived in a "culture of silence" because they did not have the literacy skills or opportunities to express their views and take action to improve their lives. In his role as an educator and a social activist, Freire sought to help workers secure living wages, decent working conditions, and opportunities to participate in government and community decisions.

While there were certainly other key contributors to the historical development of adult literacy, those mentioned above are among the most influential and best known for their specific contributions to the field. In addition, federal legislation and policy have contributed to the development and shaping of adult literacy in the United States. These influences will be examined in depth in chapter 2.

UNDERSTANDING THE DEFINITION OF ADULT LITERACY TODAY

Reviewing the various definitions of adult literacy and the contributions of pioneers in adult literacy makes it clear that the current conception of adult literacy is more complex and multifaceted than ever before. Specifically, looking at the development of adult literacy definitions over the past century makes it clear that to be deemed literate, adults are required to know much more now than they were in the past. For example, being able to sign one's name or write a simple sentence or completing five years of schooling was sufficient to identify oneself as literate in the past. Current definitions of adult literacy are broader and emphasize the application of reading and writing to work, family, and community demands; the importance of math literacy; the use of technology as a tool; and health literacy, which focuses on using literacy to understand and manage health conditions as well as implement preventative measures. Even within this broadened definition of adult literacy, functional uses of reading, writing, and other processes are still emphasized.

LEVELS AND TYPES OF ADULT LITERACY

In 2003, over two-and-a-half million adults were enrolled in adult basic education (1,056,927), adult secondary education (1,170,273), and English-as-a-second-language (453,063) programs in the United States (Institute of Education Sciences, 2005). That year, the NAAL was administered to over 19,000 adults in the United States. The NAAL included components in the following areas: demographic information for participants; prison literacy levels for adults incarcerated in state and federal prisons; state assessment of adult literacy, health literacy, fluency, and the adult literacy supplemental assessment, which measures letter and number recognition; and simple prose texts aimed at adults with the lowest levels of literacy (National Center for Education Statistics, 2005).

The 2003 NAALS categorized adult participants' literacy skills in four levels: below basic, basic, intermediate, and proficient. Adults with below-basic literacy are defined as having "no more than the most simple and concrete literacy skills." Adults at the basic level have the "skills necessary to perform simple and everyday literacy activities," while adults at the intermediate level have the "skills necessary to perform moderately challenging literacy activities." Adults who scored at the proficient level have the "skills necessary to perform more complex and challenging literacy activities" (National Center for Education Statistics, 2005, p. 3).

Adults were scored at the four levels (below basic, basic, intermediate, and proficient) in the areas of prose literacy, document literacy, quantitative literacy, and health literacy. The results are summarized in Table 1.2.

Overall, the results from the NAAL in 2003 were consistent with the findings of the National Adult Literacy Survey in 1992. The only notable change was an average increase in quantitative literacy scores of eight points from 1992 to 2003. Men and women scored similarly on the NAAL; the largest difference was in quantitative literacy, where males scored an average of seven points higher than females. Analysis of adults' performance by ethnicity indicated that white adults had the highest average scores in both quantitative and prose literacy, followed by Asians, African Americans, and Hispanics. In the area of document literacy, whites and Asians had the highest average scores, followed by African Americans and Hispanics. Adults who were 65 years of age and older had the lowest literacy levels.

Literacy can affect employment status, meaning that adults with low levels of literacy may find it difficult to secure and keep a job. Data from the NAAL indicate that 51 percent of the adults with below-basic prose literacy were not employed. Prose and document literacy levels were the highest among adults who were employed either on a part-time or a full-time basis. Quantitative literacy levels were the highest for adults employed full-time. These findings indicate that a strong correlation exists between literacy skills and employment status.

Table 1.2
Results of National Assessment of Adult Literacy (2003)

Type of literacy	Percentage of adults scoring at below-basic level	Percentage of adults scoring at basic level	Percentage of adults scoring at intermediate level	Percentage of adults scoring at proficient level
Prose	14%	29%	44%	13%
Document	12%	22%	53%	13%
Quantitative	22%	33%	33%	13%
Health	14%	22%	53%	12%

Source: National Center for Education Statistics (2005).

HEALTH LITERACY

Health literacy is defined as the ability to understand and use health-related printed information (National Center for Education Statistics, 2006). The NAAL measured health literacy by asking adults to search texts to obtain health information, to draw inferences from health-related documents, to identify and complete computations on numbers embedded in health-related documents, and to use information to make appropriate health decisions. The concern about health literacy addressed in Healthy People 2010, a U.S. Department of Health and Human Services program that is designed to improve the health literacy of adults. Health literacy is especially important for adults who have chronic health conditions or who care for other family members with such illnesses. When these conditions or illnesses are not addressed appropriately, more days of work and school are missed, which can negatively affect individuals. Fourteen percent of the adults who completed the NAAL scored at the below-basic level on adult literacy, indicating that they are unable to read and understand health-related information. Twenty-two percent of the adults scored at the basic level, meaning that they could identify, read, and use a limited amount of information about health matters. Fifty-two percent scored at the intermediate level, and 12 percent scored at the proficient level. In general, the average health literacy score for females was six points higher than for males. The age group that had the lowest overall health literacy levels was adults over the age of 65. A total of 29 percent of older adults scored at the below-basic level, and another 30 percent at the basic level. This finding is worrisome, as many older adults have health conditions that require close monitoring, medication, and other forms of treatment; however, this age group is the least likely to be able to read and use health-related information correctly.

UNDERSTANDING ADULT READING DIFFICULTIES

While the results of the NAAL indicated that many adults have limited literacy skills, additional research was needed to help adult educators and policy makers understand the types of difficulties adults have related to reading so that appropriate programs, instructional materials, and teaching techniques could be developed. To this end, the Adult Reading Component Study (ARCS) was conducted by the National Center for the Study of Adult Learning and Literacy. Approximately 1,000 adults enrolled in adult basic education (ABE) and English-for-speakers-of other-languages (ESOL) programs in the Northeast, South, and Southwest regions of the United States participated in the study. Participants were administered a battery of tests to measure their word recognition, spelling, vocabulary, silent reading comprehension, and oral reading rate. The results of the assessments were studied to identify common patterns of adult reading difficulties (Strucker & Davidson, 2003).

The ABE students in the study reported difficulty with school performance in the past. More specifically, 51 percent of the adults in this group had repeated at least one grade in school, 22 percent indicated they had difficulty reading in the early elementary school years, and 53 percent reported either receiving special education or participating in reading support classes during their school careers. On average, the ABE students had a 6th-grade-level word recognition rate, vocabulary, and oral reading skills.

The adults fit into three groups: GED/pre-GED students (group 1), intermediate students (group 2), and lower-level/beginning students (group 3). Within each of these groups several clusters were found. A summary of this information is provided in Table 1.3. Many of the adults in group 1 who are below the GED level have comprehension, reading rate, vocabulary, and background knowledge scores at the middle-school level. Because their skills are below what is needed for them to prepare for and pass the GED, they need additional reading instruction to strengthen their skills before they will be ready to embark on GED-level work. Adults at the GED level of group 1 are prepared to do work at the high school level and study for the GED.

Intermediate students represent the largest percentage of adult students. They have word identification and basic phonics skills; however, they are reading well below the middle-school level. These adults need to improve their oral reading rate and build their vocabularies and background knowledge before they will be equipped to begin work on GED preparation.

Lower-level/beginning students lack the phonics skills and word identification skills needed to read. These adults require systematic instruction in phonics and word identification. Their reading skills are at such a low level that it is unlikely they will be able to acquire the reading skills necessary to earn the GED. These adults may have learning disabilities or other disabilities that affect their ability to learn and read, chronic illnesses, and other challenges that impede their ability to acquire literacy.

The ARCS study led to the development of online resources that allow adult literacy educators to assess an adult student's reading and identify the profile that is the closest match. Once the profile has been identified, adult educators and volunteer tutors can access appropriate teaching suggestions and materials provided at the National Institute for Literacy Web site.

The ARCS study also included ESOL adult students. The majority of ESOL students in the study were Spanish speakers (78%). The findings indicate that more than 80 percent of the native Spanish speakers in the study had adequate or better literacy skills in Spanish. For these adults, the English-as-a-foreign-language approach offers greater promise for growth in English than the English-as-a-second-language (ESL) approach that is commonly used in adult

Table1.3
Adult Reading Component Study

Groups and clusters of reading skill levels	Percentage of students in ABE sample
Group 1: GED/Pre-GED	34%
Cluster 1: Strong GED	9%
Cluster 2: Pre-GED with vocabulary/background information needs	11
Cluster 3: Pre-GED with vocabulary/spelling/reading rate needs	14%
Group 2: Intermediate students	56%
Cluster 4: High intermediates with difficulties in print skills/reading rate	9%
Cluster 5: Intermediates with stronger print than meaning skills	17%
Cluster 6: Intermediates with slow reading rate	5%
Cluster 7: Low intermediates	16%
Cluster 8: Low intermediates (should be in ESOL)	9%
Group 3: Lower-level/beginning students	11%
Cluster 9: Beginners	8%
Cluster 10: Reading rate impaired	3%

Source: Strucker & Davidson (2003).

literacy programs. The ESL approach focuses on basic conversational and survival skills as opposed to the English-as-a-foreign-language approach, which teaches grammar and vocabulary to prepare the adult for the type of content instruction necessary for the GED (e.g., math, social studies, science).

The ARCS study also concluded that Spanish speakers' reading abilities in Spanish were directly related to the number of years of Spanish-language schooling they had completed. Most of these adults did not report having learning difficulties during their school careers. All the ESOL participants, regardless of reading level, were weak on English consonant sounds, indicating that phonics instruction might be appropriate for these students. Two clusters of Spanish-speaking adults who had limited schooling exhibited severe difficulties with phonics and word identification. At the present time, the National Center for the Study of Adult Learning and Literacy has not developed profiles for ESOL adult learners.

ADULT LITERACY LEARNERS

Adult literacy learners vary in terms of their racial, ethnic, and language backgrounds. A large number of low-literate adults are over the age of 65—products of an educational system from an earlier era that did not prepare them for today's literacy challenges. In addition, many adults with low literacy skills are unemployed and classified as low income. Fifty-two percent of the adults in the lowest literacy level on the National Adult Literacy Survey of 1992 were unemployed. Furthermore, the average annual income for a household headed by an adult who scored at the lowest level was $13,260, compared to an adult who scored at the highest level and earned $40,050 (Kirsch et al., 1993).

A growing number of adults with low levels of literacy are also English language learners (ELLs). These adults may or may not be literate in their native language. Sixty-four percent of adult ELLs have not participated in ESOL classes (National Institute for Literacy, n.d.b). Many factors contribute to the low level of participation in ESOL programs. The complex issue of ELL status and English language literacy will be addressed in more detail in chapter 5.

Many adult literacy learners also have affective issues that they face in the process of becoming literate. They may have negative memories of schooling that they must overcome to become engaged in adult literacy education. In addition, adults are faced with stressful situations that demand their time and energy and limit their availability to pursue literacy education. Some common challenges include working multiple low-wage jobs to make ends meet, single parenting, financial problems, housing problems, domestic violence, isolation, transportation problems, and child care problems. The challenges faced by adult literacy learners often affect their enrollment, participation, persistence, and progress in adult literacy programs (Fingeret & Drennon, 1997).

ADULT LITERACY IN PRISONS AND JAILS

Almost two million adults are in federal or state prisons or local jails. This number has increased 49 percent from the previous decade. While literacy problems do not lead directly to incarceration, a link is evident. For example, one in three inmates who participated in the National Adult Literacy Survey in 1992 scored at the below-basic level. Furthermore, 14.2 percent of inmates have an 8th-grade education or less, and another 28.9 percent did not finish high school (National Institute for Literacy, n.d.a). In Florida almost 63 percent of adult inmates scored below the level required for admission to a GED preparation program (Florida Department of Corrections, 2005). Even with such low levels of literacy as the norm, most inmates do not participate in prison education programs due to their lack of availability. Only 25 percent of state and federal prisons have adult basic education programs available to inmates (National Institute for Literacy, n.d.a). Those adult inmates who did complete an education program while incarcerated had a much lower recidivism rate (19.1%) than inmates who did not complete such a program (49.1%) (Florida Department of Corrections, 2005). The impact of prison adult literacy programming appears promising.

LITERACY INSTRUCTION FOR ADULTS

Adults who have low levels of literacy may participate in several different types of educational programs. These include ABE programs, which serve adults who need literacy instruction and preparation for the GED, and adult secondary education programs that lead to a high school diploma and are designed for students who did not complete high school and are age 16 and older. In addition, adults may participate in ESOL programs, which target immigrants. Other programs include family literacy programs, which serve adults as well as their young children, and workplace literacy programs, which focus on literacy and language skills needed for the workplace. These programs are typically offered by volunteer organizations, community organizations, community colleges, houses of worship, public schools, state and local governmental agencies, and prisons and jails. Many of these types of programs will be addressed in greater detail in the following chapters.

Within these programs, various curricular materials and approaches may be used. The Partnership for Reading examined the available research on adult literacy instruction to identify research-based principles to guide adult literacy instruction (Krudiner, 2002). These principles focus on the areas of reading assessment, alphabetics (phonemic awareness, phonics, and word analysis), fluency (the ability to read quickly, accurately, and with expression), vocabulary (understanding word meanings), comprehension (understanding what one reads), and computer technology (the use of computer-assisted instruction). The eighteen principles identified from the research literacy can be used by adult educators to develop and implement effective adult literacy instruction. These principles and other aspects of adult literacy instruction will be discussed further in chapter 3.

CONCLUSION

Adult literacy is an important issue facing the United States as well as the rest of the world. Having a literate citizenry is essential due to the increasing demands for literacy in daily life and in the workplace. While there are many competing definitions of adult literacy, the main goal of adult literacy efforts is for adults to read, write, and speak English; compute; and solve problems at the level needed to accomplish goals, function at work, and develop to one's full potential.

REFERENCES

Barton, D. (1994). Preface: Literacy events and literacy practices. In M. Hamilton, D. Barton, & R. Ivanic (Eds.). *Worlds of literacy* (pp. vii–x). Clevendon, UK: Multilingual Matters.

Chisman, F. P. (2002). *Adult literacy and the American dream.* Council for Advancement of Adult Literacy. Retrieved August 1, 2006, from http://www.caalusa.org/caaloccasionalpaper1.pdf

Demetrion, G. (2005). *Conflicting paradigms in adult literacy education: In quest of a U.S. democratic politics of literacy.* Mahwah, NJ: Lawrence Erlbaum.

Fingeret, H. A., & Drennon, C. (1997). *Literacy for life: Adult learners, new practices.* New York: Teachers College Press.

Florida Department of Corrections. (2005). *Annual report: Inmate population.* Retrieved August 15, 2006, from http://www.dc.state.fl.us/pub/annual/0405/stats/ip_grade_level.html

Foner, E. (1988). *Reconstruction: America's unfinished revolution.* New York: Harper & Row.

Freire, P. (1970). *Pedagogy of the oppressed.* New York: Seabury Press.

Hunter, S., & Harman, D. (1985). *Adult illiteracy in the United States.* New York: McGraw-Hill.

Institute of Education Sciences. (2005). *Digest of education statistics tables and figures 2005.* Retrieved August 20, 2006, from http://nces.ed.gov/programs/digest/d05_tf.asp

Kirsch, I. S., Jungeblut, A., Jenkins, L., & Kolstad, A. (1993). *Adult literacy in America: A first look at the results of the National Adult Literacy Survey.* Washington, DC: U.S. Government Printing Office.

Krudiner, J. (2002). *Research-based principles for adult basic education: Reading instruction.* Jessup, MD: National Institute for Literacy.

National Center for Education Statistics. (2005). *National assessment of adult literacy: A first look at the literacy of America's adults in the 21st century.* Retrieved September 1, 2006, from http://nces.ed.gov/NAAL/PDF/2006470.PDF#search = %22national%20assessment%20of%20adult%20literacy%20a%20first%20look%22

National Center for Education Statistics. (2006). *The health literacy of America's adults: Results from the 2003 National Assessment of Adult Literacy.* Retrieved September 15, 2006, from http://nces.ed.gov/pubsearch/pubsinfo.asp?pubid = 2006483

National Institute for Literacy. (n.d.a). *Correctional education facts.* Retrieved September 21, 2006, from http://www.nifl.gov/nifl/facts/correctional.html

National Institute for Literacy. (n.d.b). *English as a second language literacy facts.* Retrieved August 1, 2006, from http://www.nifl.gov/nifl/facts/esl.html

Newman, A. P., & Beverstock, C. (1990). *Adult literacy: Contexts and challenges.* Newark, DE: International Reading Association.

ProLiteracy. (2006a). *History.* Retrieved September 1, 2006, from http://www.proliteracy.org/about/founders.asp

ProLiteracy. (2006b). *Annual report.* Retrieved September 1, 2006, from http://www.proliteracy.org/about/annual-report.asp

Strucker, J., & Davidson, R. (2003). *Adult reading components study (ARCS).* Boston: National Center for the Study of Adult Learning and Literacy.

U.S. Army Education Division. (2006). *Prep programs: High school completion, GED, basic skills.* Retrieved September 14, 2006, from https://www.hrc.army.mil/site/education/index.html

Workforce Investment Act. Title II, 105 U.S.C. §936 (1988).

Chapter Two

THE WORLD TOUCHES THE CLASSROOM: USING "ANTHROPOLICY" TO UNDERSTAND POLITICAL, ECONOMIC, AND SOCIAL EFFECTS ON ADULT LITERACY EDUCATION

Alisa Belzer and Ralf St. Clair

This chapter explores the ways in which powerful external factors—political, economic, and social—influence adult literacy education. We define adult literacy education as instruction in basic literacy and numeracy, pre-GED and GED preparation, and English as a second language in adult education, family literacy, and workplace settings. The analysis of adult literacy is a deeply complex task because politics, social forces, and economics are intricately intertwined and together play a profound role in shaping much public policy on adult literacy education. Rather than take a top-down approach, which would begin with broad descriptions of significant political, economic, and social forces influencing the field, we take the reverse route. Our analysis focuses on descriptions of adult literacy services from the perspectives of practitioners and works its way back to the political, economic, and social forces that seem to shape the development of influential policies. We suggest that these conditions bear on policy and practice both through the legislative process and through the lived experiences of practitioners; both are within the reach of the same social forces. We also assume that the concrete and specific influences of policy on practice are not static but are highly contextualized and constantly evolving through the involvement of diverse groups of actors, such as practitioners and program managers.

Whereas many analyses focus on a horizontal interaction of policies and policy makers (with practice as simply a product of this interaction), we attempt to explore the vertical components of educational development by assuming that all stakeholders take action with regard to policies and will do so in ways specific to their own positions. In this chapter, we focus in particular on practitioners. We acknowledge that given our layered and textured assumptions about the relationships among strong external forces, policies, and practices, multiple perspectives are needed. Our analysis here, however, is centered on the idea that the lived experiences of practitioners are an important starting point. Further research and analysis are required for a deeper understanding of other layers of the system.

We call our approach to policy analysis "anthropolicy." This is a term we took from a typographical error in a conference program that intended to say "anthropology" (Plumb, 2006). We saw this new word, however, as suggesting an extremely important way to understand policy—from the perspective of the people who live it every day. By adopting this term, we are trying to suggest the importance of studying the ways in which humans interact with, make meaning from, and shape policy. This perspective denies the possibility of policy as a linear, causative mechanism and views it as essentially relational. While policy documents and legislation can be seen as reifications of intentions and aspirations making one set of ideas at one particular time the basis for creating policy, the ways in which people live and experience policy is clearly dynamic and nonlinear. By constructing narratives of practice in which practitioners tell about their experiences with, reactions to, and ways of working within policy regimes, we argue that we can learn a great deal not only about how policy affects people and how people affect policy, but also the complex and multifaceted ways in which policy can be interpreted and understood.

We begin by describing the delivery system for adult literacy education. This explanation is followed by narratives of practice constructed through interviews with three practitioners who have each worked in the field for over 20 years. These narratives represent their perspectives on the ways in which the field has changed significantly over the course of their careers. We use these stories to identify policy changes that matter to practitioners in how they do their jobs, and how they see them as changing opportunities for learning. From there, we analyze these changes in relation to key political, economic, and social changes that shape the shifting realities of the field.

THE ADULT LITERACY SYSTEM CONTEXT

Adult literacy education is funded publicly and privately through a variety of local, state, and federal sources. Federal funding for adult literacy education is estimated to address only 25 percent of total expenditures for adult literacy education (U.S. Department of Education Division of Adult Education and Literacy, 2006). Yet the federal government leverages considerable influence on how services are delivered. Federal money is allocated proportionally based on census data reflecting the total number of the target population (i.e., those age 16 and above, not in school, and without a high school diploma) residing in each state. Each state is responsible for designating an agency to distribute federal funds to local programs through a competitive grant process. In its role as grant manager, the state agency also establishes standards and expectations for program performance.

There is considerable variation in funding and governance for adult literacy programs. Programs may be funded primarily through federal money, may receive funds (beyond the required 25% match) directly from the state, or may operate strictly with private money. Some programs leverage other state and federal program funds to support a range of related programs. Many draw on a variety of sources. Governance structures are as varied as the funding sources. Nonprofits must be governed by a board of directors. Programs based in school districts generally answer to local school boards. Some of the variation in funding and governance in adult literacy education may be shaped by the nature of the state's bureaucracy. The logistics of service provision are diverse as well. Adult basic education programs can be housed in locations such as public schools, libraries, prisons, churches, community centers, community colleges, and employment centers. Programs may operate five days a week, offering classes for five hours a day, or as little as just two or three hours a week. They may focus on any number of skills and content areas, ranging from only reading instruction to a comprehensive variety of courses. Some programs may focus primarily on specific work or workforce development skills; others may emphasize working toward greater social justice, or supporting children's learning through family literacy programming.

The current legislation authorizing federal spending is Title II, the Adult Education and Family Literacy Act, of the Workforce Investment Act (WIA), of 1998. This legislation was aimed primarily at reforming the workforce development system but also addressed federal policy on adult literacy education. Some of WIA's key goals are to provide system users with more individual choice, create a better match between local training and job opportunities, eliminate duplication of services by streamlining over 70 workforce programs (Imel, 2000), provide more local control, and increase accountability. In contrast to earlier reform efforts, WIA focused more on measurable outcomes, such as standardized test results, than on improving the quality of inputs related to program components (Grubb, Badway, Bell, Chi, King, Herr, et al., 1999). For the first time, adult education was positioned within the workforce development system and collaboration was mandated between the two systems.

The National Reporting System was developed to meet WIA's accountability requirements. The National Reporting System identifies and defines skill attainment measures and establishes methods and standards for data collection and reporting. The National Reporting System is first and foremost a tool to improve access to the information available for demonstrating program effectiveness to Congress (i.e., the funder), but it can also be used to match successful outcomes with specific program and classroom practices, and as a way to track progress in improving services (National Reporting System, n.d.).

The Personal Responsibility and Work Opportunity Reconciliation Act (generally referred to as welfare reform) was initially legislated in 1996. It was not aimed at the adult literacy education system directly; however, its goal "to end welfare as we know it" (Clinton, 2006) affected many actual and potential adult learners. The basic tenets of welfare reform included a maximum five-year lifetime limit (some states elected to make the lifetime limit shorter) on availability of funds to recipients and more stringent requirements for participation regarding work-related and pre-employment activities. These changes indicated an ideological shift from an assumption that poor people are entitled to receive funds to an emphasis on helping people make transitions to work regardless of circumstances or need. The legislation's emphasis on "work first" is based on the assumption that work, rather than education, is the best preparation for job advancement and economic independence.

NARRATIVES OF PRACTICE: THE ANTHROPOLICY OF LITERACY

Typically, policy analyses focus on policy makers' intentions, the obstacles and barriers to implementing the policy, or the impact of policy in bringing about intended and unintended change. Anthropolicy, however, can help us understand policy from the perspective of those affected by the policy and can be a way to tease out important influences on policy formation itself. Anthropolicy assists us in understanding which policies matter in practice, in what ways, and why. This lens can shed light on important forces that shape policy and that might be obscured by more traditional approaches to policy analysis and directs the focus to the active construction of policy and practice by all participants. Exploring the process of construction can then help to reveal how policy can be more or less effective in attaining ends such as enhanced equity.

Our choice of narratives of practice as a tool for informing our analysis of the significant forces that shape the field confirms the assumption that "people 'make' policy through practice" (Levinson & Sutton, 2001, p. 4). Narratives are a useful tool for understanding what this means in actuality. The two key pieces of information that come from this analysis concern filtering and meaning. By "filtering," we mean the way the narratives focus attention on the changes that seem most important to the participants, and by "meaning" we mean the way the narratives frame and explain policy events. This kind of analysis helps illuminate how policy emerges within people's practice.

There are many kinds of narratives, but they are generally understood to be stories of experience that follow rhetorical patterns similar to those used in fictional stories. Most researchers who engage in narrative inquiry acknowledge that narratives are not necessarily meant to be taken literally. Schram and Neisser (1997) suggest that narratives mediate reality and that "they are not so much an artifact of a preexisting factual reality as they are constitutive of it and even written into it" (p. 5). This makes narratives valuable regardless of their relationship to some absolute standard of factuality.

We see our anthropolitical narratives as hybrids between policy narratives, which are told to explain a particular policy problem (e.g., low achievement of minority students are the fault of failing schools and teachers) or to justify a policy response (Schram & Neisser, 1997), and teachers' narratives, which locate personal experiences within broader contexts and shed light on what influences thinking (Goodson, 1992). While policy narratives are often constructed by policy elites such as elected or appointed government officials (Schram & Neisser, 1997), our narratives are told by those who live the policies. In their positions as practitioners, adult literacy educators have insider knowledge of policy, but they are less concerned with the ways in which policies are designed to address specific problems and are more concerned with how they can best do their jobs within the defined boundaries that policies create. Their narratives focus on policy in an experiential rather than explanatory manner, and the subject is the broader field as viewed through individuals' experiences of practice in relationship to policy.

The narratives were constructed through interviews with three practitioners: an executive director and two teachers who have each worked in adult literacy education for over 20 years. We believed that because of their many years of experience, we could encourage them to develop narratives that would help make clear the ways in which policies have influenced their professional lives, their perspectives on the field, and their ways of doing their work. The three narrators work in the same large community-based organization in an urban center in a Middle Atlantic state (the program and practitioner names have been changed to protect confidentiality). The organization is viewed as high quality and innovative. Its executive director and staff often present at state and regional conferences and are recognized leaders in the field. The organization offers a wide range of adult literacy services and uses an eclectic range of traditional and innovative instructional materials, formats, strategies, and service delivery modes. The organization has a well-developed infrastructure and relatively stable funding. Neither the organization nor the practitioners were selected for their typicality. Because narratives are not meant to be generalizable, extrapolating to other settings was not the intent. Rather, the practitioners were selected because they were believed to be storytellers who would be capable of positioning their experiences within the broader historical context of the field.

The narratives were constructed from transcribed interviews that were conducted in person or by telephone and lasted approximately one hour. All three interviewees had previously been colleagues of the first author of this chapter. Questions focused on ways in which the field has changed since their initial entry into it. The kinds of changes that the narrators discussed were identified by them without prompting. The narrators were then asked to talk about the specific ways in which these changes had influenced their practice. They were also asked to identify what they saw as the primary sources of change. Finally, they were asked to talk about the ways in which the changes had improved or detracted from their ability to help learners successfully meet their goals.

Michelle's Narrative

I have been the executive director of the City Literacy Program since I entered the field in 1986. Several important factors were shaping the field in the late 1980s. The Adult Performance Level Program, which claimed to measure minimum competencies needed for an adult to function successfully, was released. The findings of this study encouraged many to focus on addressing specific learning goals that related to the real-life tasks of adulthood. Concurrently, there was a lot of pressure to do phonics-based instruction. Many in the field were looking to researchers who talked about the phases of reading as if they were a straight-line progression. Now we talk about phonemic awareness, phonics, fluency, vocabulary, and comprehension, and we talk about how they're all intermixed. But then it was like you had to teach phonics before you taught how to actually read a book.

Because of my interest in policy development, I immediately got involved in advocacy at the state level so that I could advocate for programs like mine to take a more learner goal–driven and whole language approach (a contextualized, meaning-based, and integrated approach to reading and writing instruction). Similarly, I became a constant advocate for authentic assessment (when evidence of learning is demonstrated through the use of skills in the context of real-life tasks) at a time when the state was just beginning to feel the pressure of accountability and was trying to make decisions about what one test might be given. I argued that the use of specific curriculum or assessment instruments should not be mandated. Winning this battle left us free to implement the curriculum and assessment of our choice. I remember arguing that you don't have to have a standardized score to say that you are assessing and being held accountable for learner outcomes. I would say that it's a broader field than it was 20 years ago in the sense that there are now programs for family literacy and workplace literacy and other specialized needs. Now there are more full-time teachers, there is much more instructional technology available, and we have a statewide professional development system. There is more money available, but the money that's available has not kept pace with inflation, and we are now looking at actual decreases. Additionally, private-sector fund-raising has become more difficult, and as a result we spend less on instructional materials, and staff salaries have not kept up with inflation. Adult literacy education continues to be underfunded.

There's a push toward accountability, which was not part of the field 20 years ago. If you are a state- or federally funded program, you've got a mandated set of tests to demonstrate learner outcomes from which you must choose. There are clear performance standards. Because of the National Reporting System and because of the requirements of the Workforce Investment Act, states have had to enforce accountability systems. And it has enforced several things, including the use of some kind of a data management system. There are standards around pretesting, post-testing, and anticipated gains, and particular attention is paid to more specific core learner outcomes: retaining employment, attaining employment, obtaining the GED or a high school diploma, and transitioning to postsecondary education. Although we now talk a lot about student outcomes, and there are what are called secondary outcomes (but performance standards are not based around secondary outcomes), the number of people, for example, who began reading to their children, voted for the first time, or obtained their citizenship is not longer used as a performance standard. Accomplishing goals like these is not being tracked by the data system. Because of the enforcement of particular formal assessments and the amount of time that that takes, more authentic assessment goes on the back burner.

So the nature of accountability has changed. We used to set our own accountability standards and worked hard to meet them. Now they're being set by a third party—the federal government in conjunction with the state agency directors. So that has made the job more difficult. On one hand, you want to be true to yourself in your beliefs about what adult outcomes should be and how to train your teachers and your staff to achieve them. On the other hand, you're being measured by certain outcomes, and so how you justify the merger, or the division, of those is an issue. How do you make sure there is customer satisfaction at the same time you're meeting a performance standard? We work on it, but do we question the standards? Yes.

The welfare system has had an evolving impact on adult literacy education since welfare reform in 1996. Depending on how adult basic education is determined to count toward fulfilling work obligations for welfare recipients, at times the requirements have really hurt literacy programs, at times it has been supportive of literacy programs, and now I think it's somewhere in the middle. The latest initiative has already changed its requirements twice.

It began as a full-time education program for welfare recipients but has now been reduced to 10 hours per week.

I would say that the biggest contributing factor to the changes I've described is WIA. No question about that. When I say WIA, I'm really referring to the reporting requirements put in place by the National Reporting System, and the requirement that we be an integral part of the workforce development system. Collaboration is emphasized as a goal by many funders, but WIA requires us to be involved with the workforce system in new ways. I spend a lot of time in meetings with these partners but question this use of my time. Although there is a lot of talk about an emphasis on research-based practice, it has had nowhere near the impact on our work that WIA has.

In an overall assessment of the state of the field now compared to 20 years ago, I feel that more adults are receiving services because of increased funding. I believe that increased collaboration helps in terms of provision of services and information available to individuals regardless of where they enter the service continuum. From that standpoint, I think the changes have been positive. I think that data systems are critical. Administrators and teachers looking at it, and what it tells them, and what it means to inform their practice is positive. But I think only examining standardized performance data leaves out important elements of effective programs. I'm basically pro-accountability, but I do know that you end up spending more time on some goals than you ever did before. What's really important for me is how accountability is defined, what the elements are that are considered in it, and what happens to the information—how it's used. I'm not sure what the overall impact on practice is.

Kate's Narrative

I have worked in the field for 21 years. I have been a volunteer coordinator; tutor; curriculum developer; literacy, pre-GED, and GED teacher; and administrator in four different programs, including two serving women and one for out-of-school youths. Now I'm back to where I began, teaching a class that is subcontracted to the City Literacy Program. It's a class in a job-training program, most of whose clients are referred by the court for child support issues. After they go through the job-training component and begin an intensive job search, they come to me until they get a job. They don't stay long because they really can't.

When I started to think about how to describe the field when I began working, I wondered if my perception was based on the fact that I was young and vigorous and new to the work, or if the field itself changed. Is it just me looking back 21 years later? I think it's the field that has changed. Back then it was very energetic and idealistic. People had a real passion for the work. The passion was about literacy as an issue, and people's empowerment through education. It was more than a career, which it feels like now; it was almost a mission. It was creative, student-centered, grassroots. People were frustrated about money, but it felt like the sky was the limit anyway. If you could think it up, and it looked like the students would want it, and it would be good for them, you could do it. There was a lot of thinking, a lot of bright ideas.

I would definitely say the field now is less idealistic; it's less creative, and much more business-like. When I first came to one of the programs that I worked at, there was an education director. We talked about education issues and learning and teaching all the time. She was replaced by a program director, who was about making the program run smoothly and meeting the program requirements, much less about teaching and learning. This seems characteristic of the field. I think it's more cynical now. In the 1980s everyone was thinking outside the box. Now it's about staying inside the box. It seems like everyone is just thinking about what the funders want and how you can deliver that as efficiently as possible.

For my class now, student participation has a definite economic bottom line. The question always seems to be can you demonstrate outcomes to make it worth funding this program? At one point, I had a side job working at a local university coordinating an intergenerational literacy program, training college students to work with adults ages 55 and older. It was very hard to fund, and now that program is gone because there was no economic bottom line at all. I had two 90-something ladies who wanted to learn to read. For them it was just about quality of life. No one could say that there was going to be any economic payoff. That didn't matter in the 1980s, but in the 1990s it began to matter a lot.

We didn't have a lot of accountability when I started, so some people were screwing up, but now the accountability drives people's practice. Ten or twelve years ago at the end of the year, I could say students had achieved more subjective accomplishments like being more confident or increasing their self-esteem, or their parents had become more supportive. We considered that a successful outcome. But those things are irrelevant now. They don't come up at all. Now I have to pre- and post-test and show a gain. If a conversation started about relationships and it was a fruitful and productive conversation, we might let that run its course, and our social worker could run with that. Now she'd have to meet with them after class.

I think many of the changes in the field have been gradual, but when I came back after a year off when my daughter was born, that was the year when welfare reform had gone into place. I felt that in that time it had become a completely different program. I think that changed things more than anything else. I had always been working with women, and women were so profoundly affected by the welfare reform changes. Since I came back, I've never had students for a long period of time. Then, the welfare rules changed all the time. The women were really no longer focusing on their education. What was communicated to them was "Get a job and focus on your education on your own time." But the women weren't getting jobs that were pulling them out of poverty. They had to take anything to meet the 20-hour work requirement.

All this changed what their priorities were, what their goals were, and the culture of the classroom. What had been more of a support-group kind of classroom became "I'm only here for a short period of time; let's get something done." It had such a big impact because of how long people could stay. People often had to leave for a job before they met their academic goals. They had to, or they would lose their benefits. Learners' priorities changed too. People became unwilling to deal with bigger issues. People would always want to know, "What does this have to do with getting my GED?" After welfare reform it was harder to argue what this has to do with the GED. You can't talk about neighborhood crime or HIV or other concerns because they feel more pressure to perform and achieve for other people. They have less time to be there, they're more distracted with a lot of other demands on them, and we can put less of an emphasis on their individual goals. Early in my teaching, there was a focus on the learner as a whole person, and now I feel like we're really looking much more at just the academic piece.

The biggest difference probably is that early in my time in the field the focus was firmly on the students, whatever they wanted, however they wanted it. Then as we shifted over to other systems, other outside influences, other programs, the question became what does welfare want, what does WIA want, what do the funders want? It wasn't what the students wanted anymore. It's a huge ideological change, really. Ironically, with all the accountability and the pressure to document everything, there are still programs that say they are offering services that they aren't, and staff who are claiming instruction they aren't doing. I don't know sometimes if the accountability didn't backfire a little bit. By trying so hard to make sure that people are doing the right thing, people aren't being as creative as they used to be. There is creativity out there, but that and the idealism aren't as characteristic of the field anymore.

Beth's Narrative

I have worked in the field for about 28 years, always as a teacher, although I have also been involved in professional development and curriculum. When I started working, it was a very positive experience for both the teacher and the learners. Everyone was there because that's where they wanted to be. No one was mandated to be there. That's what they wanted to do. The learners participated in the hiring of the teachers. It was exciting! All these new things were happening where learners were being involved in roles that they had never been involved in before.

Not much money was being spent. People were really squeezing pennies to run programs. There was no such thing as ordering books from the Reader Resource Program, a state-funded program that provides free instructional materials. There were no professional development centers. There was very little professional opportunity other than going to conferences. Low pay. Very, very low pay. Learning environments were really rough. Sometimes you were teaching in little tiny closet rooms. I don't think there was a lot of attention back then that was being focused on quality standards. There probably weren't even any developed. I guess we reported attendance, but I can't even remember if we had a testing tool. There wasn't a lot of attention on quality or progress. It was a simple thing. You just entered a class and began working. The the state adult literacy education agency wasn't really that visible like it is now.

The field is so much bigger now. There are many more staff development opportunities. Funding has increased. Administrators have gained skills in seeking funding and have a staff. That was never the way. Back in the day, the administrator was writing all the proposals with a skeleton staff. Now we can offer all kinds of programming for many more kinds of students in a lot more settings. We didn't have on-site classes at shelters and places like that back then. And we didn't have welfare reform.

Welfare reform has had a critical impact on the field because, like all our systems that are put in place, they are set up not in a way so that people succeed, but to perpetuate failure. I think the whole main purpose of welfare reform was to get people off the welfare system, and they certainly met that goal. But they started with the wrong goal. They started with an economic goal and then plugged in the education part. If they had started with that, the economic part may have come along. So then they put the money that they saved on welfare into all these training programs that people are now going to. Many people go to many programs that may not be in their [best] interests. Then they're put in job placement programs connected with these educational training programs, and they end up having a whole group of people for low-pay frontline jobs. For $7.50 or $6 an hour, people really can't afford to take those jobs. And they're mandated to participate in the training and to work after so many months of training. I personally can't imagine getting up every day, going to a place that I hate, and not having enough money to provide health insurance to my family, along with a lot of other things. It's not like the government doesn't have the funding, but it's the way the funding is being spent. People get put into little boxes. This has changed the whole learning environment. People are really hostile, and we have a whole different population of people. Our classrooms are microcosms of the larger society. So whatever is going on in the world touches the classroom.

The welfare reform certainly changes the whole idea of participatory learner-centered approaches when you only have six months to build somebody's skills so they can pass an employment or training test. I think I've integrated into my curriculum in all my classes how to learn because I understand that I'm only a little piece in their lives as far as it connects to their learning. I'm not with them that long. If I have a learner for 50 hours, that's a pretty long time. If they meet the goals that they set coming into the classroom, then they've been successful and I've helped them to be successful. But that's only one part of it, because knowing how to learn is something that they'll take with them. I think it's important for them to think about their own learning process and the process that they're engaged in so they can get their learning needs met in the future and be in the position to evaluate [whether or not a learning situation fits with their own learning style].

Now I think there's much more data collection, much more paperwork and reporting. A lot of instructors' time today is spent on data. But the accountability doesn't really change what you do in class. It's like in the same way that the learners learn to work the system, programs and practitioners learn to work this system too. So for example, one of the core outcomes is obtain the GED. If a person comes in July and says she wants to get the GED—because everyone says they want to get a GED whether they're at the 4th- or 10th-grade level—if I check that and she comes in at the 4th-grade level, she's never going to achieve that by the end of the year. That would be a negative outcome for me and the program. In order to remedy that, if I don't think, after working with the person for awhile, that she can meet that goal at the end of the fiscal year, I'm not going to check that as a goal. I mean, look at the goals! The people who are in the position in the state capital and Washington—what do they know about this?

I think the changes have been for the better, because there's more funding available and more needs being addressed, in more specific ways. Classes are focused on different populations' needs, youths, and ESL. But at the federal level, when people are in the position to make decisions, the decisions are based on their expectations, not the expectations of those of us in the field. I think there's certain things that have never changed that really need to change. Programs are always set up where the people who know what changes need to be made are never given power to make any kind of decision. I think that's always been a contradiction. For example, teachers can give recommendations that would support higher-quality learning, yet many times throughout history, those recommendations fall in a big black hole because either organizations don't have the money to support the recommendations or the people who are in the position to know better than anybody else what kind of changes would enhance the program don't have the power to institute those kinds of changes. That hasn't changed.

NARRATIVE THEMES

It seems that there are certain areas that the informants agree strongly are key to understanding the changes in practices over the last 20 years. They break down into six themes that seem to fall into three clusters. The first is the impact of the view that literacy education is a component of workforce development, which attracts a considerable amount of focus. Next are accountability, standards, and authentic assessment, areas that are strongly related. The notions of specialized programs and changing funding patterns can also be seen as running together. The meanings practitioners attach to each of these themes emerge through closer examination of their narratives.

Both of the instructors talked about idealism and the idea of empowerment as a goal of literacy education and suggested that something was lost from the field as the structures changed over the years. In a traditional analysis, factors such as passion would not be associated with policy analysis, but the anthropolitical approach encourages such ideas to be brought forward. It brings up issues such as how things have been changed to reduce commitment to the field and points toward a key component of meaning for these practitioners. While it is not possible to link this issue with a specific policy change—and Kate raises the possibility that her perceptions may simply be an effect of aging—it certainly tells us something important about the practitioners' engagement with the field.

The key question is how external conditions, whether political, economic, or social, influence adult literacy education. These practitioners indicated that several policies have made a difference in the ways in which they interact with students, even though they resist and subvert them to some extent. Although the narratives identify specific policy initiatives, we examine these policies thematically. This approach emphasizes a changing, holistic environment with interwoven influences, rather than marking each policy as having a clearly delineated and unique set of influences.

Literacy Education as a Workforce Strategy

In the mid-1990s, adult literacy education was regarded explicitly as a component of workforce development for the first time, largely in response to concerns about the economic competitiveness of the U.S. economy and the belief that increased skills result in increased productivity. The Workforce Investment Act, which had the effect of linking literacy to workforce development more strongly than ever before, was identified as a key change. The impact of this change is hard to overemphasize—as Michelle explained, "I would say that the biggest contributing factor to the changes I've described is WIA. No question about that."

The WIA legislation promoted a standardized form of outcomes and purposes where there had previously been a far broader approach to the value of literacy education. Practitioners had mixed feelings about the effects of these changes on instructional practices. On one hand, Kate stated, "there were workers who were not doing right by the students, and they were sticking around for a long time because there wasn't accountability." On the other hand, there is concern about the loss of creativity and flexibility that was apparent before WIA. Kate stated, "I could say students had achieved more subjective accomplishments like being more confident or increasing their self-esteem, or their parents had become more supportive. We considered that a successful outcome."

Just two years before the introduction of WIA, there was a significant effort to reform the welfare system. Attendance at a literacy program was often mandated as a way for participants to show willingness to become ready for work, and failure to attend could result in reduced payments to individuals. Conversely, work was very strongly prioritized in the reforms, and individuals could be pulled out of education whenever a job became available, and the duration of their participation was limited by external regulations. Literacy educators can find this an extremely frustrating situation and may see the system as "set up not in a way so that people succeed, but to perpetuate failure," as Beth stated. Some resentment about the policy's influence on their work was expressed by Kate when she stated, "I had always been working with women, and women were so profoundly affected by the welfare reform changes." The reform's effect was seen as an externalization of control over their work, as well as having the potential for significant interference.

Overall, explicitly positioning adult literacy as a workforce development strategy can be seen as a significant move away from self-determined local programs toward a larger externally regulated system. It moved literacy from voluntary engagement to mandated service, structured according to the needs and philosophies of stakeholders who are not literacy educators or learners. In the narratives, participants linked reduced freedom in their work and a more hostile work environment with WIA and contemporary changes in welfare provision. The significance of this change, to these practitioners, is epochal, marking the end of an era.

Assessment, Accountability, and Standards

Changes in accountability systems have a profound effect on instructional practices (St. Clair & Belzer, in press). The practitioners interviewed certainly reflected this influence in their comments, and this was a substantial area of concern for them. Their understanding of accountability systems was profound and insightful. For example, Michelle stated, "What's really important for me is how accountability is defined, what the elements are that are considered in it, and what happens to the information—how it's used."

When Michelle started her career, she advocated authentic assessment, arguing that no one test or one curriculum would be best for all students. Her efforts kept the field open for local programs and practitioners to develop and implement their own models. This has since changed. Michelle reported, "There are standards around pretesting, post-testing and anticipated gains, and particular attention is paid to more specific learner outcomes: retaining employment, attaining employment, obtaining the GED or a high school diploma, and transitioning to postsecondary education." Programs have become accountable for providing a narrow range of services in ways that were not always compatible with learner goals or effective teaching and learning practices.

While Michelle refers to standards as coming from the federal government, most of the specific implementation structures are actually decided and driven at the state level. The state agency has raised its profile within the field and has started to require specific forms of assessment in response to the demands of the National Reporting System. Alongside these assessment requirements, perhaps inevitably, come demands to use standardized assessment tools that contribute to determining instruction in ways that are less likely to be customized to individual needs and interests. While testing has always been a significant issue in schooling, there is no comparable history in adult literacy education—the tradition has been based on collaborative learner-centered teaching and learning interactions. This means that not only have systems been built from almost nothing over the last 10 years, but that practitioners in the field may not have a great deal of experience in challenging the way such systems are constructed.

The meaning attached to these developments is a reduction in freedom for practitioners and, perhaps more tellingly, a sense that responsiveness to the needs and desires of students is significantly reduced. Assessment systems can very easily reorient instruction. Michelle underlined this by stating, "I do know that you end up spending more time on some goals than you ever did before." This statement, however, should not be read as suggesting that practitioners simply comply with centralized demands. As Michelle puts it, "We work on it, but do we question the standards? Yes." Beth makes it clear that she simply subverts the system. These comments demonstrate the ways that practitioners may reconfigure and resist policy imperatives in the service of the values they see as important to maintain within literacy education.

Funding and Specialization

Current funding for the field seems good compared to what has been available in the past. Lower levels of funding led to some frustration. Kate shared, "There wasn't enough money, so you could have all the bright ideas in the world, but there wasn't any money. There was never enough money for the projects you wanted to do, so people were frustrated about that, so they needed to leave, and it was hard to hire people." There was general agreement across the narratives that there has been some degree of improvement. One of the benefits of increased funding over the last few years has been an increasing emphasis on specialized programs for specific types of learners. Beth stated, "Now we can offer all kinds of programming for many more kinds of students in a lot more settings." This development can be viewed very positively.

As Michelle pointed out, however, "adult literacy education continues to be under-funded. This has led to the devotion of considerable amounts of people's time, and other resources, to the pursuit of funding. Michelle stated, "As we have pursued funding opportunities, it has changed what I do and how I spend my time." Conscious thought is devoted to positioning the City Literacy Program appropriately—including within the right partnerships—to pursue funding when it becomes available. Money can become a determining factor in shaping provision at both the organizational and classroom levels. Kate stated, "At the program where I work now, student participation has a definite economic bottom line. The question always seems to be can you demonstrate outcomes to make it worth funding this program?"

In summary, changes in resources are seen as having a beneficial effect because, as Beth reports, "there's more funding available and more needs are being addressed, in more specific ways." The significance of these changes in resource patterns resides in the programs' abilities to aim services at underserved learners even though the overall support for adult literacy education is still regarded as fundamentally insufficient. It is important to note as well that from the perspectives of practitioners, increased funding seems to come with many strings attached that are not always palatable to them or learners.

LINKING DOWN AND LINKING UP

When adult literacy education is examined using some of the approaches suggested by the notion of anthropolicy, a vibrant portrayal of the way practices react to, react against, and reformulate policy results. This discussion suggests that only some policy initiatives actually reach teaching and learning practices in any direct way. It is also notable that the significance of the initiatives is reinterpreted at the practitioner level in terms of their actual effects on their professional lives, their practice, and the learners with whom they work rather than ideologically or on the basis of intention. For example, the Workforce Investment Act is seen as producing a less pleasant working environment with little room for maneuvering on the part of practitioners, which can make the experience of learning less relevant and inspiring for learners.

These narratives of practice tell the story of a field that has both benefited from and paid a price for increased funding and attention. While there is more money for professional development, infrastructure, and materials, and programs can provide more diverse services for a greater number of learners in an expanding range of settings, some important opportunities for teaching and learning have been reduced. The political, economic, and social outcome of this loss is unknown, but these practitioners express ambivalence at best, and cynicism and doubt at worst, about these changes. At the same time, decision making regarding purposes and valued outcomes for learning has shifted from learners, teachers, and program managers to third parties at the state and federal levels. This shift translates into a shift in practitioners from feeling accountable to learners to feeling accountable to funders. These three narratives suggest that the field has matured in many ways by clarifying performance goals and accountability systems, but the changes have also shifted practitioner attention away from teaching and learning and toward externally constructed, not always meaningful measures. At the same time, these practitioners identify a shift in learners' attitudes away from motivation for literacy learning toward a sometimes resentful compliance with external expectations.

If we view the developments from the top down, it is possible to link up to the practitioner perspectives by identifying the policy interventions that have affected their working context so radically. The policies that seem to drive these shifts are state and federal increases in funding (accompanied by increased expectations for demonstrated returns on investment), welfare reform (with mandated participation in specified programs for predetermined lengths of time), and the Workforce Investment Act (with mandatory collaboration with the workforce system and standardized accountability and performance standards). Each of these policy initiatives shares economic, social, and political characteristics implicated in the changes in practice identified in the narratives of Michelle, Kate, and Beth. These include a market view of investments in education as necessitating demonstrable economic returns, and standardization determined by a top-down approach that assumes a unitary definition of literacy.

As adult literacy education has been brought further into the mainstream, there has been increased emphasis on centralized approaches to performance standards. When adult literacy was seen as having relatively low stakes, there was little interest, or perceived need, to manage the system as a coherent whole. Localization was the norm and seemed to present few problems. The increasing investment in adult literacy has started to make the field a more high-stakes endeavor, resulting in the promotion of more consistent approaches to measuring the quality of services, even though it is far from clear that quality will mean the same thing in every context or with every learner. Nonetheless, adult literacy education can no longer avoid the current push toward unified models of practice and accountability.

The reasons for the increased interest in adult literacy are complex, and it is hard to identify direct causes in a reliable way. There are a number of critical elements that seem to have come together around the same time, however.

One is the assumption that low literacy is linked to dependence on social services. The independent American worker and citizen is a literate one, and the notions of illiteracy and dependency are strongly linked in national cultural myths (Sandlin & St. Clair, 2002). So, even though many problems have to do with intractable poverty and racism, adult literacy education is expected to produce solutions.

Another condition that sits in some tension with the last is the promotion of narrow educational goals as the desirable outcome. The narrower the goal, the easier it is to measure, and one effect of the push for accountability has been the inadvertent acceptance of the idea that outcomes must be measurable in standardized and narrow ways to be real (Merrifield, 1998). This perception works alongside an interest in the efficiency of education to prioritize a set of simple outcomes that can be easily achieved and demonstrated—in the current context it is in nobody's interest to invest resources in less demonstrable soft outcomes such as those that have been historically important to the field.

Literacy education, then, is expected to address massive social problems while maintaining a tight focus on externally defined educational outcomes. To some extent, it may be that the field has gotten itself into this position by expressing willingness to engage with contradictory expectations, but there may have been little choice open to literacy educators. As the educational field as a whole has had to accommodate the movement in social policy priorities away from welfare toward market-centered responsibility, it is perhaps inevitable that adult literacy education should have to move in the same direction.

CONCLUSIONS

In this discussion, we have attempted to approach the links between adult literacy education as a field of practice and a policy area by using an analytic approach rooted in the narratives of those who have lived the changes. By doing so, we were able to show how those lived experiences both filtered policy initiatives and provided meaning for them. The picture that we end up with is that of a field experiencing significant shift over the last 20 years in direct response to political, economic, and social pressures. It is certainly possible to present this shift as an example of responsive evolution within an educational area, but it is equally possible to suggest that the endeavor has lost its way to some extent.

The current mission of adult literacy education seems to be simply impossible—it will never ameliorate poverty on a large scale or even ensure the existence of a universally well-educated workforce. Yet these are the claims that the field has been encouraged to make despite the discomfort of those involved in practice. Adult literacy education seems to be forced away from what practitioners believe they do well—respectful and effective work with learners based on their identified needs and interests—toward areas where they may feel they can never do well enough. The meaning of this for the practitioners informing the present discussion seems clear. The world not only touches the classroom; it floods in and changes everything.

REFERENCES

Clinton, B. (2006, August 22). How we ended welfare, together. *New York Times*. Retrieved December 5, 2005, from http://www.nytimes.com/2006/08/22/opinion/22clinton. html?ex = 1313899200&en = fc65ae4741105227&ei = 5088&partner = rssnyt& emc = rss.

Goodson, I. F. (1992). Studying teachers' lives: An emergent field of inquiry. In I. F. Goodson (Ed.), *Studying teachers' lives* (pp. 1–17). New York: Teachers College Press.

Grubb, W. N., Badway, N., Bell, D., Chi, B., King, C., Herr, J., et al. (1999). *Toward order from chaos: State efforts to reform workforce development systems.* Berkeley, CA: National Center for Research in Vocational Education.

Imel, S. (2000). *Welfare to work: Considerations for adult and vocational education.* (ERIC Digest No. 216). Columbus, OH: ERIC Clearinghouse on Adult Career and Vocational Education. (ERIC Document Reproduction Service No. ED 440 253).

Levinson, B.A.U., & Sutton, M. (2001). Introduction: Policy as/in practice—a sociocultural approach to the study of educational policy. In M. Sutton & B.A.U. Levinson (Eds.), *Policy as practice: Toward a comparative sociocultural analysis of educational policy* (pp. 1–22). Westport, CT: Ablex.

Merrifield, J. (1998). *Contested ground: Performance accountability in adult basic education.* Cambridge, MA: National Center for the Study of Adult Learning and Literacy.

National Reporting System (n.d.). *National reporting system for adult education (NRS).* Retrieved January 6, 2006, from http://www.nrsweb.org/default.asp

Plumb, D. (2006, May). *The nature and archaic origins of lifelong learning processes: The relevance of anthropology to adult education.* Paper presented at the meeting of the Adult Education Research Conference, Minneapolis, MN.

Sandlin, J. A., & St. Clair, R. (2002, July). *The unlettered state: Illiteracy and intrusion in North American social policy.* Conference paper presented at the Standing Committee on University Teaching and the Education of Adults Conference, Stirling, Scotland.

Schram, S. F., & Neisser, P. T. (1997). Introduction. In S. F. Schram & P. T. Neisser (Eds.), *Tales of the state: narrative in contemporary U.S. politics and public policy* (pp. 1–4). Lanham, MD: Roman & Littlefield.

St. Clair, R., & Belzer, A. (In press). National accountability systems. In P. Campbell (Ed.), *Accountability in adult basic education.* Edmonton, AB: Grass Roots Press.

U.S. Department of Education Division of Adult Education and Literacy. (2006). *Adult Education and Family Literacy Act, program year 2003–2004.* Report to Congress on state performance. Washington, DC: Author.

Part Two

ADULT LITERACY INSTRUCTION AND ASSESSMENT

Chapter Three

TEACHING AND LEARNING IN ADULT BASIC EDUCATION

M. Cecil Smith

Although it is commonly assumed that the adults who enroll in adult basic education (ABE) programs are illiterate, this is rarely the case. Most ABE participants have completed several years of schooling; despite their school attendance, they were unsuccessful at learning to read. Often this lack of reading achievement is due to factors that are largely outside of the control of the individual. They may have had poor role models who did not demonstrate good reading practices, such as reading to them at home when they were young. They may have had inadequate reading instruction in school. Or they may have one or more undiagnosed learning disabilities—among a myriad of other problems (Corley & Taymans, 2002).

Despite these challenges, most individuals who have had some schooling can read at least a few simple or commonly used words and can often use the context to figure out other words in books, documents, and newspapers. Most scholars and many literacy practitioners recognize that literacy is not an all-or-nothing skill but constitutes a continuum of abilities (Barton, 1994). Therefore, it is preferable—and more accurate—to refer to adult participants in ABE programs as low literate in regard to their reading and writing, rather than illiterate.

This chapter describes teaching and learning in adult literacy education. The chapter begins by providing a context for understanding important characteristics of adult learners in literacy programs. Because adult basic education is a fundamentally different system from that of the pre-K–12 education system, the preparation and qualifications of adult literacy teachers are somewhat different from those found in elementary and secondary schools. Thus, some background is provided about the preparation of ABE teachers and the roles and responsibilities of the volunteer tutors who are the backbone of the ABE system. The next section of the chapter describes reading instruction in ABE classrooms in terms of practices and activities that are aimed at developing both the component skills of reading and the cognitive strategies that enable more effective reading. In addition to teaching reading, many ABE programs also help adult learners to write and to use basic math or numeracy skills. Therefore, writing and math instruction are also described, as is computer-assisted instruction that is used to supplement adults' reading, writing, and numeracy abilities. Finally, learning in ABE programs is discussed, with particular emphasis on learners' perceptions of the benefits derived from their participation in basic skills programs.

THE CONTEXT FOR TEACHING AND LEARNING IN ABE

Many children and adults who struggle to read—slowly and without enjoyment—simply avoid reading. This lack of exposure to the printed word serves to further compound their reading problems, as they do not practice using the reading abilities that they have. This condition is called aliteracy. Reading is a significant contributor to the growth of vocabulary and, therefore, one's knowledge. Nagy and Anderson (1984) estimated that the least motivated middle school students read perhaps 100,000 words per year. Yet highly motivated middle school readers may read more than 10 million words per year! Thus, children who do not read very much do not see a variety of words in print and are, therefore, less likely to learn them. Because vocabulary knowledge directly contributes to reading comprehension (Stahl, 1983), the academic achievement gap between good and poor readers grows ever wider.

In many cases, adults who are not native English speakers also participate in ABE programs. Generally, these individuals are immigrants to the United States. Some of these adults have been well educated in their home countries and are fully literate in their native language, but not in English. Others may have had little or no schooling in their country of origin and can be said to be either low literate or illiterate in both their native language and English. Adults in both groups participate in English-as-a-second language (ESL) literacy programs. ESL programs are described in chapter 5.

Many children and adolescents who struggle with reading eventually drop out of school, and some then attempt to earn a General Educational Development diploma. The GED is a high school equivalency examination that is taken by thousands of older adolescents and adults each year. The GED test assesses reading and writing skills, as well as knowledge of school subjects such as math and history. Those adults whose reading skills are not sufficient to study for the GED attend classes in ABE programs.

ABE programs focus on teaching adults to read and write. ABE students may also learn basic math skills. State-funded ABE programs are typically offered through community colleges. Other ABE programs are provided by community-based or religious organizations at neighborhood centers, YMCAs, and local churches. Enrollment in ABE programs is typically free and open ended, meaning that adults can drop in and drop out of these programs at will. This is an important characteristic of ABE programs, because many low-literate adults lack the financial means to pay for classes, and they may have transportation or child-care problems that are barriers to their consistent participation. Because ABE participants are usually not required to attend classes, teachers are challenged to develop motivating instructional activities that can help adults learn to read. It is estimated that more than 100 hours of instructional time is required to increase an adult's reading skills by one full grade level (Sticht & Armstrong, 1994). Unfortunately, many ABE participants receive much less than this amount of instruction. Often, adults quit programs because they are bored with the instruction or frustrated by their lack of progress. Because of the attrition problem, some ABE programs require enrolled students to regularly attend classes.

Adults' motivations for participating in ABE programs are varied. Many individuals, of course, want to improve their reading and writing skills. They are often prompted to do so to get and hold on to a job, or to assist their children with homework. Many low-literate parents want to be positive role models for their children. By showing their children that they are learning to read, they hope to inspire them to work hard and to persist in school. Other adult learners profess a desire to read the Bible or the newspaper, or to read letters from family members or correspondence from businesses such as utility companies. For many older adults in ABE programs, learning to read has been a lifelong desire that they are finally able to pursue.

It is not unusual to find a wide age range of adult participants in ABE classrooms. Coupled with the diversity of ages is a range in reading ability. Such diversity of skills, knowledge, and life experiences owing to differences in students' ages creates special demands for ABE teachers in these multilevel classrooms. Smaller class sizes, greater structure and enforcement of rules guiding classroom behavior, and individualized learning plans are some of the strategies that ABE teachers have employed to meet the needs of youth and adult learners (Hayes, 2000).

ABE instruction is typically provided in two ways. First, many formal programs, such as those offered through community colleges, employ teachers to provide literacy instruction in classrooms of a dozen or more students. Many ABE teachers are hired on a part-time basis, although most programs have at least a few full-time teachers. Second, some programs rely exclusively on volunteer tutors to provide one-on-one instruction to adult learners.

Typically, volunteer-based literacy programs are run by community groups or religious organizations. Literacy tutors often receive their training through federally funded programs such as AmeriCorps and the Peace Corps. Others may receive training from literacy advocacy groups such as ProLiteracy Worldwide, the oldest and largest nongovernmental literacy organization in the world. Many ABE programs employ a mix of professional teachers and volunteer tutors. Federal legislation embodied in the 1998 Workforce Investment Act has increased program accountability, however, and now requires measurable outcomes for adult learners. These changes have prompted calls for increasing the professional profile of ABE teachers and tutors (Sabatini, Ginsburg, & Russell, 2002).

ABE TEACHER PREPARATION

The majority of ABE teachers have elementary or secondary school teaching experience or credentials. Their teaching experiences provide valuable knowledge that they can draw upon to help them to effectively manage the ABE classroom and create interesting activities and assignments that are engaging for adult learners. Yet a significant portion of the ABE teacher population has little or no teaching experience prior to teaching adult learners (Smith & Hofer, 2003). These individuals are often drawn to ABE teaching out of a desire to help others, or because they enjoy working with adults. Many but not all states require ABE teachers to be certified teachers in elementary or secondary education. Only one state, Alabama, requires a master's degree in adult education for ABE teachers. Because the majority of states do not require ABE teachers to have professional preparation in adult education, there is no guarantee that these teachers are well equipped to effectively teach adult learners.

Generally, only a modest amount of preparation or training is provided to ABE teachers before they begin teaching adult learners. Smith and Hofer (2003) surveyed ABE teachers and found that more than half (53%) had no formal coursework in adult education. To compensate for this lack of teacher preparation, some ABE programs offer orientation programs for new teachers. These programs provide descriptions of adult learners' characteristics, information about how to teach reading, and a few basic concepts of classroom management. Thereafter, the opportunities for ABE teachers to improve their skills and knowledge are mostly confined to professional development programs that are offered by state adult education offices (Smith & Hofer, 2003). Such programs often include off-site workshops, although ABE teachers may lack the means to participate in them if transportation and other costs are not covered by their ABE program. Therefore, there is little uniformity in the skills and knowledge of ABE teachers, and few professional standards that they are required to achieve and maintain.

Tutors

Classroom instruction in ABE programs is frequently supplemented by one-on-one tutoring that is provided by a volunteer literacy tutor. The tutor may work closely with the ABE teacher to design a program of independent learning for the adult. Frequently, tutors provide the only reading instruction that the adult learner receives, as some ABE programs have no formal classes for literacy instruction. One-on-one instruction can be intensive and provides an opportunity for the tutor and tutee to establish a close relationship. Adult learners are often ashamed of their poor reading skills, so having a trusting relationship with a tutor who is encouraging and nonjudgmental is deemed to be very important to adults' success in reading. Yet many literacy tutors feel unprepared to teach reading and report feelings of frustration at the slow progress of their tutees (Belzer, 2006c). Because the tutors are generally very able readers themselves, they may hold unrealistic expectations about adult tutees' abilities to learn to read. While many literacy tutors can achieve much success with their adult students, it is evident that the preparation of tutors is even more inconsistent than that of ABE teachers. Belzer (2006c) found that tutors used only a few instructional strategies and that these were largely ineffective in helping their tutees learn to read.

Literacy Instruction in ABE

Despite the fact that the purpose of ABE is to teach adults to read, often very little explicit reading instruction takes place in ABE classrooms. Teachers may lead large-group lessons in which students complete letter and word identification drills, or the teacher may read aloud while students listen. Teachers often cannot provide individualized instruction for learners because of large class sizes and the wide range of learner abilities that are typical within ABE classrooms.

Robinson-Geller and Lipnevich (2006) surveyed 695 ABE teachers in 12 states to determine their instructional practices. Three types of instruction were identified. These were teacher-led groups, where teachers initiate and terminate class discussions, utilize commercially published instructional materials, and emphasize basic skills; individual group instruction, where basic skills are emphasized and all learners work on the same materials but at their own pace while the teacher works with individual students; and meaning making, where learners' interactions are encouraged, learning is connected to their lives, they learn about topics of personal interest, and they make decisions about classroom content and activities. They found that 14.9 percent of teachers reported using some combination of all three approaches in their classrooms. Another 14.5 percent reported using meaning-making approaches. A slightly smaller percentage (13.7%) reported using a combination of meaning making and individualized group instruction with a basic skills emphasis. Nearly 10 percent (9.5%) reported using other approaches not captured by the above three categories. Thus, teachers appear to pick and choose what seems to work best for them and their students.

ASSESSMENT

Teachers rarely engage in systematic assessment of learners' needs or evaluate if their instruction has met individual learners' or groups' needs (Beder & Medina, 2001). Scores from standardized test, such as the Test of Adult Basic Education, which many ABE programs use, do not tell the teacher what the learner's skills deficits are or how to teach to remediate these deficits. Until recently, ABE teachers had few guides as to what kinds of skills to teach and lacked information about the best methods for teaching adults to read.

The best assessment practices are ongoing processes that enable both teachers and learners to gather and analyze data to inform instructional decisions. ABE teachers are encouraged to use a variety of assessment tools to identify and diagnose learners' skill deficits and to then design instruction to address these deficits. Assessment serves three purposes (McShane, 2005). The first purpose is to identify learners' goals, strengths, and needs. The information derived from this assessment is used for instructional planning. The second purpose is to monitor the learner's progress. The third purpose is to determine the outcomes for the learner. Simply put, has the student learned to read at a given level of proficiency?

Ideally, assessments of learners' progress are an important dimension of teaching, but assessment is an area in which most ABE teachers have little preparation or experience. Learner assessments in ABE programs—if they occur at all—tend to happen only two times: upon initial entry into the program (to determine the learner's grade-level reading ability) and at the end of the program (i.e., when the learner takes the GED test). Ongoing learner assessment to track progress or for the purposes of diagnosing learning deficits, or to modify instruction, is uncommon.

Programs that receive federal funding are required to gather standardized test data on students to assess their progress, as mandated by Title II of the 1998 Workforce Investment Act. The WIA established the National Reporting System for Adult Education, a national accountability system for adult education programs. ABE programs satisfy National Reporting System requirements by reporting both pre- and post-test data. However, there is some indication that enrollment began to drop when ABE programs implemented more widespread testing more to comply with the National Reporting System (Sticht, 2004).

TEACHING READING

The National Reading Panel (2001) has identified five components of reading ability: phonemic awareness, decoding, fluency, vocabulary, and comprehension. Phonemic awareness is the ability to detect individual speech sounds within words, which is necessary to accurately decode words. Decoding refers to word identification, and it involves making letter-to-sound correspondences to recognize printed words. Fluency means rapid, accurate reading. Nonfluent readers read slowly and stumble over words. They often have difficulty comprehending what they read because they focus their attention on accurately decoding individual words rather than getting the gist or meaning of the text. Phonemic awareness, decoding, and fluency are considered print-based skills. Vocabulary refers to the person's knowledge of word meanings. Vocabulary growth occurs best through print exposure—that is, reading—rather than through direct instruction or oral language (e.g., watching television). Comprehension is the goal of reading—to understand the ideas conveyed in the written text. Comprehension requires knowledge of words and of the world (Hirsch, 2003). Vocabulary and comprehension are considered meaning-based skills.

During the 1990s, the U.S. government took a significant interest in improving adult literacy education. For example, the National Research Council, which is part of the National Academies, advocated adult reading instruction emphasizing mastery of both print-based and meaning-based skills so that all five reading components are addressed. Also, the Partnership for Reading—a collaborative effort among three federal agencies (the National Institute for Literacy, the National Institute of Child Health and Human Development, and the U.S. Department of Education)—was established in 2000. The Partnership for Reading brought together findings from reading research to better inform the educational community and to help all people—children, youths, and adults—learn to read well.

Subsequently, during the George W. Bush administration, the partnership was authorized by the No Child Left Behind Act, which was enacted by Congress in 2001. That year, the Partnership for Reading produced materials for dissemination to ABE teachers that informed them about instructional approaches and strategies that may be useful for teaching the five reading components. More recently, however, the Bush administration has shown little interest in adult literacy education, preferring to focus on reading improvement in the early school years. Also, despite the efforts of the Partnership for Reading to produce guidelines for teaching that are helpful to ABE teachers, there is no comprehensive body of research that has distinguished between effective and ineffective reading instruction methods for adults.

Having little research to guide them, both ABE teachers and tutors tend to be unsystematic in their approaches to reading instruction. Under the best of circumstances, adult literacy teachers and tutors draw upon what they know about reading instruction as it is practiced in the primary grades. ABE teachers' knowledge of reading instruction may be based upon their experience as elementary teachers, or drawn from professional development workshops or their recollections of their own experiences in school.

Phonemic Awareness Instruction

Because adult nonreaders have little awareness of phonemes (the individual sounds of spoken English) and beginning readers have difficulty manipulating phonemes (Curtis & Kruidenier, 2005), it is believed that they require specific instruction in phonemic awareness. Such instruction has been shown to increase reading achievement for some adult learners (Gold & Johnson, 1982). Generally, explicit instruction—that is, the direct and sequenced teaching of letter-sound relationships—is recommended. In this way, students learn the different sounds that are associated with letters (/ c / a / t /) and letter combinations (/ sh / ph / ous /). A disadvantage of direct instruction is that lessons tend to be drill-and-skill activities that are dull and devoid of meaning for learners.

Some scholars argue that direct instruction is not a useful approach to reading development. Krashen (1993), for example, claims that language is too complex to be taught one phoneme or word at a time, that people can and do learn to read without receiving formal instruction, and, further, that the evidence supporting direct instruction is modest. The effects of direct instruction tend to be very small and to disappear over time, according to Krashen.

Decoding Instruction

The National Reading Panel (2001) recommends that decoding or word analysis be taught together with phonemic awareness in the primary grades. This recommendation has also been applied to adults, although there is little research on adult learners to determine if this approach is effective. One of the activities that teachers can use to promote decoding ability is to have learners convert both individual letters and letter combinations into their phonemes, blending them together to form words (/ c / + / a / + / t / + / ch / = catch). These activities can be done both orally and in writing. Alternatively, new readers can look at new, unfamiliar words and break down the letters and associated sounds and then put them back together. Creative ABE teachers find ways to make these learning activities interesting and fun, often through the use of games and classroom contests.

Fluency Instruction

Repeated practice at reading—both silently and orally—is recommended to promote fluent reading for adult beginning readers (Curtis & Kruidenier,

2005). The more exposure new readers have to the printed word, the more familiar and comfortable they will become with reading. This approach is consistent with Krashen's (1993) view that people (both children and adults) learn to read by reading. An advantage of repeated reading practice is that the teacher can provide immediate corrective feedback about the reader's accuracy and reading rate (i.e., how quickly he or she is reading) and can quickly determine where the reader is experiencing difficulty (e.g., lengthy words, unfamiliar words). A potential disadvantage is that it is time consuming for the teacher to observe the reader. Having the student use a tape recorder to audio-record his or her oral reading for later playback is a timesaving method that teachers sometimes use to assess readers' fluency and provide individual feedback.

Vocabulary Instruction

Curtis (2006) describes four typical approaches to vocabulary instruction: direct instruction, differentiating word meanings, promoting word consciousness, and engaging in wide reading. Direct instruction is both intensive and systematic. Teachers provide learners with numerous exposures to new words and opportunities to use these words when speaking and writing. Using new words in speaking and writing enables learners to extend the meanings of words, that is, the uses of words in new contexts. Teachers often rely upon established word lists that contain common, everyday vocabulary, along with more abstract words, and low-frequency words.

ABE teachers help adult learners to differentiate word meanings when they highlight distinctions among words (e.g., *capital* versus *capitol*). Word comparisons, classifications, and analogies are all useful activities. For more advanced students, semantic mapping can be used—students make visual representations of the relationships that exist among vocabulary words, using lines and arrows to show connections among the word and related concepts.

The promotion of word consciousness entails nurturing students' awareness of and interest in words and word meanings. One such activity is having students generate creative but accurate uses of specific vocabulary words in sentences. Another approach is to have students investigate word meanings by using dictionaries and other printed materials.

Although these direct instruction approaches are widely used, Stanovich (2000) notes that direct instruction is not an effective means for extensive vocabulary learning. Nagy, Herman, and Anderson (1985) argue that learners acquire word meanings ten times faster by reading alone than through intensive vocabulary instruction. Still, reading by itself may not be sufficient to ensure that new readers acquire a rich and varied vocabulary. ABE teachers must supplement adult learners' free reading activities by creating opportunities for students to practice using the new words they have encountered in their reading (e.g., writing and talking about what they have read).

Reading Comprehension Instruction

The language experience approach is a commonly used method in which learners orally recite a story that is transcribed by the teacher or tutor. The story may be about something that the individual has experienced firsthand, or it could be a fictional tale. The transcribed narrative is then used as instructional material for reading, writing, speaking, and listening activities (Taylor, 1993). Thus, the learner's own words are used, which provides powerful motivation for word recognition, vocabulary development, and comprehension. Such an approach also conveys to learners that their ideas are important and valued (Purcell-Gates, 1987).

Direct instruction of reading comprehension, like the teaching of phonemic awareness and decoding, involves teacher-led instructional procedures. Typically, students are given specific task instructions, and the teacher directs students' practice and skill building and provides immediate corrective feedback. The direct instruction of reading comprehension has been demonstrated to be effective with some young learners (Stevens, 1991). Less evidence is available regarding the effectiveness of direct instruction approaches with adults. Alamprese (2001) has reported preliminary observations, but not yet the results, of a study of five ABE programs in which reading is explicitly taught in structured, organized classes, and the instructional content is sequenced.

In these programs, an organized series of exercises and activities provides the instructional content. The ABE teachers use reading passages that have highly relevant content for adults for different comprehension exercises. The passages are also judged by their teachers to be reading-level appropriate. Other activities are aimed at developing phonemic awareness, reading fluency, and vocabulary skills and knowledge. The teachers foster high levels of learner engagement by involving all students in instruction, such as by having them take turns working when completing whole-class exercises and by encouraging their participation in discussions. Finally, the teachers also give concrete feedback and verbal praise when students correctly respond to prompts and questions, and they elicit praise from other learners.

Little evidence exists that ABE teachers actively encourage adult learners to read books and other print materials, such as newspapers and magazine, outside class. This lack of encouragement to participate in authentic reading (and to practice one's reading skills) tends to reinforce the notion that students should only read school materials (e.g., workbooks) and that real-life reading is somehow different from the kinds of reading activities that take place in the classroom (Belzer, 2006a). Adult learners cannot improve their reading comprehension and increase their vocabularies if they do not practice reading a variety of text materials. Further, they are unlikely to acquire a positive attitude about reading and will avoid reading for pleasure.

Strategy Instruction

It is also important for new adult readers to develop reading comprehension strategies. A strategy is a conscious activity that is initiated to improve one's cognitive performance, as when reading. An example of a simple comprehension monitoring strategy is to ask oneself, "How well do I understand this passage?" If the reader determines that he or she has not fully comprehended the text, then one of several possible actions may follow. The reader might ignore this lack of understanding and continue to read the text, assuming that the meaning will become clear. Alternatively, the reader might go back and reread the passage to try to get the gist of it. Or the reader might ask for assistance from the teacher. Most new readers do not possess such strategies and fail to spontaneously adopt them; they must therefore be taught strategies that will aid their comprehension. Teachers can demonstrate and model these strategies and have learners practice using them and then provide corrective feedback as needed.

Prepackaged Programs

Another approach to teaching reading in ABE programs is to employ one of four varieties of commercially available programs or instructional systems. These four programs are the Lindamood-Bell Learning Process, which is designed for learners with reading disabilities who also have poor auditory skills and teaches them alternate ways to perceive the various sounds in English; the Orton-Gillingham method, which is a multisensory structured language approach that adheres to direct, explicit teaching of English phonology; the Slingerland Approach, which is also a multisensory, structured language approach to teaching language skills; and the Wilson Reading System, which teaches students word structure and language through 12 sequenced steps. The Wilson program targets students with specific language learning disabilities such as dyslexia. Proponents of all four programs claim that these work well for learners who have been unsuccessful in other reading programs.

An advantage of these programs is that they are highly structured and systematic and provide good instructional materials. Typically, teachers learn the instructional scope and sequence of the programs' curricula through participation in professional development workshops and other training sessions. A significant weakness of these programs is that none have been proven in independent research to be effective for reading instruction in the general population of nonliterate adults. No randomized trial studies wherein students are randomly assigned to the commercial programs and to other forms of instruction have been conducted. Further, there is no way to determine if teachers who use these programs adhere faithfully to the established methods and procedures. Therefore, literacy researchers do not know if these commercial programs are truly better for teaching reading than teachers' idiosyncratic methods.

Other Instructional Activities

Having students complete reading tasks in commercially produced workbooks is a staple of most ABE classrooms. These workbooks provide an organization and structure for teaching that might otherwise be missing in many classrooms. Students can complete letter and word identification tasks, learn new vocabulary, and read brief passages and respond in writing to questions about what they have read. While students are completing assignments in their workbooks, the teacher can move around the classroom and provide individual assistance to those who need it. A limitation of workbooks is that the materials and tasks are typically neither interesting nor motivating for the student. Also, because students are working independently in their books, they have few opportunities to share what they are learning with others.

WRITING

In addition to reading instruction, some ABE classes also focus on developing adult learners' writing skills. Learning to write can help to reinforce reading ability. Writing provides the first opportunity many low-literate adults have ever had to read the words that they, not others, have produced (Purcell-Gates, 1987). Thus, writing is a tremendously powerful activity for ABE students. Perhaps even more than learning to read, being able to write imbues the adult learner with a sense of personal identity as a literate person.

Unfortunately, as Belzer and St. Clair (2005) point out, we do not know very much about how writing is taught to adult learners because there has been little research on ABE writing instruction. Generally, ABE writing instruction appears to be even less systematic than the teaching of reading. The focus of instruction is often on the mechanics of writing—spelling, punctuation, and grammar—which are, of course, important but lower-order skills. Attending primarily to these basics of writing does little to encourage adult learners to actually write. There is some evidence that when ABE writing instruction occurs, it focuses on helping learners attain the minimum skills necessary to pass the GED writing test (Halbrook, 1999). Again, such a limited mastery approach does little to promote independent writing activities among adult learners.

Despite the pervasiveness of the mechanics-based approach to writing, a few ABE writing teachers do encourage adult learners to write extended and creative texts. Some ABE teachers allow learners to write about topics of their own choice. These teachers encourage personal, expressive writing in which students commit their thoughts, wishes, feelings, and personal goals to paper. Students' writings may take the form of correspondence, autobiographies, or daily journal writing. Keeping a personal journal is often encouraged as a way for students to regularly practice their writing skills.

An approach called process writing has gained favor over the past two decades in K–12 and higher education and has made some inroads into ABE writing instruction. A process-oriented writing approach takes the view that writing is a problem-solving activity and, therefore, the writer should engage in planning prior to writing . Students are encouraged to define their purpose for writing, identify their audience, and employ a variety of writing strategies. Prewriting (e.g., thinking about the audience, creating an outline) is also emphasized. Students receive carefully crafted corrective feedback from the teacher and then have multiple opportunities to revise their work. In doing so, they discover that any kind of learning—whether a skill such as writing or a content area such as history—involves recursive rather than linear thinking processes.

Some progressive ABE instructors develop writing workshops in their classrooms, often incorporating process writing and other creative writing activities. Learners not only practice their basic writing skills but also read the stories, poems, and other narratives that they have written before audiences of fellow students, teachers, family members, and friends. They also read and critique the writing of their fellow students. In some workshops, students' writing is assembled in a book that is printed and disseminated to others, providing further confirmation to students of the value of their own words and ideas.

NUMERACY

Numeracy is defined by the U.S. Department of Education (n.d.) as "the ability to interpret, apply, and communicate mathematical information." Numeracy is synonymous with math literacy. Generally, adults who are learning to read and write also need to improve their basic math skills. Numeracy instruction typically focuses on improvement in four areas: understanding numbers, data analysis (statistics and probability), geometry and measurement, and algebraic patterns and functions.

Unfortunately, aside from those ABE teachers who have professional backgrounds as math teachers, ABE teachers often have no formal training in math education (Schmitt, 2002). As Belzer and St. Clair (2005) note, math instruction is often ignored altogether in ABE classrooms, as it is not considered as essential to adults' success as reading. This is indeed unfortunate, as most adults today are constantly faced with everyday tasks that require some basic math skills.

Commercially prepared materials tend to predominate in ABE math instruction. Students engage in skill-and-drill activities, solving problems out of workbooks, and getting corrective feedback from the instructor. While there is nothing wrong with getting lots of practice at math problem solving, the kinds of math problems found in workbooks are highly decontextualized and encourage routinization in problem solving and an understanding of mathematics that is rooted in external authority and rules rather than personal experience (Tout & Schmitt, 2002). Learning research has shown, however, that adults learn more quickly and effectively when they work on problems that are embedded in real-life situations and activities and when they can create their own problem-solving procedures.

The Adult Numeracy Network advocates the adoption of the following approaches for improving adult learners' numeracy skills and knowledge: First, math should be taught in the context of real-life and workplace situations to which most adults can easily relate. Second, learner-centered approaches should be used so that learners see the personal relevance of what they are learning. Third, an interdisciplinary approach should integrate math with other content areas. Fourth, new learning should be linked to previous learning and promote learners' interests in math. Finally, math concepts should be taught before math rules. Effective numeracy instructors use models, examples, and learners' real-world experiences to convey concepts before they teach them formulas and equations.

COMPUTER-ASSISTED INSTRUCTION

Because there are few effective guides for using technology to enhance ABE instruction, most ABE teachers employ computers and other technologies (i.e., audiovisual media) in a trial-and-error fashion. A survey of programs conducted a decade ago (Sabatini & Ginsburg, 1998) found that only about one-third of ABE programs in the Midwest described themselves as significant users of computers for any purposes, including instruction. It is likely, however, given the rapid and extensive infusion of computing technology into all kinds of social and educational institutions, combined with greater affordability of the hardware and software, that computer-assisted instruction (CAI) is more common in ABE classrooms today.

CAI may be either supplemental or stand alone. Supplemental use occurs when the teacher incorporates CAI into teacher-led instruction and the computer is then used to reinforce students' learning. CAI is frequently used in situations where adult learners can work independently on drill-and-skill activities (i.e., learning vocabulary) or self-tests (e.g., GED practice examinations).

In stand-alone usage, the computer is the principal vehicle for instructional delivery. Lessons and activities might be embedded in instructional software that is used by the students. More advanced software offers interactive features, which gives some control to the learner but also features some of the structure and content that a teacher would otherwise provide. Effective software programs provide consistent corrective feedback for learners. Learners might access other online literacy-related lessons, such as those offered by the Public Broadcasting System's *PBS LiteracyLink*. An advantage of stand-alone uses of technology is that learners can work at their own pace, pausing or stopping the program at any time, rather than trying to keep up with the pace of the teacher's instruction.

Using technology in adult literacy instruction opens up a world of possibilities that go beyond basic literacy. Students can, for example, be taught to use computer programs such as word processors, databases and spreadsheets, desktop publishing, Web page authoring, and presentation software (i.e., PowerPoint). These programs are very useful in that they provide opportunities for adult learners to practice writing; play with written language; use numbers and math; combine text with graphics, animation, and video; and develop skills that are valued in the workplace.

ABE teachers can also take advantage of the numerous instructional videotapes and CDs and streaming videos on the Internet that demonstrate lessons and activities that have been developed to support adult literacy instruction. Creative and imaginative teachers find exciting, innovative ways to use these media in their ABE classrooms either alone or in combination with CAI. Kruidenier (2001) reports that CAI has been found to be at least as effective as non-CAI for increasing learners' reading achievement. CAI appears to be most effective for somewhat more advanced ABE students (i.e., those who read at the pre–secondary school level). Finally, CAI makes it possible to more readily integrate the multiple components of reading instruction—word recognition, vocabulary, and comprehension.

Aside from teaching adults reading, writing, basic math, and computer applications, a variety of other activities and programs that support adult literacy learning may be found in ABE classrooms and programs. Adult learners often come to ABE programs with a number of problems in their lives, only some of which are directly related to their low literacy. These problems may include domestic abuse, drug and alcohol use, and chronic unemployment. Thus, the provision of personal counseling can be an important component of a comprehensive ABE program. While teachers typically do not provide formal counseling, they may often give informal guidance by being good listeners or suggesting possible solutions to problems.

STUDENTS' LITERACY LEARNING

There are numerous reports in the literature with adult learners' testimonials as to the personal and educational benefits they have derived from participating in ABE and other literacy development programs. These testimonials are powerfully persuasive in suggesting that low-literate adults benefit in several important ways from their participation in such programs. Yet evidence from more objective studies paints a very different picture of the effects of ABE programs on adult literacy. These studies raise important questions about the extent of adults' literacy learning as a result of ABE instruction.

Two large studies provide compelling evidence that ABE programs may not be helping adults to improve their literacy abilities. Friedlander and Martinson (1996) compared the literacy proficiencies of adults in California who were randomly assigned to ABE classes to the proficiency of adults who were not. Both ABE students and non-ABE students were school dropouts and recipients of Aid to Families and Dependent Children benefits. Following ABE instruction (a period of several months), the standardized reading measures of participants were found not to differ from those of non-ABE adults, although more ABE participants had earned a GED than had the non-ABE adults.

Sheehan-Holt and Smith (2000) used data from the 1992 National Adult Literacy Survey to determine if participation in adult basic skills programs is associated with higher literacy proficiency scores and more extensive reading practices (e.g., reading books and newspapers). Adults who reported having ever participated in a basic skills program to improve their reading, writing, and/or math skills were compared to adults who were similar in terms of age, native language, educational attainment, and other important background variables. Adults who had participated in basic skills programs did not differ from adults who had not taken part in such programs in regard to their reading abilities. There were a few differences in regard to reading practices, as those who had participated in a basic skills program in the workplace had more extensive document reading practices than other groups of adults. Combined, the findings from these two studies raise serious questions about the literacy benefits that adults might gain through their participation in basic skills programs.

Thus, on one hand, individual participants offer impassioned testimonials that they have greatly benefited from their time in ABE programs. On the other hand, large-scale studies comprised of representative samples of adults show that the benefits are small to nonexistent. What, then, might explain the discrepancy between these two kinds of results?

One explanation is that the kinds of personal benefits that individuals derive from participating in an adult education program cannot be easily or adequately captured by objective tests of literacy proficiency. As noted previously in this chapter, adults enroll in ABE programs for many reasons. While most participants do want to learn to read or to improve their existing reading skills, many may exit programs satisfied that they can read a few simple texts or that they have expanded their intellectual or social boundaries. Thus, ABE participants may acquire just enough reading ability to do the things that they want to do, but not so much to show statistically meaningful changes from pre- to post-test.

Success and failure in regard to literacy learning are therefore relative concepts. Learners' perceptions of their experiences and outcome is every bit as valid as the evidence obtained from a standardized test of reading (Belzer, 2006b). What might objectively appear to be an adult's failure to improve his or her reading skills might, for that adult, represent a success because the individual attended class every week, made new friends, and learned to feel less ashamed of his or her poor reading ability. Certainly, other conditions are also related to ABE students' literacy learning as well as their failure to improve their performance on standardized literacy tests. These conditions include participants' persistence in attending and completing an ABE program in spite of myriad obstacles to their success. The quality and the kinds of instruction that adults receive play a large role in their success, as suggested previously in this chapter. Adults' persistence or success in ABE is related to the extent to which the literacy tasks they encounter in the classroom are similar to and connected with the literacy tasks that they face in their everyday lives.

CONCLUSIONS

ABE teachers and tutors engage in a wide variety of instructional practices and activities to assist low-literate adults who are learning to read and write and to use basic math skills. Because there is no single path to becoming an ABE teacher, and few educational requirements, adult literacy teachers often feel challenged and frustrated in helping learners improve their literacy skills. Although adult learners are often faced by numerous barriers to participating and learning in ABE classes, many are successful in acquiring the literacy skills they need to function effectively in their homes, workplaces, and communities. Often, however, these successes cannot be objectively determined from standardized literacy tests.

REFERENCES

Alamprese, J. A. (2001). *Strategies for teaching reading to first-level ABE learners.* Paper presented at the Commission on Adult Basic Education Conference, Memphis, TN.

Barton, D. (1994). *Literacy: An introduction to the ecology of written language.* Oxford: Blackwell.

Beder, H., & Medina, P. (2001). *Classroom dynamics in adult literacy education* (NCSALL Report No. 18). Retrieved August 22, 2006, from http.//www.ncsall.net/fileadmin/resources/research/report18.pdf

Belzer, A. (2006a). Influences on the reading practices of adults in ABE. *Focus on Basics, 8*(B). Retrieved August 22, 2006 from http://www.ncsall.net/?id = 1103.

Belzer, A. (2006b). Learners on learning to read. *Focus on Basics, 8*(B). Retrieved August 22, 2006, from http://www.ncsall.net/?id = 1110.

Belzer, A. (2006c). What are they doing in there? Case studies of volunteer tutors and adult literacy learners. *Journal of Adolescent & Adult Literacy, 49*(7), 560–572.

Belzer, A., & St. Clair, R. (2005). Back to the future: Implications of the neo-positivist research agenda for adult education. *Teacher's College Record, 107*(9), 1393–1412.

Corely, M. A., & Taymans, J. M. (2001). Adults with learning disabilities: A review of the literature. In J. Comings, B. Garner, & C. Smith (Eds.), *The annual review of adult learning and literacy* (Vol. 3, pp. 44–83). San Francisco: Jossey-Bass.

Curtis, M. E. (2006). The role of vocabulary instruction in adult basic education. In J. Comings, B. Garner, & C. Smith (Eds.), *Review of adult learning and literacy: Connecting research, policy, and practice* (Vol. 6, pp. 43–70). Mahwah, NJ: Erlbaum.

Curtis, M. E., & Kruidenier, J. (2005). *A summary of scientifically based research principles.* Washington, DC: National Institute for Literacy.

Friedlander, D., & Martinson, K. (1996). Effects of mandatory education for adult AFDC recipients. *Educational Evaluation and Policy Analysis, 18,* 327–337.

Gold, P. C., & Johnson, J. A. (1982). Prediction of achievement in reading, self-esteem, auding, and verbal language by adult illiterates in a psychoeducational tutorial program. *Journal of Clinical Psychology, 38*(3), 513–522.

Halbrook, A. (1999). Formulaic writing: Blueprint for mediocrity. *GED Items, 3,* 8–9.

Hayes, E. (2000). Youth in adult literacy education programs. In J. Comings, B. Garner, & C. Smith (Eds.), *The annual review of adult learning and literacy* (Vol. 1, pp. 74–110). San Francisco: Jossey-Bass.

Hirsch, E. D. (2003, Spring). Reading comprehension requires knowledge—Of words and the world. *American Educator, 10,* 12–13, 16–22, 28–29, 44–45.

Krashen, S. (1993). *The power of reading: Insights from the research.* Englewood, CO: Libraries Unlimited.

Kruidenier, J. (2001). *Research-based principles for adult basic education reading instruction.* Washington, DC: Partnership for Reading.

McShane, S. (2005). *Applying research in reading instruction for adults: First steps for teachers.* Washington, DC: National Institute for Literacy.

Nagy, W. E., & Anderson, R. C. (1984). How many words are there in printed school English? *Reading Research Quarterly, 19,* 304–330.

Nagy, W. E., Herman, P. A., & Anderson, R. C. (1985). Learning words from context. *Reading Research Quarterly, 20,* 233–253.

National Reading Panel. (2001). *Report of the National Reading Panel: Teaching children to read.* Washington, DC: National Institute of Child Health and Human Development.

Purcell-Gates, V. (1987). *Other people's words: The cycle of low literacy.* Cambridge, MA: Harvard University Press.

Robinson-Geller, P., & Lipnevich, A. A. (2006). Instructional practices of ABE and GED teachers. *Focus on Basics, 8*(B). Retrieved August 22, 2006, from http://www.ncsall. net/?id = 1103

Sabatini, J., & Ginsburg, L. (1998). *Instructional technology utilization survey of mid-western adult literacy programs* (NCAL Report No. 98–01). Philadelphia: National Center on Adult Literacy.

Sabatini, J., Ginsburg, L., & Russell, M. (2002). Professionalization and certification for teachers in adult basic education. In J. Comings, B. Garner, & C. Smith (Eds.), *Annual review of adult learning and literacy* (Vol. 3, pp. 203–247). San Francisco: Jossey-Bass.

Schmitt, M. J. (2002, July). Seeking interventions to improve adult numeracy instruction in the United States: Hybrids only need apply. *Mathematics education in the South*

Pacific: Proceedings of the annual conference of the Mathematics Education Research Group of Australasia Incorporated (Vol. 1). Auckland, New Zealand.

Sheehan-Holt, J. K., & Smith, M. C. (2000). Does basic skills education affect adults' literacy proficiencies and reading practices. *Reading Research Quarterly, 35*(2), 226–243.

Smith, C., & Hofer, J. (2003). *The characteristics and concerns of adult basic education teachers* (NCSALL Report No. 26). Cambridge, MA: National Center for the Study of Adult Learning and Literacy.

Stahl, S. A. (1983). Differential word knowledge and reading comprehension. *Journal of Reading Behavior, 15,* 33–50.

Stanovich, K. (2000). *Progress in understanding reading: Scientific foundations and new frontiers.* New York: Guilford Press.

Stevens, R. J. (1991). The effects of cooperative learning and direct instruction in reading comprehension strategies on main idea identification. *Journal of Educational Psychology, 83*(1), 8–16.

Sticht, T. G. (2004). The year 2001 in review. In J. Comings, B. Garner, & C. Smith (Eds.), *Review of adult learning and literacy: Connecting, research, policy, and practice* (Vol. 4, pp. 1–16). Mahwah, NJ: Erlbaum.

Sticht, T. G. & Armstrong, W. B. (1994). *Adult literacy in the United States: A compendium of quantitative data and interpretive comments.* San Diego, CA: San Diego Community College District.

Taylor, M. (1993). *The language experience approach and adult learners.* ERIC Document No. ED350887. Washington, DC: National Clearinghouse on Literacy Education. Retrieved August 22, 2006, from http://www.ericdigests.org/1993/approach.htm

Tout, D., & Schmitt, M. J. (2002). The inclusion of numeracy in adult basic education. In J. Comings, B. Garner, & C. Smith (Eds.), *The annual review of adult learning and literacy* (Vol. 3, pp. 152–202). San Francisco: Jossey-Bass.

U.S. Department of Education. (n.d.). *Frequently asked questions—ALL.* Retrieved August 22, 2006, from http://nces.ed.gov/surveys/all/faq_all.asp

Chapter Four

ADULT LITERACY EDUCATION PROGRAMS

Hal Beder

Adult literacy programs are the organizations that organize, manage, and conduct the work of adult literacy education at the local level. The Adult Learning Center (ALC) is an example of an adult literacy program. The ALC is located in the mid-Atlantic state of New Jersey and serves about 3,600 students each year. In 2004, the program employed 57 teachers and 28 support staff, making it a comparatively large program. The ALC has three full-time counselors, four full-time teachers, and three full-time administrators. It has classes in basic education, English as a second language, and GED preparation. In GED preparation classes, adult students prepare to pass the GED tests, and if they are successful, they are awarded high school certification. The ALC also has an adult high school program through which students can earn a school district diploma by meeting state standards and school district requirements. The ALC is open from 8:30 A.M. to 8:30 P.M. Monday through Thursday and 8:30 A.M. to 4:30 P.M. on Fridays. It is located in an urban neighborhood in a building that also houses the local school district's administrative offices.

Prospective students typically learn about the ALC through word of mouth or by referral from other community agencies, although the ALC does advertise through a brochure. New students seeking to enroll in the ALC first stop at the office, where they are greeted by the program director if she is in, or by a teacher if she is not. The director is very active in the community and is often away attending meetings.

Following a friendly greeting, new students are introduced to one of the counselors, who conducts the intake interview. One purpose of the interview is to determine the student's goals. This is an important step, because ALC staff members are very aware that their students are voluntary learners who come in order to meet their personal goals. If students can meet them, they will persist; if they cannot, they are likely to drop out. Establishing student goals is also a step in the National Reporting System, the accountability system that is mandated by the federal legislation that funds most of the ALC's classes. Next, students take the Test of Adult Basic Education, a literacy skills test. Although the Test of Adult Basic Education is commonly used by adult literacy programs, other tests are also used.

The Test of Adult Basic Education has two purposes. First, it is used as a diagnostic to determine students' skill levels in reading and math. Second, it is used as a pretest in the National Reporting System–mandated accountability standard for tested learning gain. Students who score at an 8th-grade level or higher on the Test of Adult Basic Education are typically assigned to a GED preparation class. Instruction in these classes is individualized. Students are assigned instructional materials appropriate to their grade level, and they work independently to complete the workbook exercises. The materials are geared to passing the GED tests. Students' work is corrected when they are finished, and if it is correct, the teacher supplies the student with more difficult materials and assistance, if needed. When a student is able to pass a GED practice test, the teacher recommends that he or she register to take the GED tests.

The ALC is a real program. Although it is larger and better funded than most programs, and although it has the reputation of being one of the best programs in the state, the process described above is typical of many adult literacy programs.

PROGRAM CHARACTERISTICS

Understanding adult literacy programs is important for at least two reasons. First, because these are the programs that organize, manage, and conduct the work of adult literacy education at the local level, understanding how they operate is critical to an understanding of how adult literacy education functions. Second, adult literacy programs are very different from the K–12 and higher education institutions with which most educators and policy makers are familiar. When educators make decisions that are based on the assumption that adult literacy programs are like K–12 or higher education institutions, their decisions are often inappropriate.

When most literacy education professionals speak of programs, they are referring to state and federally funded classroom-based operations that educate students in groups. This type of program will be the focus of this chapter. It must be acknowledged, however, that there is a large volunteer-based adult literacy sector that educates students through one-on-one tutoring, typically in homes and libraries. The largest volunteer agency, ProLiteracy America, has 1,200 affiliates and operates in all 50 states; it served 202,834 students in 2004–2005 (ProLiteracy America, n.d.). There are also many developmental skills programs maintained by community colleges. Students in developmental skills programs pay regular tuition and are considered to be enrolled at the community college. Although developmental skills courses generally do not count toward graduation requirements, students are eligible for financial aid and have access to all the services the college offers. As Chisman (2002) notes,

> Approximately one million adults attend developmental education classes nationwide each year. The content and method of instruction varies, and there has been no authoritative research comparing developmental courses with those supported by Title II funds. However, the existing evidence indicates that the goal of most developmental instruction is to upgrade the literacy, math and English language skills of students who would be placed in the middle or upper levels of Title II ABE, GED, or ESL programs. In many cases, developmental classes are virtually indistinguishable from adult education classes supported by Title II. (p. 10)

There are several factors that influence how adult literacy programs operate and cause them to differ from K–12 and higher education institutions. These include funding, organizational sponsorship, enrollment and attendance patterns, staffing, and structural marginality.

Funding

The great majority of adult literacy programs are grant funded. The largest federal source of funding is Title II of the Workforce Investment Act of 1998, the Adult Education and Family Literacy Act (AEFLA). In 2005, AEFLA funding was $560 million dollars (U.S. Department of Education, 2005). Under AEFLA, federal funds are dispersed to the states, which then allocate the funds to local programs through a competitive grants process. AEFLA programs are sometimes referred to as Title II programs.

The grant funding of adult literacy programs has major implications for how they operate. AEFLA, for example, stipulates that service is to be provided to those who are age 16 and older and are not enrolled or required to be enrolled in secondary school. It further stipulates that those served must "lack sufficient mastery of basic educational skills to enable the individuals to function effectively in society; … not have a secondary school diploma or its recognized equivalent, and have not achieved an equivalent level of education; or are unable to speak, read, or write the English Language" (Workforce Investment Act of 1998). These eligibility requirements translate into the three services most adult literacy programs provide: adult basic education, which is analogous to elementary education; adult secondary education, which generally focuses on teaching the skills needed to pass the GED tests; and English as a second language.

According to AEFLA, all states must match federal funding at the amount of at least 25 percent of their federal allocation, but some states allocate considerably more than the mandated minimum. State funding for California, Connecticut, Florida, Maine, Minnesota, and Oregon pays for 80 percent or more of their programs' costs. In contrast, Kansas, Mississippi, Nebraska, South Dakota, Tennessee, and Texas provide the minimum required to meet the AEFLA match (U.S. Department of Education, 2005).

While some adult literacy programs receive only AEFLA funding, others acquire grant funding from other sources as well. A 2001 New Jersey study found that there were 23 separate and independent sources of public funding that supported adult literacy programs in the state, and that these funds were administered by four state agencies (State Council on Adult Literacy Education Services, 2001). The report also found that while New Jersey's AEFLA funding stood at $13,396,286, the funding from all the grant sources that funded adult literacy education was approximately $100 million, of which $32 million came from Department of Education grants, $29 million came from the Department of Labor, and $35 million came from Department of Human Services grants. In other states, the situation is similar. In Massachusetts, programs may receive funding from AEFLA, Even Start, Special Education, Welfare, Head Start, Community Development Block Grants, the McKinney-Vento Homeless Assistance Act, and the Massachusetts Education Reform Act (Comings & Soricone, 2005).

For programs that have multiple grant funding streams, the result can be chaotic. The New Jersey report noted:

> Resource allocation and distribution is clearly an issue when we look at the impact of funding from 23 different programs in four state departments. Bureaucratic fragmentation produces disjointed resource allocation and this reeks havoc at the provider level. As one provider put it, "Currently we are operating 15 different grant programs to maintain the variety of programs we have here. This means 15 different funding streams, 15 different goals and objectives and targeted programs, plus 15 different reporting systems…. Each has different calendars, reporting forms and requirements. All of these are operating to provide basic skills instruction. The needs are the same, but because money is targeted, we must recruit different populations. But what we are teaching is very similar. Depending on the funding source and how people (clients) are labeled, if they are from one economic level you can serve them. If they are from another they cannot be serviced. If they are a certain age they go to one class. If they are over an age, they go somewhere else." (State Council on Adult Literacy Education Services, 2001, p.14)

The grants that a program seeks and is successful in acquiring determine who the program serves and, to some extent, how it serves them. Grant eligibility requirements target services to a multiplicity of populations, including the general low-literate public, welfare clients, the incarcerated, the homeless, low-literate families, and the employed at their worksites.

Under AEFLA, states have a considerable amount of latitude in how they spend their federal allocations. For that reason, the adult literacy education system varies from state to state. Some states have invested substantially in professional development—for example, Ohio, Pennsylvania, and Illinois have developed a system of resource centers that provide professional development—while other states do very little in professional development.

Grants also determine how much funding programs will receive, and because receiving a grant is not a certainty, programs face funding insecurity. In 2005, for example, the president's budget recommended that AEFLA funding be cut from $569 million to $207 million. Had not the funds been restored due to a massive advocacy campaign mounted by the adult literacy community, programs would have been decimated. Moreover, there is little doubt that adult literacy education programs are underfunded, at least in comparison to elementary and secondary education (Beder, 1996). In 2002, adult literacy education programs spent an average of $803 per participant, compared to $9,941 for elementary and secondary education (National Center for Educational Statistics, 2005).

Grant funding also requires that programs seek and administer grants. This adds significantly to the burden of administering programs. Grant applications have to be written, and reporting and accountability requirements must be met. Under Section 233 of AEFLA, programs are restricted to an expenditure of 5 percent for administrative costs. As Chisman (2002) notes, lack of resources for program administration severely constrains programs:

> Moreover, the management resource problem is at the program level because most programs in most states have at best one full-time staff member, the Program Director. With such limited managerial resources, it is virtually impossible for Title II programs to meet their managerial challenges as they should—it is remarkable that they meet them at all. (p. 22)

Belzer (2003) studied the impact of changes caused by welfare reform and the advent of the Workforce Investment Act in two grant programs on how programs operate. In 1996, the Personal Responsibility and Work Opportunity Reconciliation Act, which radically reformed how welfare was administered in the United States, was passed. As Belzer notes, prior to welfare reform, many states had adopted an education-before-work policy in the belief that those on welfare needed enhanced skills before they could be successful in the workforce. Although the specifics varied by states, grants from welfare-funded programs provided adult literacy education, and these grants were a major source of funding for many programs. Because welfare clients were not working, many welfare classes were conducted during the day and were able to meet 20 hours per week. Welfare reform, however, put work first, and many of the welfare clients who had attended literacy classes were slotted into jobs. As a result, some adult literacy programs were decimated. Their only recourse was to expand their evening classes to meet the needs of those who were now employed, but that hardly compensated for the decline of enrollment and program income.

In 1998, the Workforce Investment Act was passed, and the Adult Education Act, which had changed little since its inception in 1966, became section 2 of the Workforce Investment Act, also known as the Adult and Family Literacy Act. The AEFLA had a new requirement for accountability. Under the new accountability provisions, programs were now required to collect and report data on students' outcomes. One stipulated outcome was leaning gain, which meant that programs now had to pretest and post-test their clients if they wished to receive an AEFLA grant. Some states anticipated the new accountability requirements and established systems to deal with the requirements. Other states were caught nearly unaware. Collecting and reporting the data, especially the testing, placed a severe administrative burden on programs that lacked the staff to manage the accountability system and knew little about the fundamentals of testing. Responses to the accountability requirements noted by Belzer (2003) included turning away the least skilled students, who were less likely to show gains on the tests; focusing instruction more on workplace topics; and hiring new staff to collect accountability data. In respect to the shift in emphasis to the workforce, the director of one large program remarked:

> [The Workforce Investment Act is] looking for outcomes that are not necessarily relevant to all adult literacy programs. What are the outcomes on the reporting system that the feds want? How many people got jobs. Well, a program such as ours is not always looking to get a person a job, and the person is not necessarily coming into our program to look for a job. The student might need literacy because their family found out they don't have a high school diploma, for their self-esteem. They want to be able to help their children with school. They never had a high school diploma and it's a dream they want. A person could come in saying, "I can't read and I'm fondly admitting I can't read. Help me." The students in our school have different reasons why they're here. The feds would like us to get everyone a job with benefits and so that they can get out and help the economy of the country. It's not one size fits all. (Beder & Medina, 2005a)

Belzer (2003) categorized each program, depending on how the programs reacted to the vicissitudes of changes in grant requirements, as a refiner, a reinventor, or a resister. Refiner programs took the changes in grant requirements in stride and made minor changes to comply with the requirements. Most refiner programs had the capacity to make the mandated changes without major dislocation. In contrast, reinventor programs operated in ways that made compliance with mandated requirements difficult, and responding to the changes in the Workforce Investment Act funding necessitated major change.

Resister programs decided either to abandon AEFLA funding or not to comply with the new regulations in the hope that they would not be sanctioned.

Organizational Sponsorship

Adult literacy education programs are sponsored by several types of organizations. Programs sponsored by public schools predominate, with 54 percent in 2003, followed by community-based organizations at 24 percent, community colleges at 17 percent, and prisons at 7 percent (U.S. Department of Education, 2005). Thus, most adult literacy programs are not free-standing educational institutions like public schools or universities. They are attached to parent organizations, and they serve functions that are ancillary to the primary objectives of the organizations that sponsor them. This means that adult literacy programs are influenced by the regulations and policies of their sponsoring organizations. For example, in New Jersey, all teachers who work in public schools must be certified in a K–12 area. Consequently, all adult literacy teachers who work in public school–sponsored programs must be certified, even if their K–12 certification is in an area that has nothing to do with what they teach in adult literacy. The program director at a large mid-Atlantic program explained how being sponsored by a public school district influenced her program:

> How much space you have is determined by your local superintendent and so forth, so if you have limited space, you know, that determines certain kinds of decisions that you make in terms of how you allocate space. As you see by our room charts, we just about fill every slot for every hour of the 56 hours we are open per week. The pressures that are on the school district affect us. For example, you know, No Child Left Behind. One concrete thing I can say is that we have really shifted our focus to trying to actively recruit parents, because we feel that as far as school district goes, the one way we can really help them with the achievement of their kids is by, you know, educating the parents. So, certainly we've always recruited parents in the past, but this year in particular we doing this more actively, really trying to reach parents. (Beder & Medina, 2005b)

Enrollment and Attendance Patterns

Adult students who participate in literacy education are constrained by a multitude of problems that adults who live on marginal incomes face. Lack of transportation, arranging for child care, and shifting job schedules are just some of them. The result is a high dropout rate. When students drop out, spaces are left in the classroom. Due to attrition, an adult literacy class can simply evaporate. Given this situation, when new adult students arrive, they are typically immediately slotted into the spaces vacated by dropouts. The result is open enrollment. Open enrollment is abetted by the reality that funding is often predicated on the number of students served, and open enrollment maximizes the number served. The open-enrollment environment, then, is one in which students are constantly dropping out or stopping out, and new students are constantly enrolling in classes. This makes the traditional classroom instruction typical of the K–12 system problematic, as newly enrolled students are not privy to the subject matter teachers presented before they arrived. In essence, in open-enrollment programs that employ traditional classroom instruction, new students are behind before they even start.

Because of the same constraints that adult students will face and that sometimes lead them to drop out, tardiness and absenteeism are common. Individualized group instruction is a common response to open enrollment, absenteeism, and tardiness (Robinson-Geller, 2005). Describing individualized group instruction in a mid-Atlantic program, Beder, Tomkins, Medina, Riccioni, and Deng (2006) explain:

> In [individualized group instruction], students are tested at intake to assess their skill levels in reading and math. Then they are assigned to a classroom, where after a brief orientation, they are given materials appropriate to their diagnosed skill level. The materials are kept in large envelopes with the students' names written on them. They are deposited in file crates, picked up by the students when they come to class, and put back when the when the students leave. Students work independently on their materials. When they have completed an exercise, the teacher corrects the work and provides help if needed. If the work is essentially correct, the teacher assigns more difficult materials. Thus in [individualized group instruction], materials are the focus of teaching and learning, and students progress by completing progressively more advanced materials. (p. 2)

Since individualized group instruction students work at their own skill levels, they can begin and end work at any time and can pick up where they left off if they miss a class. Thus, individualized group instruction compensates for open enrollment, tardiness, and absenteeism (Robinson-Geller, 2005). Students' enrollment and attendance patterns are important factors that shape the teaching and learning technologies of adult literacy programs. These patterns also have significant implications for research on adult literacy education, since high attrition confounds many research designs.

Although participation in adult literacy is sometimes mandated for welfare clients, and although the courts sometimes mandate participation for offenders, by and large participation in adult literacy is voluntary. This means that programs are under pressure to satisfy the needs of their students, because if they do not, students will simply cease to attend.

Staffing

Eighty percent of the staff who work in adult literacy programs are part time (Chisman, 2002). Programs are typically headed by a director who reports to an official employed by the sponsoring agency. In public school–sponsored programs, this would usually be the school principal or superintendent. Part-time teachers typically arrive, teach their classes, and leave. For this reason, intercommunication among teachers is constrained, and this thwarts the ability of teachers to learn from each other.

Use of part-time staff is related to program size. In small programs that operate only in the evening, all staff, including the director, may be part time. In larger programs, the director is typically full time; some of the teachers may be full time, and the program operates both during the day and the evening. About half of the programs in the United States might be classified as small, operating on budgets of $200,000 or less (U.S. Department of Education, 2005).

Certification requirements for adult literacy teachers vary considerably by state. Kutner, Webb, and Matheson (1996) reported that 24 states require no certification to teach adult literacy, 15 states require K–12 certification, and 12 states require certification in adult literacy.

Structural Marginality

Due to conditions such as funding insecurity, underfunding, serving a function that is ancillary to the function of the sponsoring agency, and use of a part-time workforce, adult literacy programs tend to be structurally marginal. In other words, adult literacy programs experience a weak power position in relation to other organizations that seek to acquire educational resources.

Structural marginality begins at the state level. In most states, the official who is responsible for adult literacy, typically called the state director, is at the third or fourth level in the state department of education bureaucracy and has limited access to the centers of power. Because K–12 education is the business of most state departments of education, adult literacy frequently gets little attention (Chisman, 2002). When states are successful in acquiring additional resources for adult literacy programs, it is usually because of an idiosyncratic and fortuitous situation—a supportive governor, for example, or a supportive coalition of legislators. If, however, these external supporters leave the scene, or if the state finds itself in a financial crisis, everything gained can be lost. In one New England state, for example, the governor decided that adult literacy education would be one of his new initiatives. While policy staff made sound progress on reforms favorable to adult literacy, a serious budget crisis developed. Consequently, 13 agencies were completely defunded and the adult literacy initiative was quickly abandoned.

ISSUES FACING PROGRAMS

Quantity versus Quality

Because funds are limited, states and the programs to which they allocate funds are faced with two strategic options. The can emphasize service by serving as many students as possible or they can emphasize quality by serving fewer students and using the funds that are saved to invest in things that promote program quality, such as full-time teachers, professional development, and support staff (Comings & Soricone, 2005). Programs that emphasize service have lower costs per student because the funds are spread out among more students. Programs that emphasize quality have higher costs per student. In 2002, Georgia had the lowest cost per student ($208), while Vermont had the highest ($2,683), followed by Michigan ($2,301) (U.S. Department of Education, 2005). The disparity is striking.

Massachusetts has led the way in promoting the quality policy—that is, serving fewer students with more resources per student. In 1988, the cost per student in Massachusetts was $150 and the state served 40,000 students. By 2002, however, the state served 12,000 students and the cost per student was $1,904 (Comings & Soricone, 2005). When the number of students served declined in Massachusetts, programs that previously had full-enrollments now had waiting lists. This created a demand for increased service that was parlayed into a grass-roots campaign aimed at the state legislature. The campaign was successful, and state funding for adult literacy programs increased dramatically.

PROVIDING PROFESSIONAL DEVELOPMENT

As noted previously, nearly half the states require no certification to teach in adult literacy education; another fifteen states require K–12 certification, but not certification in adult literacy. This means that the largely part-time teaching force for adult literacy is often ill equipped to do the job, and for this reason, professional development is a critical issue for programs. This is particularly true for new and inexperienced teachers. Teachers who have certification and/or experience in K–12 education at least have foundational knowledge about teaching, but they lack knowledge about how to teach in adult education programs.

Smith and Hofer (2003) found that adult literacy education teachers faced three challenges that created needs for professional development: developing curriculum, organizing instruction, and assessing skills and progress. They found that while the majority of teachers had to develop their own curriculum, many lacked an understanding of either what a curriculum is or how to develop one. In organizing instruction, the major challenge was responding appropriately to the enrollment patterns that we previously described. Sixty-nine percent of the teachers in Smith and Hofer's study taught open-enrollment classes and had to learn how to cope with a student population that was constantly changing. Since experience in K–12 education provided little guidance for dealing with this situation, simple trial was common strategy teachers used for coping with the challenge of being underprepared to teach adults. Teachers also had difficulty using the results of diagnostic tests to design instruction and to meet accountability requirements. Despite the emphasis on assessment, the teachers in Smith and Hofer's study felt that they lacked the skills, time, and tools to administer and interpret formal assessments.

The need for professional development is not easily met. Part-time teachers who are employed full time elsewhere generally owe their primary professional allegiance to their full-time profession and are less likely to invest in professional development in adult literacy. Moreover, scheduling professional development for a part-time workforce that is paid by the hour is extremely difficult. Teachers who are working both full time and part time are understandably reluctant to devote the little free time they have to professional development activities.

MANAGING HIGH STUDENT ATTRITION

Dealing with student attrition is a significant challenge for adult literacy programs. According to Development Associates (1993), 20 percent of the adults who enroll in adult basic education drop out before 4 weeks of instruction and 50 percent drop out before 16 weeks of instruction. Although these figures are dated, there is no evidence that the dropout problem has improved.

As we have noted, dropout leads to continuous enrollment, which in turn frequently leads to individualized instruction. Although there is no evidence to suggest that individualized instruction is an ineffective approach, it is clear that dropout does shape the instructional system of adult literacy education programs in major ways. Moreover, when students drop out of adult literacy programs, their social and financial investment in their education is largely lost.

There are two primary factors that influence students' persistence: motivation and the prevalence of constraints to persistence. Adult literacy students are motivated by many conditions, including the desire to be better parents, obtain better jobs, earn the GED, and shed the stigma of being illiterate. At the same time, adult literacy education students face many constraints to persistence, including changes in work schedules, arranging child care, lack of transportation, and fear of failure. These barriers are exacerbated by the fact that most adult literacy education students have low incomes and therefore have fewer resources available to overcome barriers.

In considering motivation and constraints to persistence, it is possible to divide the population of adults who need adult literacy education into three groups: the demand population, the constrained, and the no demand population. The demand population is comprised of those who are highly motivated to enroll and are relatively free of constraints. They are individuals who attend adult literacy education and persist as long as motivation is maintained and new constraints do not arise. The second population, the constrained, consists of those who are motivated to attend but also experience significant constraints. They are less likely to enroll in programs and much more likely to drop out. The final group, the no-demand population, consists of those who are not motivated to attend and/or are highly constrained. Lack of motivation is sometimes caused by a low perception of need for literacy. Quigley (1997) notes that negative attitudes toward schooling develop through negative experiences in K–12 education, which is also a demotivator.

For program staff, the second group—the constrained—should be the primary concern in reducing attrition. The problem for this group is maintaining or enhancing motivation while reducing the constraints. Beder and his colleagues (2006) found that students who persisted in a large adult learning center were highly motivated and engaged in their studies. Motivation is enhanced when students understand that they are progressing toward the attainment of their goals. There are two categories of constraints: material and psychological (Comings, Parrella, & Soricone, 1999). Material constraints include such things as child care and transportation. The appropriate response is support services, such as child care and counseling, but unfortunately, few programs can afford comprehensive support services.

As Comings, Parrella, and Sorcione (1999) found in their study of persistence, lack of self-efficacy was a major psychological constraint. Self-efficacy can be enhanced through the provision of mastery experiences that allow students to be successful and to have real evidence of that success, the showcasing of successful student role models, verbal support, and addressing negative physiological and emotional states such as tension, stress, and fear of failure.

ACQUIRING OPERATING RESOURCES

Unlike in public schools, basic operating resources for adult literacy programs are not guaranteed. Funding is contingent on success in grant acquisition. Students are voluntary students and have to be recruited. Classroom space has to be negotiated with the parent organization. Thus, if programs are to grow and prosper, administrative staff will have to adopt a decidedly entrepreneurial orientation with the network of organizations that provide resources. Mezirow, Darkenwald, and Knox (1975) published one of the first comprehensive studies of adult literacy education. In discussing programs' resource acquisition activities, they stated that for adult basic education,

> This means linking up with a variety of specific organizations, community groups, and target populations. Through them the operator recruits the players [i.e., students], space and support without which he is out of business. His style in hustling the community will depend on its size and composition, past experience of adult education in the schools, and his own professional orientation. (Mezirow et al., 1975, p. 119)

Although the study is over 30 years old, conditions have not changed much regarding resource acquisition. For example, a recent study showed that the director of a large adult learning center understood how important her relationships were with the urban public school system that sponsored her adult literacy program; her program was dependant on the school system for both space and a significant portion of the program's funds (Beder & Medina, 2005a). To build and maintain productive relationships with the school district, she attended K–12 back-to-school nights and administrators' meetings and asked K–12 teachers to refer their students' parents to the adult literacy program. She also placed articles about her program in the PTA newsletter.

CONCLUSIONS

Adult literacy education programs are in many ways very different from the K–12 and higher education institutions with which most educators are familiar. To survive, adult literacy programs must acquire grant funding. The nature of the grants they receive shapes who they serve and to some extent how they serve them. Unlike free-standing organizations that control their own facilities, they are attached to parent organizations that influence how they operate. Their staff is primarily part time, and they are structurally marginal compared to more mainstream educational institutions. Professional development is a major concern, but difficult to provide. The student attrition rate is very high; this influences enrollment patterns and the type of instruction provided.

To many, the characteristics of adult literacy education programs highlighted here may seem to be weaknesses, and to a certain extent they are. Clearly, sufficient and stable funding, more full-time staff, reduction in marginality, more and better professional development, and reduction of attrition would enhance program success.

REFERENCES

Beder, H. (1996). *The infrastructure of adult literacy education.* Philadelphia: National Center on Adult Literacy.

Beder, H., & Medina, P. (2005a, March). Unpublished raw data.

Beder, H., & Medina, P. (2005b, June). Unpublished raw data.

Beder, H., Tomkins, J., Medina, P. Riccioni, R., & Deng, W. (2006). *Students' engagement in adult literacy education* Cambridge, MA: National Center for the Study of Adult Learning and Literacy.

Belzer, A. (2003). *Living with it: Federal policy implementation in adult basic education.* Cambridge: MA: National Center for the Study of Adult Learning and Literacy.

Chisman, F. (2002). *Leading from the middle: The state role in adult education and literacy.* New York: Council for the Advancement of Adult Literacy.

Comings, J., Parrella, A., & Sorcione, L. (1999). *Persistence among adult basic education students in pre-GED classes.* Cambridge, MA: National Center for Adult Learning and Literacy.

Comings, J., & Soricone, L. (2005). Massachusetts: A case study of improvement and growth of adult education services. In J. Comings, B. Garner, & C. Smith (Eds.), *Annual review of adult learning and literacy* (Vol. 5, pp. 85–123). Mahwah, NJ: Lawrence Erlbaum.

Development Associates. (1993). *National evaluation of adult education programs second interim report: Profiles of client characteristics.* Arlington, VA: Author.

Kutner, M., Webb, L., & Matheson, N. (1996). *A review of statewide learner competency and assessment systems.* Washington: Pelavin Associates.

Mezirow, J., Darkenwald, G., & Knox, A. (1975). *Last gamble on education.* Washington, DC: Adult Education Association of the USA.

National Center for Educational Statistics. (2005). *Digest of educational statistics tables and figures: Total and current expenditure per pupil in public elementary and secondary schools: Selected years, 1919–20 through 2002–03.* Retrieved September 7, 2006, from http://nces.ed.gov/programs/digest/d05/tables/dt05_162.asp

ProLiteracy America. (n.d.). *2004–2005 statistical report.* Retrieved September 7, 2006, from http://www.proliteracy.org/proliteracy_america/asr05.asp

Quigley, A., B. (1997). *Rethinking literacy education: The critical need for practice-based change.* San Francisco: Jossey-Bass.

Robinson-Geller, P. (2005, March). Individualized group instruction: A common model. *Focus on Basics, 7.* Retrieved September 8, 2006, from http://www.ncsall.net/?id = 733

Smith, C., & Hofer, J. (2003). *The characteristics and concerns of adult basic education teachers.* Cambridge, MA: National Center for Adult Learning and Literacy.

State Council on Adult Literacy Education Services. (2001). *Preliminary report on the adult literacy funding and delivery system.* Trenton, NJ: State Employment and Training Commission.

U.S. Department of Education. (2005, December). *Adult Education and Family Literacy Act: Program facts.* Washington, DC: Author. Retrieved September 7, 2006, from http://www.ed.gov/about/offices/list/ovae/pi/AdultEd/aeflaprogfacts.doc

Workforce Investment Act , 112 U.S.C. § 936 (1998).

Chapter Five

ADULT ESL IN THE UNITED STATES

John Strucker

English as a second language (ESL), also known as English for speakers of other languages, is the fastest-growing sector of adult education in the United States, primarily because of dramatic increases in immigration over the last three decades. The percentage of foreign-born individuals in the total population was at its highest during the decades from 1870 to 1910, when foreign-born individuals averaged nearly 15 percent of the population. Over the next 60 years, that percentage gradually declined to a low point of 4.7 percent in 1970 (U.S. Census Bureau, 1999), but from 1970 on, the percentage of foreign born began to rise again, and in 2002 it was an estimated 11.8 percent (U.S. Census Bureau, 2003).

How many foreign-born adults in the United States are potential candidates for adult ESL instruction? To arrive at an estimate of this target population, the U.S. Department of Education commissioned an analysis of English language proficiency from the 2000 U.S. Census Population and Housing Survey (Lasater & Elliott, 2005). In that survey, all adults who were not native speakers of English were asked whether they spoke English "very well," "well," "not very well," or "not at all." Those answering anything less than "very well" were considered potential candidates for English language instruction. Using this criteria, it was estimated that 11.5 percent of the adults age 16 and over—approximately 21.9 million people in 2000—could be considered the maximum target population for adult English language instruction.

A small number of foreign-born individuals are business professionals, who usually pay for English instruction at colleges, universities, or private language schools. This chapter will focus on what is by far the largest category of ESL learners: those who enroll in the free and publicly funded adult basic education (ABE) system. That system is mandated to serve adults age 16 and older who either lack a high school diploma or lack high school–level academic skills. According to the U.S. Department of Education's Office of Adult and Vocational Education (2006a), 44 percent of all students in the ABE system are enrolled in ESL classes.

WHY IS ESL IMPORTANT?

It is important for immigrants to know English so that they can improve their employment prospects and income. Studies have consistently shown a strong relationship between the English speaking and reading ability and income (Park, 1999). According to 1999 U.S. Census Bureau figures, the average income of immigrants who reported speaking English "not at all" was $16,345, $20,595 for those who answered "not well," $29,595 for those who answered "well," and $40,741 for those who answered "very well" (Sum, Kirsch, & Yamamoto, 2004).

Limited English proficiency also adversely affects the health of immigrants (Derose, 2000) and their children (Flores, Abreu, & Tomany-Korman, 2005). People with limited English tend to visit doctors less frequently, and they are less likely to be aware of preventive health-care procedures like vaccinations and screenings. In the workplace, adults with limited English proficiency and their coworkers face additional safety risks if immigrant workers do not understand safety rules and procedures explained to them in English (Hong, 2001). Finally, studies suggest that the children of immigrants are more likely to be successful in school if their parents can communicate in English (Pastore, Melzi, & Krol-Sinclair, 1999; Weinstein-Shr & Quintero, 1995). Parents who can speak English are better able to advocate their children's needs with school officials and better able to support their children with their homework and out-of-school learning.

WHERE DO IMMIGRANTS AND ADULT ESL STUDENTS RESIDE?

In the nineteenth and early twentieth centuries, immigrants tended to be concentrated in the big cities of the Northeast, the upper Midwest, and the West Coast. States like New York, Illinois, and California continue to be home to the largest numbers of immigrants. From 1990 to 2000, however, states that had not been traditional immigrant destinations experienced rapid increases in their percentages of foreign-born individuals, including North Carolina (274%), Georgia (233%), Arkansas (196%), and Nebraska (165%) (Center for Adult English Language Acquisition, 2006).

This dispersed settlement pattern for immigrants reflects the dispersed employment opportunities in many areas of the U.S. economy. If an employer establishes a plant that attracts immigrant workers in a rural or suburban area, that locality can soon have dozens or even hundreds of foreign-born families residing within it. This can present challenges to the entire local infrastructure, including K–12 schools, health care, public safety, and ABE programs charged with providing ESL instruction.

WHAT ARE THE NATIVE LANGUAGES SPOKEN BY ESL STUDENTS?

In the 2000 census, of the 47 million residents who reported speaking a language other than English at home, about 60 percent, or an estimated 28 million people, spoke Spanish. After English and Spanish, the U.S. language picture quickly becomes very diverse. Chinese, the third most common native language, was spoken by about 2 million people, or about 4 percent of non-English speakers, followed by French (including Cajun Creole), German, Tagalog, Vietnamese, Italian, Korean, Russian, Polish, Arabic, Portuguese, Japanese, French Creole (mostly Haitian), Greek, Hindi, Persian, Urdu, Gujurathi, and Armenian. Together, these 17 languages accounted for an additional 25 percent of the "other than English-speaking" population. The remaining 10 percent spoke dozens of other languages. These trends have continued: by 2005, Spanish was the native language of 62 percent, and Chinese 4.4 percent, and Korean had moved past Italian into 5th place (U.S. Census Bureau, 2005).

ALL ESL IS LOCAL

Spanish speakers are likely to be present in ESL classes almost anywhere in the United States. They do not necessarily make up the majority or even a plurality of ESL learners, however. Taking a cue from the late House Speaker Tip O'Neill's aphorism "All politics are local," it can also be said that all ESL is local. Consider, for example, the Hmong people from Southeast Asia, who settled in the United States after the Vietnam War. The Hmong make up only 0.3 percent of the total national non-English-speaking population (U.S. Census Bureau, 2005), but they are heavily concentrated in a few areas: 50,000 Hmong live in or near Minneapolis–St. Paul, 25,000 in Fresno, and 10,000 in Milwaukee, as well as in smaller cities such as Modesto, California (3,500); Appleton, Wisconsin (2,000); and Hickory, North Carolina (5,000) (Hmong Information Center, 2006).

Haitian Creole speakers, who make up only 1.1 percent of the "other than English-speaking" population, provide another example of local concentration (U.S. Census Bureau, 2005) but are a significant presence in ESL classes in Miami; Washington, D.C.; New York; Boston; and other East Coast cities. Immigrants, especially those who are refugees, are now likely to show up in seemingly unlikely parts of the United States, sometimes because of a particular employment opportunity, or sometimes because a local church or community organization has agreed to sponsor them and help them to resettle.

WHAT DO WE KNOW ABOUT THE NATIVE LANGUAGE LITERACY AND EDUCATION OF ESL ADULTS?

An adult's level of native language education and literacy plays an important role in his or her ability to acquire English oral and literacy skills because people with higher levels of native language literacy usually acquire literacy in English faster than those with lower levels of native language literacy. In addition to allowing learners to use tools such as dictionaries and grammar texts, being able to read can also support oral language acquisition. When one is learning a foreign language, it is not easy to segment or separate the words in sentences spoken by native speakers because they frequently run the words together, as in "Wannuh goferuh cuppuh coffee?" If learners can read speech written down, they have time to analyze it and note where words start and end. This advantage for more educated adults holds even when their native language employs a written script that is very different from English, such as Cambodian, Korean, or even Chinese (Carlo & Skilton-Sylvester, 1994; Solorzano, 1994).

According to 2000 U.S. Census data, 33.0 percent of the entire foreign-born population were not high school graduates, 25.0 percent were high school graduates, 16.2 percent had some college education (but did not earn a bachelor's degree), and 25.8 percent had a bachelor's degree or more. Little information is available about immigrants' actual levels of native language literacy, however. It is very difficult, for example, to know what high school completion means in terms of literacy skills, since many immigrants come from developing countries where the quality of schooling is uneven at best. Of the adults who enroll in publicly funded ESL classes, only 25 percent reported completing high school and 50 percent reported not having completed high school (National Center for Education Statistics, 2005). The 50 percent reporting that they did not finish high school includes everyone from those with some high school education to those who never had the opportunity to attend school at all. Some ESL students speak native languages that do not have writing systems. Speakers of nonwritten languages make up a small percentage of the ESL population, but, like the Hmong and Bantu-speaking Somali refugees, they can be quite significant locally.

THE U.S. ABE SYSTEM

In the late nineteenth and early twentieth centuries, new immigrants learned English in so-called evening schools provided by public schools, as well as in churches and settlement houses, such as Jane Addams's Hull House in Chicago. Some immigrants paid for instruction at private business colleges and secretarial schools. These earlier forms of ESL education still exist today: free or low-cost English classes are offered by public school systems, churches, settlement houses, and community-based organizations, while private language schools, joined by community colleges, offer fee-based instruction. In addition, the federal government's Even Start family literacy program provides ESL education to parents of young children, and many employers offer ESL instruction in the workplace (Sticht, 2002).

HOW IS THE ABE SYSTEM FUNDED?

The modern framework for funding adult education was laid down in the Economic Opportunity Act of 1964, the centerpiece of President Lyndon Johnson's Great Society programs. From the beginning, states were given many options as to how to use this money. They could use it for specified populations, such as Native Americans, migrant workers, immigrants, or unemployed young adults, or for teacher training and administration, as well as direct instructional service. Programs could be operated by public schools, community organizations and agencies, or private nonprofit and for-profit groups. Collaborations combining funding from various federal initiatives (e.g., Model Cities and the Job Corps) and tapping into the federally funded Volunteers in Service to America (VISTA) were encouraged at the both the local and national levels (Sticht, 2002).

Over the ensuing 30 years, targeted funds were added to ABE to serve clients of Temporary Assistance to Needy Families, formerly known as Aid to Families with Dependent Children, or welfare; immigrant refugees; and employment training programs such as the Job Partnership Training Act. In 1998, all federal funding for adult education and ESL was incorporated into the Workforce Investment Act, which continues to be the overall statute providing funds to the states for adult basic education and ESL (Office of Adult and Vocational Education, 2006a).

In 2002, $494.8 million in federal funds, with an additional $70 million earmarked for ESL, was distributed to the states. That year, the average expenditure, including federal, state, and local, and other sources, was $803 per adult learner (Office of Adult and Vocational Education, 2005). In comparison, in 2002 the average per-pupil expenditure for elementary students was $8,049 and $9,098 for secondary students (Organization for Economic Cooperation and Development, 2006). This tenfold difference between K–12 and adult education funding is not quite as disproportionate as it appears, because adult learners usually attend class six or fewer hours per week, while children normally attend school for 35 hours per week.

Of the $803 per adult learner in 2002, the federal contribution averaged only $206, with the remaining $597 coming primarily from state funds, and some very small additional amounts contributed by local and private sources. The national funding average masks great disparities among the states: at the upper end, Vermont spent $2633 per learner, while at the lower end, Mississippi spent only $248 (Office of Adult and Vocational Education, 2005).

Public schools are obligated by state constitutions to provide education for school-age children, but this is not the case with regard to ABE and ESL. In lean budget years, state legislatures are free to slash adult education funds, forcing local programs to cancel class offerings and thus deny education to many students. ESL students in many areas face waiting lists from six months' to a year's duration, even in states that do not normally tolerate long waiting lists for ABE students (Tucker, 2006), a situation that a 1993 report termed "a national disgrace" (Chisman, Wrigley, & Ewen, 1993). Other states disguise their failure to provide enough classes by encouraging over-enrollment: they allow up to 30 to 40 adults to enroll in each beginning ESL class, knowing that large and unwieldy classes will discourage students and cause more than half to drop out within a few weeks.

WHERE DOES ADULT ESL INSTRUCTION TAKE PLACE?

The typical adult ESL classroom in the United States could be anything from a church basement staffed by a volunteer teacher to a modern high school or community college classroom staffed by a certified teacher with a master's degree in ESL. Nationally, 54 percent of the federally funded programs are operated by local school districts, 24 percent by community-based organizations, 17 percent by community colleges, and 5 percent by corrections institutions (Office of Adult and Vocational Education, 2005). Some states, like Oregon, deliver almost all their ABE and ESL instruction through community colleges, and others, like Texas, Connecticut, and California, rely heavily on local school districts, while Massachusetts delivers the majority of its instruction through community-based organizations.

According to the Office of Adult and Vocational Education (2005), 80 percent of the federally funded adult education programs across the United States are small, with annual total budgets under $200,000, but since small programs serve fewer people, most students attend programs that are somewhat larger. In any event, when it comes to instructional effectiveness, the key factor is the size of the sites where classes are actually held. Large urban programs can be made up of dozens of small sites that may not differ in terms of capacity and scope from more isolated rural programs.

Separate national figures for teachers of adult ESL are not available, in part because some individuals teach both ABE and ESL, but the figures for all adult education indicate that the workforce is composed overwhelmingly of part-time teachers and unpaid volunteers. Of the 92,309 teachers who worked in federally funded programs in 2005, 14 percent were employed full time, 58 percent were employed part time, and 28 percent were unpaid volunteers (Office of Adult and Vocational Education, 2007). Part-time employees are used because they are cheaper because they do not receive benefits, and adult education runs on a split-shift schedule that makes the most use of part-timers as possible. Unlike the seven-hour K–12 day, adult education classes are usually offered in a morning shift for adults who work nights or are unemployed, and an evening shift for those who work days.

The fact that only 14 percent of the teachers are full time does not necessarily mean that 14 percent of the teaching is done by full-time teachers, since they average more total contact hours with students than part-timers. Many part-timers actually work the equivalent full-time contact hours by teaching at two or three different programs to piece together a full-time income. Part-timers have rates of turnover above 13 percent per year, more than double those for K–12 teachers (Smith, Hofer, & Gillespie, 2001). Administrators and full-time teachers report spending inordinate amounts of time replacing part-timers who quit, and much time in orienting and training a constant stream of new hires (Smith et al., 2001). Most volunteers work only a few hours per week, usually in tutorials with one or two students at a time. As a result, their actual student contact time is probably quite a bit less than their 28 percent representation in the ABE workforce would suggest.

Given that states establish their own guidelines for the formal qualifications and training of adult ESL teachers, it is difficult to generalize about teacher qualifications in the country as a whole. ESL teachers include people with master's degrees and formal adult ESL certification and people with bachelor's degrees in various disciplines, as well as people who have taught English abroad. Because of the high percentage of part-time teachers, states have been reluctant to insist on high levels of formal education such as master's degrees for their adult ESL teachers. Over the last 20 years, many states have increased in-service training for ESL teachers, usually in the form of workshops and study circles. The federal government has also funded research and dissemination centers that develop distance learning training materials for ESL teachers, such as the National Clearinghouse for English Language Acquisition and the Center for Applied Linguistics.

ADULT ESL INSTRUCTION

Since 1998, the U.S. Department of Education's Office of Adult and Vocational Education has operated the National Reporting System to track students' progress and participation in ABE and ESL in terms of attendance, academic growth, and a range of additional outcomes, including employment, U.S. citizenship, and attainment of personal goals. The National Reporting System levels for ESL learners provide a thumbnail description of the stages of language learning of ESL students. Each level is identified by score ranges on any of three standardized norm-referenced tests of oral and written English authorized by Office of Adult and Vocational Education. In addition to test score ranges, each level is also identified by qualitative descriptions of learners' skills.

Beginning ESL literacy students make up 21 percent of the ESL enrollment in the United States. These individuals cannot speak or understand English and have no or minimal reading or writing skills in any language. They function minimally in English, communicating only through gestures or a few isolated words, and can handle only very routine entry-level jobs that do not require oral or written communication in English (Office of Adult and Vocational Education, 2006b).

Some beginning ESL literacy students, like the Hmong, speak native languages that do not exist in written form. A larger proportion of beginning literacy students come from the rural areas of developing countries or are members of minority populations or females who were denied access to formal schooling in their native countries. Still others come from countries where war and famine disrupted what schooling existed. Such students may also suffer from cognitive difficulties that are the result of trauma and prolonged malnutrition. Others come from societies where limited education was available, but they were learning disabled and their teachers were not trained to help them.

Beginning literacy adults face the difficulty of learning to read in a language that they barely speak or do not speak at all. Mastering the alphabetic principle, the relationship between spoken language and its written form, can be especially difficult for them. When children or adults are taught to read in their mother tongue, they know both the spoken representations and the meanings of the written words that they are attempting to decode. It is much more difficult to make this leap between spoken language and print for the first time in a foreign language.

ESL beginning literacy students usually require classes of 10 or fewer students, not only because of their literacy needs, but because many of them have had so little experience with formal education that they don't know how to "do" school. They may not know how to hold a pencil or book, or the basic rules of classroom etiquette, such as paying attention to the teacher. Teachers who work with beginning literacy students require specialized training in methods of teaching reading that are similar to those used with English-speaking dyslexics. They also need training in how to present English oral skills very concretely, using realia, that is, objects such as foods, items of clothing, and tools, as well as pictures and drawings (Wrigley, 2003).

Beginning literacy learners pose a challenge to small programs because they may not have teachers trained to meet their needs. Even under ideal circumstances, beginning literacy students are not easy learners to serve, as 32 percent drop out before completing a class (Office of Adult and Vocational Education, 2007). Those who persist make slower progress than other learners because they are starting farther behind.

Low-beginning learners are individuals who can understand basic greetings and simple phrases and respond to simple questions, but they speak slowly and with little control over grammar. With regard to reading and writing, they can read numbers, letters, and common words and may be able to sound out simple words but have limited understanding of connected prose. Writing is restricted to basic personal information (e.g., name, address, and telephone number). With regard to functional and workplace skills, they can provide limited personal information on simple forms and can handle routine entry-level jobs that require very simple written or oral English communication and for which the job tasks can be demonstrated (Office of Adult and Vocational Education, 2006b).

High-beginning learners are individuals who can understand common words, simple phrases, and sentences containing familiar vocabulary and are able to respond to simple questions with simple sentences showing a limited control of grammar. With regard to reading and writing, they can read most sight words—or words that are instantly recognized on sight by most readers without having to be sounded out and that cannot be decoded (*the* and *is*, for instance)—but have limited understanding of connected prose. Writing shows very little control of grammar, capitalization, and punctuation and contains many spelling errors. With regard to functional and workplace skills, they can function in familiar social situations and recognize common forms of print found around the home, workplace, and community. They can handle routine entry-level jobs requiring basic English and may have limited knowledge or experience using computers (Office of Adult and Vocational Education, 2006b).

Low beginners and high beginners together make up 29 percent of ESL enrollment nationwide. Low beginners are made up of people who are studying English for the first time, while high beginners may be thought of as people who have had some previous instruction or people who have lived in the United States long enough to acquire minimal speaking and listening abilities informally. These students range from people who have very basic literacy in their native language to those with considerable native language literacy and education. If their native languages are written in alphabetic form, like the 62 percent or more who are Spanish speakers, these adults may be able to transfer some of their knowledge of the alphabetic principle to English. Teachers working with low and high beginners are not as dependent on using realia as those working with beginning literacy students. With these literate students they are able to use workbooks, charts, signs, and word lists as springboards for oral language practice and discussion.

Low intermediates and high intermediates are similar in their listening and speaking skills in that they can participate in most basic English conversations, while the high intermediates are distinguished by their control of more complex grammar. With regard to reading and writing, low intermediates can understand paragraphs and texts on familiar material, while high intermediate can begin to understand longer and less familiar texts if they have a clear structure. The latter group may also have sufficient English vocabulary to use context to guess at the meanings of unknown words. In regard to functional and workplace skills, low intermediates can interpret simple written materials such as signs, schedules, and maps and handle some entry-level jobs that involve some written as well as oral English skills. In addition, high intermediates can communicate on the telephone, write basic messages and notes, and complete medical forms and job applications (Office of Adult and Vocational Education, 2006b).

The low and high intermediates, who make up 34 percent of the ESL enrollees, are on their way to having functional competence in many areas of English. Functional competence allows an individual to perform many important day-to-day tasks in the workplace and the community in English. Because these learners are developing English reading skills, their classroom work involves reading of stories, poems, and simplified stories from the newspaper. For the high intermediate learners, reading is beginning to become one of their main sources for learning new English vocabulary.

There is a sharp falloff in enrollment between low and high intermediates from 21 percent to 13 percent of total enrollment. Some of this falloff is due to low intermediates transferring to intermediate levels of adult basic education within the same program, particularly if their goal is to earn a GED. The falloff may also indicate that many immigrant adults are satisfied with acquiring functional levels of English competence. For young single adults who plan to pursue postsecondary education in the United States, it may make more sense to invest the considerable time needed to achieve more advanced levels of English. For those who do not aspire to higher levels of education, however, it may make more sense to spend that time at home with one's family or working overtime or taking a second job.

Moving beyond functional oral competence to being able to read and learn in English involves acquiring far more English vocabulary knowledge than intermediate students possess. Their tested vocabulary can be quite limited, often the equivalent of a 2nd-grade vocabulary (Davidson & Strucker, 2002). When it comes to acquiring vocabulary, an ESL learner's level of native language education plays a key role. Adults with high levels of native language education and vocabulary are faced only with learning the English words for concepts they already know, but those with low levels of native language education are faced with having to learn both the words *and* the concepts for the first time in English. Spanish speakers with higher levels of native language education possess an additional advantage in learning vocabulary because of the high number of Latin-based cognates in higher-level English texts.

The terms "advanced" and "high advanced" are used in ESL to refer to individuals who can communicate orally in a variety of contexts related to life and work, including some more formal informational communication. They can read moderately complex texts, make inferences and predictions, and contrast information presented in multiple texts. They are able to write organized multiparagraph texts using some complex grammar, a variety of sentence structures, and a range of vocabulary. They can understand radio and television, and in the workplace they can handle nontechnical oral and non-written instructions and routine interactions with the public, use common computer software, and learn new applications (Office of Adult and Vocational Education, 2006b).

The 16 percent of ESL students who fall into the advanced ESL levels are distinguished by their ability to use English to learn more English. They are capable of understanding and using English that is more formal, academic, and abstract. As they near the end of the advanced levels, many educational options are become available to them. Those who wish to acquire a U.S. high school credential can transfer to adult secondary education, the designation within the ABE system for GED preparation classes. Those who already have a high school credential may want to study to take the Test of English as a Foreign Language, which is required for admission to many U.S. colleges, universities, and technical schools. Still others may choose to enroll directly in community colleges and continue to hone their advanced English skills while pursuing a career education.

HOW LONG DOES IT TAKE FOR ADULTS TO LEARN ENGLISH?

It can take ESL children who attend school 35 hours a week two to three years to develop functional English ability and seven years or more to catch up to their English-speaking classmates in academic achievement in English (Collier, 1989). Mainstream English Language Training (1985) estimated that it can take from 500 to 1,000 hours of instruction for an adult who knows no English but is literate in his or her native language to develop sufficient functional ability in English to cover the basic workplace and social interactions. Thus, if an adult could attend ESL class four hours per week and never miss a class, it could take a minimum of 125 weeks, or nearly two-and-half straight years of instruction to reach a functional level. Based on likely rather than maximum attendance, three to five years from beginning to intermediate is probably a more accurate estimate (Chisman et al., 1993).

EXPOSURE TO ENGLISH OUTSIDE THE CLASSROOM

For adult ESL students in the United States, exposure to English outside the classroom can play an important role, but the amount and character of that exposure varies a great deal. For example, some ESL adults interact almost exclusively with English speakers during their workdays, while others work exclusively with speakers of their native language. Those with school-age children may encounter English through their children's homework and English conversation at home, while elderly adults or those who remain at home to care for young children may have little exposure to spoken English. Adults have considerable discretion over the amount of English they encounter in social, religious, and recreational settings, as well as through television, radio, movies, and the Internet. In the past, only Spanish speakers enjoyed access to native-language media in the United States, but satellite television and the Internet have brought native-language news and cultural programming to many other immigrant groups, freeing them of the need to acquire English for those purposes.

CHALLENGES AND OPPORTUNITIES FACING ESL

Improving Assessment of Learners' Skills

Research on children and adult ESL students highlights the critical need for diagnostic assessments of learners' strengths and needs (August & Shanahan, 2006; Wrigley, 2003). It is not unusual to find great differences across adults' levels of skills in English Some have strong reading skills but little oral language ability in English, while others are fluent conversational speakers with almost no English reading ability.

The tests mandated by the National Reporting System have helped to improve teachers' knowledge of students' strengths and needs in English, but information about students' native language literacy is still generally lacking. Other than those for Spanish speakers, there are no widely available tests of ESL students' native language literacy abilities. Brief computer-administered and scored tests of native language reading comprehension would tell teachers whether an adult has low, medium, or high literacy in his or her native language. In a promising development, UNESCO and ETS are conducting a pilot study called the Language Assessment and Monitoring Program to develop basic reading assessments in a number of languages spoken in developing countries (UNESCO, 2005).

Assessment isn't just a matter of tests; it's also a matter of having the time to give them and the staff trained to interpret them. Even though many ESL programs in the United States have Spanish-speaking teachers and staff, and even though reliable Spanish reading tests are available, too few programs have the money and time to invest in buying and using those tests.

Improving Attendance and Persistence of ESL Students

Despite the fact that ESL adults are highly motivated to learn English, their attendance tends to be erratic (Sticht, MacDonald, & Erickson, 1998), and 20–25 percent end up dropping out before completing the levels they enroll in (Office of Adult and Vocational Education, 2006). They do not usually miss classes or drop out of school for frivolous reasons: like other adults in our society, they have car problems, or their employer asks them to work late, or their child-care arrangements fall through, or their family members get sick (Comings, Parrella, & Soricone, 2000).

Given that some attendance and persistence problems are unavoidable, a partial solution might be to offer on-site ESL classes that are accompanied by parallel online versions. If a student has to miss classes or even drop out for a time, he or she could follow the class and at least participate in some of the activities at home. Online learning would probably not be effective with low-skilled beginning literacy students, but it could benefit those with basic functional skills and some familiarity with computers

Increasing the Intensity of Instruction

Wrigley (2003) found that ESL students who attended a higher percentage of their classes for the period they were enrolled made better progress than students who attended a greater number classes but attended more sporadically. In other words, intensity of study appears to be more important than total hours. It would be useful to know whether ESL students would achieve better results if shorter, more intensive courses were offered to them. What if, instead of the typical semester of 48 hours of instruction spread over three months, some students could receive 48 hours of instruction in one month? Some students might find it easier to commit to attendance over a shorter period.

Using Technology to Improve Instruction

Since the 1980s, ESL teachers have made extensive use of low-cost computer software programs for drill and practice in vocabulary, grammar, and spelling. Such programs allow students to work at their own pace on skills, while at the same time acquiring some basic computer literacy skills. Videos have also been effective with ESL learners because they offer exposure to natural language presented in a structured sequence, and they can be replayed for multiple exposures (Burt, 1999). In the past few years, computer language learning programs employing text-to-speech and speech recognition have become commercially available from several sources, aimed primarily at English-as-a-foreign-language learners. Their potential for ESL students has yet to be explored. But in a recent study, intermediate ESL students reported high levels of engagement and satisfaction with a speech recognition reading tutor. In the future these technologies might be used to create self-study language labs for ESL students or as part of the online support for on-site classes.

Making Use of Native Language in Adult ESL Classrooms

Total English immersion in the classroom was once considered to be best practice, but recent research with both K–12 and adult ESL students suggests that the "judicious use of native language" can be highly effective (Huerta-Macias, 2003). This could be relatively easy to implement in programs where adult ESL students who are native speakers of Spanish make up all or nearly all of the students, but it would obviously not be possible for the many classes in the United States in which multiple native languages are represented among the students.

Addressing the Need for Structural Reforms in Adult ESL

This point serves as a fitting conclusion, because key structural weaknesses in the adult basic education ESL delivery system undermine the best efforts of administrators, teachers, and the students themselves. As discussed earlier, funding for adult ESL is inadequate and inconsistent. Inadequate funding is the direct cause of long waiting lists and class sizes that are too large to be effective and contributes to an overreliance on part-time teachers. Inconsistent funding at the state level leads to fluctuations from year to year in services and further exacerbates workforce turnover.

It takes skill, training, and experience to be an effective ESL teacher. Minimally trained volunteers can provide opportunities for ESL students to perfect their conversational ability, but it takes specialized training to teach English grammar, vocabulary, and literacy skills to the diverse learner population in adult ESL. Despite federal support for state teacher training initiatives, the 13 percent annual turnover rate among part-timers severely undercuts in-service teacher education efforts.

One reform that is not dependent on increased funding is the consolidation of smaller sites and programs into larger entities capable of providing a better range and quality of ESL instruction and better access to technology. Small sites have too few teachers and too little space to offer the range of classes needed by the diverse multilevel adult ESL population. At larger sites teachers are better able to specialize in the various learner types and develop expertise in assessment and technology. Small sites are unavoidable in rural or exurban areas, but there is no educationally justifiable reason for small sites in urban areas.

CONCLUSION

Despite these challenges and limitations, adult ESL programs remain among our most important centers of civic culture. Every morning and night, in thousands of classrooms across the country, work-weary adults from 100 different countries come together to learn English in safe, supportive environments, places where nobody makes fun of their accents and where teachers and volunteers are understanding and patient. Like generations of immigrants before them, they come to learn English, but in the process they also experience much of what is good and enduring about America.

REFERENCES

August, D., & Shanahan, T. (Eds.). (2006). *Developing literacy in second-language learners: Report of the national literacy panel on language-minority children and youth.* Mahwah, NJ: Lawrence Erlbaum.

Burt, M. (1999). *Using video with adult English language learners.* Washington, DC: Center for Applied Linguistics, National Center for ESL Literacy Education.

Carlo, M. S., & Skilton-Sylvester, E. E. (1994). *A longitudinal investigation on the literacy development of Spanish-, Korean-, and Cambodian-speaking adults learning to read English as a second language* (Unpublished manuscript). Philadelphia: National Center on Adult Literacy.

Center for Adult English Language Acquisition. (2006). *Where do adult English language learners live?* Retrieved from http://www.cal.org/caela/esl_resources/faqs.html#Five

Chisman, F., Wrigley, H., & Ewen, D. (1993). *ESL and the American dream: Report on an investigation of English as a second language service for adults.* Washington, DC: Southport Institute for Policy Analysis.

Collier, V. P. (1989). How long? A synthesis of research on academic achievement in a second language. *TESOL Quarterly, 23*(3), 509–531.

Comings, J., Parrella, A., & Soricone, L. (2000). Helping adults persist. *Focus on Basics, 4*(A), 1–6.

Davidson, R., & Strucker, J. (2002). Patterns of word-recognition errors among adult basic education native and nonnative speakers of English. *Scientific Studies of Reading, 6*(3), 299–315.

Derose, K. P. (2000). Limited English proficiency and Latinos' use of physician services. *Medical Care Research and Review, 57*(1), 76–91.

Flores, G., Abreu, M., & Tomany-Korman, M. S. (2005). Limited English proficiency, primary language spoken at home, and disparities in children's health and healthcare: How language barriers are measured. *Public Health Reports, 120*(4), 418–430.

Francis, W. N., & Kucera, H. (1982). *Frequency analysis of English usage.* Boston: Houghton Mifflin.

Hirsh, D., & Nation, P. (1992). What vocabulary size is needed to read unsimplified texts for pleasure? *Reading in a Foreign Language, 8*(2), 689–696.

Hmong Information Center. (2006). *Hmong population by state and major state cities.* Retrieved from http://www.hmongcenter.org/hmonpopbysta.html

Hong, O. S. (2001). Limited English proficiency workers: Health and safety education. *American Association of Occupational Health Nurses Journal, 49*(1), 21–26.

Huerta-Macías, A. (2003). Meeting the challenge of adult education: A bilingual approach. *Journal of Adult and Adolescent Literacy, 47*(3), 218–226.

Lasater, B., & Elliott, B. (2005). *Profiles of the adult education target population.* Washington, DC: U.S. Department of Education, Division of Adult Education and Literacy, Office of Vocational and Adult Education.

Mainstream English Language Training. (1985). *Competency-based mainstream English language training resource package.* Washington, DC: Department of Health and Human Services, Social Security Administration, Office of Refugee Resettlement.

National Center for Education Statistics. (2005). *National household education survey (NHES).* Washington, DC: Author.

Office of Adult and Vocational Education. (2005). *Adult education and family literacy act program facts.* Washington, DC: Author.

Office of Adult and Vocational Education. (2006a). *Adult Education and Family Literacy Act program year 2003–2004: Report to Congress on state performance.* Washington, DC: Author.

Office of Adult and Vocational Education. (2006b). *Implementation guidelines: Measures and methods for the national reporting system for adult education.* Washington, DC: Author.

Office of Adult and Vocational Education. (2007). *National reporting system reports and tables.* Washington, DC: Author.

Organization for Economic Cooperation and Development. (2006). *OECD in figures 2006–2007.* Paris: Author.

Park, J. H. (1999). The earnings of immigrants in the United States: The effect of English-speaking ability. *American Journal of Economics and Sociology, 58*(1), 43–56.

Pastore, J. R., Melzi, G., & Krol-Sinclair, B. (1999). *What should we expect of family literacy? Experiences of Latino children whose parents participate in an intergenerational literacy project.* Newark, DE: International Reading Association.

Smith, C., Hofer, J., & Gillespie, M. (2001). The working conditions of adult literacy teachers: Preliminary findings from the NCSALL staff development study. *Focus on Basics, 4*(D). Retrieved from www.ncsa11.net/?id=1291

Solorzano, R. W. (1994). *Instruction and assessment for limited-English proficient adult learners* (NCAL Report No. TR94–06). Philadelphia: National Center for Adult Literacy.

Sticht, T. (2002). The rise of the adult education and literacy system in the United States: 1600–2000. In J. Comings & C. Smith (Eds.), *Annual review of adult learning and literacy* (Vol. 3, pp.

Sticht, T., MacDonald, B., & Erickson, P. (1998). *Passports to paradise: The struggle to teach and learn on the margins of adult education.* El Cajon, CA: Applied Behavioral and Cognitive Sciences.

Sum, A., Kirsch, I., & Yamamoto, K. (2004). *A human capital concern: The literacy proficiency of U.S. immigrants.* Princeton, NJ: Educational Testing Service.

Thomas, W. P., & Collier, V. (1997). *School effectiveness for language minority students.* Washington, DC: National Clearinghouse for Bilingual Education.

Tucker, J. T. (2006). *The ESL logjam: Waiting times for adult ESL classes and the impact on English learners.* Los Angeles, CA: National Association of Latino Elected Officials.

UNESCO. (2005). *Report of the governing board of the UNESCO Institute for Statistics on the activities of the institute (2004–2005).* Paris: Author.

U.S. Census Bureau. (1999). *U.S. abstracts.* Washington, DC: Author.

U.S. Census Bureau. (2005). *American community survey.* Washington, DC: Author.

Weinstein-Shr, G., & Quintero, E. (Eds.). (1995). *Immigrant learners and their families: Literacy to connect the generations.* McHenry, IL: Delta Systems and Center for Applied Linguistics.

Wrigley, H. (2003). What works for ESL students. *Focus on Basics, 6*(C). Retrieved March 2, 2006, from www.ncsa11.net/?id=189

Chapter Six

ADULT LEARNERS IN A CHANGING AMERICA

Irwin Kirsch, Marylou Lennon, and Claudia Tamassia

In many ways, the challenges faced by adult education programs and the learners they serve are more complex than ever before. In America today, the rewards for higher levels of educational attainment and skills are large and growing. Those in our society with below-average skills are finding it increasingly difficult to earn above-average wages in a global economy. They cannot hope to fully participate in an evolving society where individuals are being required to take on additional responsibility for more aspects of their lives: from planning their careers to nurturing and guiding their children, navigating the health-care system, and assuming more responsibility for their financial future. Policy makers and others are coming to recognize that in modern societies, human capital, or what one knows and can do, may be the most important form of capital (Becker, 2002).

In this changing America, the skills that participants in adult education programs do or do not develop have increasingly important implications in terms of their workforce participation, long-term self-sufficiency, acculturation, and citizenship. A growing body of data shows that literacy and numeracy skills are associated with the likelihood that individuals will participate in life-long learning, keep abreast of social and political events, and vote in state and national elections, in addition to obtaining and succeeding in a job (OECD & Statistics Canada, 2005; Sum, Kirsch, & Taggart, 2002). These data also suggest that literacy is likely to be one of the major pathways linking education and health and may be a contributing factor to the disparities that have been observed in the quality of health care in developed countries. Thus, the noneconomic returns to literacy in the form of enhanced personal well-being and greater social cohesion are viewed by some as being as important as economic and labor market returns (Friedman, 2005; OECD, 2001). Given the social and economic stakes involved, it might reasonably be argued that adult education programs have a more critical role to play in today's society than ever before. Recognition of this fact has led some to believe that it is important to gather national data about both these programs and their participants to stimulate and inform a conversation about the needs of adult learners and the ways in which those needs might best be met to ensure that both individuals and society as a whole can reach their full potential.

OVERVIEW OF THE ADULT EDUCATION PROGRAM STUDY

The Adult Education Program Study (AEPS) was sponsored by the Office of Vocational and Adult Education. The study was designed and conducted by the Educational Testing Service and Westat, in conjunction with staff from the Office of Vocational and Adult Education and the National Center for Education Statistics. Westat is an employee-owned research corporation that conducts national surveys for various agencies of the U.S. government. The overall goal of the AEPS was to provide nationally representative information about adult education programs and their participants through the use of two surveys (Tamassia, Lennon, Yamamoto, & Kirsch, 2007).

The Program Survey consisted of a detailed questionnaire designed to collect information about the characteristics of adult education programs, including size (in terms of number of programs, sites, and participants and budget), staffing profiles, the types of learners served, the kinds of assessments employed, and the extent to which various technologies were used by learners and staff. The questionnaire covered the program year (July 1, 2001–June 30, 2002) and was completed by administrators from a nationally representative sample of adult education programs.

The focus of this chapter is on the second of the two surveys—the Learner Survey. This survey was designed to provide a profile of the literacy and numeracy skills of a nationally representative sample of adult learners enrolled in federally supported adult education programs. The Learner Survey administered between March and June of 2003 and assessed the skills of participants in three domains: prose literacy, document literacy, and numeracy. The definition of literacy for this survey followed that used in the Adult Literacy and Life Skills Survey (ALL), the International Adult Literacy Survey (IALS), and the National Adult Literacy Survey (NALS): "Literacy is using printed and written information to function in society, to achieve one's goals, and to develop one's knowledge and potential" (Kirsch, Jungeblut, Jenkins, & Kolstad, 1993, p. 2).

The definition of each domain also followed that used by other large-scale literacy assessments. Prose literacy was defined as the knowledge and skills needed to understand and use information from texts such as editorials, news stories, brochures, instruction manuals, poems, and fiction. Document literacy was defined as the knowledge and skills required to locate and use information presented in various formats, including job applications, payroll forms, transportation schedules, maps, tables, and charts. Numeracy was defined as the knowledge and skills required to effectively manage and respond to the mathematical demands of diverse situations. While the ALL and AEPS surveys employed the numeracy scale as it is defined here, the earlier NALS and IALS assessments used a quantitative literacy scale that dealt primarily with arithmetic skills embedded in texts. The numeracy scale focuses more on mathematical reasoning and, as such, represents a broader construct that is important in today's society.

The AEPS Learner Survey instrument was derived from the ALL , an international large-scale assessment of adults conducted in 2003. The ALL was a household survey that examined the characteristics and levels of literacy and numeracy of the general adult population in the United States and six other countries. Assessment tasks were based on real-life materials taken from a variety of sources, including newspapers, brochures, and magazines. The tasks were presented in an open-response format; that is, rather than respond to multiple-choice questions, participants were asked to respond to questions by writing brief responses, completing portions of an order form, circling numbers in a table, and so forth. Like the ALL, the AEPS survey was administered by a trained administrator. Because the AEPS survey used instruments and methodology derived from the ALL, the results of the AEPS and ALL surveys are directly comparable and able the adult learner population to be compared with the general adult population in the United States.

The Learner Survey also included a detailed background questionnaire that was used to collect information about various learner characteristics. Like the ALL, the AEPS background questionnaire addressed areas including language background, educational background and experiences, labor force participation, and other activities, as well as general demographic information such as gender and age. The background questionnaire not only added to the interpretability of the AEPS data but, as was true with the assessment instruments, allowed for direct comparisons with the general adult population.

One important research question addressed in the AEPS focused on the impact that language of assessment has on the performance of English language learners. In previous large-scale assessments that were conducted with English-language tasks, it was important to qualify the results as not capturing the literacy skills and knowledge that some respondents might possess in other languages. To investigate this issue, the AEPS oversampled the Hispanic population enrolled in adult education programs and randomly assigned these learners to either a English or Spanish version of the AEPS prose and document instruments. This aspect of the study design allowed for an analysis of the extent to which the language of the assessment influenced performance on literacy tasks.

In summary, the data derived from the AEPS Learner Survey provided information about the skills and characteristics of participants in federally funded adult education programs. This information is important and unique for several reasons.

- It was the first time comparable literacy measures have been used to assess the skills of adult education participants in the United States in a nationally representative sample.

- It was the first time such a measurement allows comparisons with a household sample, through comparison of the Learner Survey results with those from the ALL.

- It was the first time this type of large-scale assessment has been conducted in both Spanish and English.

THE ADULT EDUCATION POPULATION

Throughout the history of adult education, a range of groups—both public and private, state and federal—have been involved in educating a diverse group of adult learners. While diversity within the field persists, the past 40 years have been characterized by a sustained federal and state partnership. In 1964, as part of the federal War on Poverty, Congress passed the Economic Opportunity Act, which introduced the Adult Basic Education Program. This legislation established a program of federal grants to states and focused on setting up basic education classes for adults who had not completed secondary education. In 1966, the program expanded beyond basic education with the passage of the Adult Education Act. The 30 years that followed saw an increase in the commitment of federal dollars to adult education, and a concomitant increase in the number of adults enrolled in federally supported programs.

Adult education programs in the United States are currently governed by the Adult Education and Family Literacy Act, Title II of the Workforce Investment Act of 1998, which defines the target population for adult education. According to that legislation, individuals are eligible to participate in federally funded adult education programs if they are at least 16 years of age; are not enrolled or required to be enrolled in secondary school under state law; and either lack sufficient mastery of basic educational skills to function effectively in society, do not have a secondary school diploma or its recognized equivalent, or are unable to speak, read, or write the English language.

Table 6.1 shows the distribution of participants in adult education programs by selected demographic characteristics. At 53 percent, women continue to represent more than half of the participants in adult education, although the difference between males and females is smaller than it was in 1970, when women accounted for some 57 percent of participants (Sticht, 1998). Adult learners also tend to be younger than the general population, on average, with some 35 percent reporting that they were 16–24 years of age at the time of the survey. In fact, 80 percent of the participants in adult education programs reported that they were 44 years of age or younger. Only 17 percent of participants in adult education programs were 45 years of age and older.

Not only are participants in adult education programs young, but they are increasingly non-native. Some 43 percent reported being born outside the United States, with Hispanic adults representing some 35 percent of program

Table 6.1
Demographic Characteristics of the AEPS Learner Population

	Learner population	Percent of learner population
Total	2,429,531[1]	100
Gender		
Male	1,137,353	47
Female	1,291,601	53
Age		
16–18	106,738	4.4
19–24	732,236	30.1
25–44	1,114,259	45.9
45–59	378,458	15.6
60+	42,130	4
Born in United States		
Yes	1,389,754	57
No	1,036,756	43
Ethnicity		
Hispanic	852,474	35
Non-Hispanic	1,577,057	65
Program		
ABE	1,033,454	42
ASE	505,290	21
ESL	890,336	37

[1] This figure is the weighted sample of individuals who participated in the Learner Survey. The Program Survey data found that 2,720,512 learners participated in federally funded adult education programs during the period from July 1, 2001, to June 30, 2002. While all learners were included in the Program Survey data, learners enrolled in the lowest-level ESL classes were not included in the sample for the Learner Survey because it was judged they would not have the English language skills necessary to complete the assessment tasks.

participants. This percentage is up from the 21 percent that has been esti-mated for 1979 (Sticht, 1998).

To help address this changing population and meet the broad range of educational needs of adult learners, federally funded adult education pro-grams provide instructional services categorized according to the skill level or language background of learners. These include the following three types of instructional programs.

- Adult basic education (ABE) programs are designed for adults "who lack compe-tence in reading, writing, speaking, problem solving or computation at a level nec-essary to function in society, on a job or in the family" (National Reporting System for Adult Education, 2001, p. 25). ABE learners participate in adult programs to acquire basic literacy and numeracy skills.
- Adult secondary education (ASE) programs are intended to help adults "who have some literacy skills and can function in everyday life, but are not proficient or do not have a certificate of graduation or its equivalent from a secondary school" (National Reporting System for Adult Education, 2001, p. 25). Typically, these learners are attending ASE classes to obtain a GED or adult high school cre-dential.
- English-as-a-second-language (ESL) programs are designed "to help adults who are limited English proficient achieve competence in the English language" (National Reporting System for Adult Education, 2001, p. 25).

Table 6.1 shows that 37 percent of the learners participated in ESL pro-grams while another 42 percent were in ABE programs. ASE programs addressed the needs of 21 percent of participants in adult education pro-grams. It is important to keep in mind that these percentages are slightly different from what was found in the Program Survey because learners at the lowest ESL level were not included in the Learner Survey, as it was thought that they would not have the requisite language skills to respond to either part of the assessment. Nevertheless, enrollment in the two larg-est groups shows that some 80 percent of adult learners were enrolled in programs designed to help participants with the lowest skills—both basic literacy and numeracy skills and English language skills. In addition, level 1 ABE, as defined by the National Reporting System, increased by 70 percent between 2000–2001 and 2004–2005 (National Reporting System for Adult Education (n.d.). With so many learners needing to develop foundational skills, these data clearly show one set of challenges that adult education pro-grams and their participants strive to meet.

The remainder of this chapter will look more closely at the AEPS's learner data, first presenting the distribution of skills in the overall adult education population. Literacy and numeracy skills will be further investigated by pro-gram type and then by selected background characteristics of adult learners. Given the central role that English-language learning plays in adult education, we will give ESL learners particular emphasis and will look at the ways in which nativity, language, and educational background interact with literacy and numeracy proficiencies. Because the AEPS survey design included the assessment of a representative sample of the Hispanic population in either English or Spanish, the impact of testing language on the performance of Hispanic learners will also be discussed. Finally, we will place findings from the AEPS survey in the context of the economic and labor force changes arising in this country and discuss the challenges these raise for our adult education system now and in the future.

PROFILING THE SKILLS OF ADULT EDUCATION PARTICIPANTS

Results of the AEPS Learner Survey are reported on the prose literacy, document literacy, and numeracy scales, each ranging from 0 to 500 points. Scores on each scale represent degrees of proficiency in that particular dimension. While most respondents tend to obtain similar, although not identical, scores on the three scales, this does not mean that the underlying skills involved are the same. Each scale provides some unique information, especially when comparisons are made across groups defined by variables such as gender, age, and nativity.

Performance on each scale is divided into five levels, of which level 1 represents the lowest skills and level 5 the highest. These levels were determined not as a result of any statistical property of the scales, but rather as a result of shifts in the information-processing skills and strategies required for one to succeed on various tasks along the scales. Thus, individuals who perform at level 1 on the prose and document scales tend to be restricted to using familiar materials to perform simple tasks such as locating information. At level 2, individuals typically are able to make low-level inferences and compare and contrast information. Individuals at level 3 are generally able to integrate multiple pieces of information found in documents and texts. Performance in levels 4 and 5 reflect the ability to apply increasingly specialized knowledge and use increasingly complex texts and displays of information.

On the numeracy scale, individuals performing at level 1 tend to be able to complete simple tasks in concrete, familiar contexts, such as sorting dates in a list or counting objects in a photograph. Individuals at level 2 are still restricted to fairly simple tasks but can typically solve problems involving more than a single step. At level 3 in numeracy, individuals are typically able to understand mathematical information in a range of different forms, including symbols, graphs, and drawings, and can solve problems that require knowledge of mathematical patterns and relationships. Numeracy levels 4 and 5 reflect an understanding of an increasingly broad range of mathematical information and the ability to understand complex representations.

Of particular significance for the interpretation of data from the Learner Survey is the fact that a number of national and state organizations, including the National Governor's Association, identified level 3 as a standard of minimum proficiency for success in today's labor market (Comings, Sum, & Uvin, 2000). The identification of level 3 was based on judgments made after an examination of the relationships between performance on the NALS and IALS scales and its connection to social, educational, and labor market outcomes (Sum, Kirsch, & Yamamoto, 2004). One factor that influenced this judgment was the relationship between the average literacy scores on the NALS and educational attainment. Adults who were performing at levels 1 and 2 demonstrated proficiencies that were below those of the average high school graduate and, for the most part, below the proficiencies of those who graduated but reported they did not pursue any postsecondary education. This comparison was thought to be important because in all states those who are 16 years of age and older and have not earned their high school diploma or GED are eligible to participate in adult education programs.

What also concerned those researchers about these data was not just that large percentages of adults were found to have limited skills but that the association between these skills and opportunities is strong and growing. Collectively, what data from the NALS and IALS indicate is that literacy is a currency. Just as adults with little money have difficulty meeting their basic needs, those with limited literacy skills are likely to find it more challenging to achieve their goals, whether these involve seeking or advancing in a job, making consumer decisions, pursuing educational opportunities, or participating actively in civic affairs. Moreover, as information and technology continue to increase in importance, and as our economic competitors continue to invest in human capital, even those adults in this country with average skills may experience increased difficulty obtaining better-paying jobs and understanding the many complex issues facing our society.

OVERALL RESULTS FOR THE ADULT LEARNER POPULATION

Not surprisingly, data from the Learner Survey show that, overall, the overwhelming majority of adult education participants performed at the two lowest levels of the literacy scales. Over 80 percent performed at level 2 or below in prose and document literacy, and over 90 percent performed similarly on the numeracy scale (see table 6.2). The performance of adult learners was consistently lower in numeracy than their performance in prose and document literacy.

Data from the Learner Survey showing the distribution of performance across program types also confirmed what might be expected given the learning needs of populations in those programs. In all three domains, learners in

Table 6.2
Proficiency Distribution on the Prose, Document, and Numeracy Scales by Program

	Overall Score		Level 1 (0-225)		Level 2 (226-275)		Level 3 (276-325)		Level 4 (326-375)		Level 5 (376-500)	
	Mean	SE	%	SE	%	SE	%	SE	%	SE	%	SE
Prose literacy	219	(1.9)	48.8	(1.3)	35.5	(1.0)	14.3	(1.4)	1.3	(0.3)	0.1	(0.1)
ABE	240	(3.5)	35.5	(2.7)	46.8	(2.0)	16.2	(2.8)	1.2	(0.6)	0.2	(0.2)
ASE	255	(3.3)	23.6	(3.0)	45.2	(1.9)	28.3	(3.0)	2.9	(0.6)	0.1	(0.1)
ESL	175	(3.1)	78.6	(1.6)	16.8	(1.3)	4.2	(0.5)	0.4	(0.1)	0.0	(0.0)
Document literacy	228	(1.9)	44.3	(1.5)	37.4	(1.0)	16.7	(1.3)	1.5	(0.4)	0.0	(0.0)
ABE	244	(3.7)	30.7	(3.1)	47.9	(2.3)	19.5	(2.6)	1.9	(1.0)	0.0	(0.0)
ASE	258	(3.0)	19.2	(2.3)	46.0	(2.4)	32.0	(2.9)	2.8	(0.7)	0.0	(0.0)
ESL	192	(2.5)	74.5	(1.7)	20.5	(1.2)	4.7	(0.6)	0.3	(0.1)	0.0	(0.0)
Numeracy	203	(2.1)	66.4	(1.8)	25.3	(0.9)	7.7	(1.1)	0.7	(0.1)	0.0	(0.0)
ABE	210	(4.4)	65.5	(3.9)	26.4	(2.0)	7.5	(2.5)	0.6	(0.3)	0.1	(0.1)
ASE	229	(3.3)	46.9	(3.2)	38.2	(1.8)	13.7	(2.0)	1.2	(0.4)	0.0	(0.0)
ESL	182	(2.7)	78.5	(1.6)	16.7	(1.2)	4.3	(0.5)	0.5	(0.1)	0.0	(0.0)

ASE programs performed significantly higher, on average, than learners in ABE and ESL programs. These findings are not surprising, as ASE learners are expected to have completed basic educational requirements and are enrolled in programs to receive help to obtain secondary education certification. Similar results were found for ABE programs compared with ESL programs. As shown in table 6.2, the largest percentage of ABE learners performed at level 2 on the prose and document literacy scales, whereas the largest percentage of learners in ESL programs performed at level 1. For each group of learners, the largest percentage performed at level 1 on the numeracy scale.

One finding of interest was the fact that, overall, 16–18 percent of adult learners performed at level 3 and higher on the prose and document literacy scales, while some 8 percent did so on the numeracy scale. Among participants in ASE programs, more than 30 percent demonstrated performance at level 3 and above on the prose and document scales, while only 15 percent did so on the numeracy scale. A number of studies discuss the skills of individuals performing at these levels on the literacy scales. For example, a study looking at the percentage of test-takers who passed the GED showed that 88 percent of those with document literacy scores at level 3 passed the GED, while 98 percent at levels 4 and above passed the GED (Baldwin, Kirsch, Rock, & Yamamoto, 1995). Thus, these data raise interesting questions outside the scope of the AEPS Learner Survey about these higher-performing participants with respect to their particular purposes for attending adult education programs and their learning goals. Given their relatively lower performance on the numeracy scale and the fact that numeracy skills are critical across a range of adult contexts, including performance on the GED, one hypothesis is that these adult learners were attending adult education programs to improve their skills in the numeracy domain.

As noted previously, the AEPS survey was designed so that results from this study could be compared with those for the general household population in the ALL. As table 6.3 shows, the performance of the general adult population was 42 points higher on the document literacy scale than participants in adult education programs, 49 points higher on the prose literacy scale, and 59 points higher on the numeracy scale. In terms of performance by proficiency levels, the largest percentage of the general population performed at either level 2 or 3, while the largest percentage of the AEPS population performed at level 1.

It is equally important to examine the performance gaps that exist between the most and least skilled adults (e.g., 10th and 90th percentiles). These gaps provide a measure of inequality of outcomes for these populations. This analysis reveals findings that are not consistent across domains. The performance gap between the two populations were approximately equal on the document literacy scale, while the gap for the AEPS population was 24 points wider on the prose literacy scale and 10 points narrower on the numeracy scale—still

Table 6.3
Skills in Prose Literacy, Document Literacy, and Numeracy among the AEPS and ALL Populations

	Mean		Percentiles					Distribution by proficiency levels			
Scales	Score (SE)	SD	10th Score (SE)	25th Score (SE)	50th Score (SE)	75th Score (SE)	90th Score (SE)	Level 1 % (SE)	Level 2 % (SE)	Level 3 % (SE)	Levels 4/5 % (SE)
Prose literacy scale											
AEPS	219 (1.9)	60.3	134 (4.3)	186 (3.4)	229 (1.8)	262 (2.5)	290 (5.5)	48.8 (1.3)	35.5 (1.0)	14.3 (1.4)	1.3 (0.3)
ALL	269 (1.3)	51.9	200 (2.1)	235 (1.1)	272 (2.4)	306 (2.7)	332 (1.4)	20.0 (0.8)	32.6 (1.1)	34.6 (1.2)	12.8 (1.0)
Document literacy scale											
AEPS	228 (1.9)	52.5	153 (3.2)	196 (2.6)	232 (1.8)	268 (3.6)	292 (2.9)	44.3 (1.5)	37.4 (1.0)	16.7 (1.3)	1.5 (0.4)
ALL	270 (1.5)	53.9	199 (1.5)	236 (1.8)	273 (1.6)	308 (2.2)	337 (1.6)	20.2 (1.0)	32.3 (1.4)	32.6 (1.1)	15.0 (1.0)
Numeracy literacy scale											
AEPS	203 (2.1)	53.6	134 (2.3)	170 (2.7)	205 (1.9)	238 (3.7)	272 (3.7)	66.4 (1.8)	25.3 (0.9)	7.7 (1.1)	0.7 (0.1)
ALL	261 (1.4)	57.5	186 (2.6)	223 (2.4)	264 (1.1)	302 (2.1)	334 (2.6)	26.8 (0.9)	31.8 (1.1)	28.8 (1.0)	12.7 (1.1)

equivalent to 2.6 standard deviations. The fact that prose showed the widest performance gap is most likely related to characteristics of the domain. Prose literacy requires a greater knowledge of language structure, including grammar, syntax, text schemata, and prosodic elements. Thus, these results could have been affected by the larger percentages of non-native adult learners in the AEPS population who had a mother tongue other than English.

Overall, about one in two adults in the general population and four in five adults in the AEPS population performed below level 3. Of course, it would be expected that adults participating in programs to improve their skills would demonstrate lower skill levels than the general adult population, and these results from the Learner Survey and comparable measures across the adult learner population confirm that assumption. The large proportion of adult learners in level 1 suggests that adult education programs are, in fact, serving adults who are most in need of educational services. It also points to the fact that their educational needs are significant and varied. Previous studies have shown that adults in level 1 are a particularly heterogeneous group who not only have limited literacy skills but also tend to have poor language skills and/or lack component skills such as decoding, vocabulary, and fluency that one must possess in order to become a proficient reader. A recent study by Strucker, Yamamoto, and Kirsch (2006) found that many participants in adult education programs who performed at levels 1 and 2 on the literacy scales also demonstrated difficulties with one or more of these component skills. These characteristics highlight the challenges to be faced by learners and programs if the skill levels of these level 1 learners are to be raised to a point that will allow them to fully participate in today's society.

RESULTS BY GENDER

Results from the Learner Survey showed no differences between male and female learners on the AEPS on either the literacy or numeracy scales (see table 6.4). In addition, the percentage of learners performing at each proficiency level was similar for males and females across the three domains. While these findings contrast to those of surveys of school-age populations, which generally find performance differences between girls and boys (Freeman, 2004; OECD, 2004), they are similar to the findings of other surveys such as the International Adult Literacy Survey (OECD & Statistics Canada, 2000) and the National Adult Literacy Survey (Kirsch, Youngblood, Kolstad, & Jenkins, 1993), which found no important differences between the performance of males and females.

The AEPS results on the numeracy scale, however, stand in contrast to those found for the household population in the ALL. While, as noted, there were no significant differences between males and females on the numeracy scale in the AEPS, a significant 16-point difference in favor of males was found in the ALL

Table 6.4
Gender and Skills on the Prose Literacy, Document Literacy, and Numeracy Scales
for the AEPS and ALL Populations

| | Mean score | | | Distribution by proficiency levels | | | |
| | | | Level 1 | Level 2 | Level 3 | Levels 4/5 |
	Mean SE	SD	% (SE)	% (SE)	% (SE)	% (SE)
Prose literacy scale						
AEPS						
Male	219 (2.6)	59.5	49.0 (2.2)	36.0 (1.8)	14.2 (1.5)	0.9 (0.3)
Female	220 (2.1)	60.9	48.7 (1.4)	35.1 (1.2)	14.5 (1.5)	1.8 (0.4)
ALL						
Male	266 (1.8)	53.1	21.0 (1.0)	33.0 (2.0)	34.0 (1.0)	12.0 (1.0)
Female	271 (1.6)	50.5	19.0 (1.0)	32.0 (2.0)	36.0 (2.0)	14.0 (1.0)
Document literacy scale						
AEPS						
Male	229 (2.2)	51.3	42.9 (2.2)	38.9 (1.7)	17.2 (1.5)	0.9 (0.2)
Female	228 (2.3)	53.4	45.6 (1.6)	36.2 (1.2)	16.2 (1.4)	2.1 (0.6)
ALL						
Male	272 (2.1)	55.7	20.0 (1.0)	31.0 (2.0)	32.0 (1.0)	17.0 (2.0)
Female	268 (1.6)	52.2	20.0 (1.0)	34.0 (2.0)	33.0 (2.0)	13.0 (1.0)
Numeracy scale						
AEPS						
Male	205 (2.3)	53.0	64.6 (2.0)	27.0 (1.5)	8.0 (1.2)	0.4 (0.1)
Female	202 (2.4)	54.0	67.9 (2.0)	23.8 (1.1)	7.3 (1.2)	1.0 (0.3)
ALL						
Male	270 (1.8)	58.5	23.0 (1.0)	29.0 (2.0)	31.0 (1.0)	17.0 (1.0)
Female	254 (1.9)	55.3	30.0 (2.0)	34.0 (2.0)	27.0 (2.0)	9.0 (1.3)

(OECD & Statistics Canada, 2005). This may reflect the fact that, relative to the prose and document literacy scales, and in comparison to the general adult population, the performance of adult education participants is weakest on the numeracy scale. This more uniform weakness may well wash out any performance differences between males and females on the numeracy scale in the AEPS.

There were also no significant differences found between males and females participating in the three types of adult education programs. That is, the performance of males and females in ASE, ABE, and ESL programs was similar, which corresponds to the general finding that, across the adult education population, gender does not affect performance on the prose literacy, document literacy, or numeracy scales.

RESULTS BY AGE

Adult education programs target learners ages 16 and older and therefore are attended by individuals across a wide age span. In the background questionnaire for the Learner Survey, respondents were asked to indicate their year of birth, which allows literacy and numeracy skills to be examined across age groups. Forty-six percent of adult learners were between the ages of 25 and 44. An additional 35 percent of adult learners were between the ages of 16 and 24. For all three types of programs, a negative relationship existed between performance and age, with younger age groups performing better, on average, on each of the three scales.

As shown in table 6.5, average scores in prose and document literacy for the two youngest groups—ages 16 through 18 and 19 through 24—were at proficiency level 2 (226–275), compared with scores at level 1 (0–225) for the older cohorts. The largest differences were found in prose literacy, for which the youngest age group—ages 16 through 18—scored 34 points higher than participants between 25 and 44 years of age, and some 40 points higher than participants ages 45 to 59. Performance in numeracy was not only more uniform across age groups, but it was also the only domain in which all age groups had average scores at level 1.

Table 6.5
Percentages and Average Proficiencies of Adult Education Participants: Overall, by Type of Program, and by Age

	Age				
	16–18	**19–24**	**25–44**	**45–59**	**60 +**
Percentage					
Overall	4.4 (0.9)	30.1 (2.0)	45.9 (1.9)	15.6 (1.4)	1.7 (0.3)
ABE	4.3 (1.4)	36.9 (3.8)	42.2 (3.4)	14.2 (2.4)	1.3 (0.3)
ASE	11.9 (2.9)	45.7 (3.0)	27.8 (3.3)	10.9 (2.5)	0.8 (0.4)
ESL	0.2 (0.1)	13.4 (1.0)	60.4 (2.7)	19.8 (1.5)	2.7 (0.6)
Prose literacy scale					
Overall mean	248 (5.2)	236 (3.2)	214 (2.5)	208 (5.2)	164 (7.3)
SD	42.9	50.7	59.4	66.7	63.6
ABE mean	247 (5.2)	241 (4.7)	242 (3.5)	236 (7.3)	184 (10.3)
ASE mean	252 (7.3)	257 (4.0)	251 (4.9)	263 (6.8)	237 (16.8)
ESL mean	137 (28.7)	177 (4.2)	181 (3.2)	168 (5.5)	141 (8.3)
Document literacy scale					
Overall mean	250 (5.7)	245 (2.2)	222 (2.3)	218 (4.5)	182 (6.6)
SD	41.1	45.6	51.6	55.3	50.4
ABE mean	251 (4.8)	250 (4.5)	244 (3.9)	238 (6.8)	190 (9.6)
ASE mean	253 (8.0)	262 (3.3)	256 (4.7)	260 (8.6)	242 (15.9)
ESL mean	159 (36.3)	195 (3.3)	195 (2.6)	189 (4.5)	167 (6.4)
Numeracy scale					
Overall mean	218 (8.2)	212 (2.8)	201 (2.3)	199 (4.7)	165 (6.4)
SD	53.0	49.9	51.9	57.9	54.4
ABE mean	219 (8.1)	211 (4.9)	209 (4.8)	210 (7.8)	162 (10.1)
ASE mean	220 (11.3)	231 (4.1)	224 (5.7)	239 (8.8)	231 (18.4)
ESL mean	134 (44.4)	179 (3.9)	187 (3.1)	178 (5.6)	156 (6.2)

To what extent is this relationship between age and proficiency similar among adults in the three types of instructional programs? Data in table 6.5 show that when we look at it by type of program, the relationship between performance and age is different from the negative relationship found for the total adult education population. A relatively flat relationship was demonstrated among learners between ages 16 and 59 in ABE and ASE programs, while those participants 60 years of age and older performed at a significantly lower level on each scale. Data for the ESL participants revealed a more curvilinear relationship, with the youngest and oldest cohorts performing at a somewhat lower level than adults between 19 and 24 and 25 and 44 years of age.

Care should be taken when we interpret these results because they in part reflect differences in the percentages of adults in each age group participating in each type of program. For example, while the youngest cohort (those 16–18 years of age) represented some 4 percent of the overall adult education population, they represented 4 percent of those in ABE classes, 12 percent of those in ASE classes, and less than 1 percent of those in ESL classes. In contrast, while those between 25 and 44 years old represented some 46 percent of adult learners, they represented 42 percent of those in ABE classes, 28 percent of those in ABE classes, and 60 percent of those in ESL classes.

RESULTS BY SOURCES OF INCOME

The background questionnaire of the Learner Survey asked respondents about their labor force status as well as about their sources of income during the previous program year. Sources of income included wages or salaries; income earned through self-employment; interest, dividends, or investments; pensions; and government transfers. These variables were examined through latent class analysis, which is a statistical tool for clustering subjects based on categorical variables. The analysis yields a classification for each survey participant that represents a tendency to respond to a set of questions in a particular way (Lazarsfeld & Henry, 1968; Patterson, Dayton, & Graubard, 2002). The analysis of these variables resulted in the identification of three classes that associate performance with sources of income and can be looked at by labor force status. We can also compare the results for the AEPS learner population with those of the general household population.

- Class 1 represents 15 percent of participants in adult education programs and 9 percent of adults in the general population. In general, this group of learners had a low likelihood of reporting any income, but when they did, it was likely to come from a combination of wages or salaries, Social Security benefits, and SSI payments.

- Class 2 represents 85 percent of participants in adult education programs and some 65 percent of adults in the general population. For adults in this group there was a high likelihood that their only source of income was wages or salaries (including commissions, tips, and bonuses).

- Class 3 is almost nonexistent in the adult education population but represents about 25 percent of adults in the general population. This group was likely to have income from wages or salaries or to be self-employed. What distinguishes them from the other two groups is that they reported receiving additional income from interest, dividends, capital gains, or other investments.

Table 6.6 shows the results of the latent class analysis using sources of income for participants in adult education programs and for adults in the general population. Before examining these results, it is important to remember that participants in adult education programs are there to improve their language skills as well as their literacy and numeracy skills. Many are also there to increase their labor market opportunities and hence their wages and incomes. Overall, some 50 percent of the adult learners reported they were employed, while some 33 percent indicated they were unemployed but looking for work, compared to the 69 percent of the general ALL population who reported they were employed and the 9 percent who indicated they were unemployed but looking for work. As the AEPS learner population is both younger and less skilled than the general population, it is not surprising that the probability of adult learners receiving income from interest, dividends, capital gains, or other investments (class 3) was close to zero, compared to some 25 percent of adults in the general population.

The AEPS and ALL groups differed not only in terms of how they are distributed across the three latent classes but also in terms of their performance on the three scales. The ALL data for the general population shows that adults in class 3 demonstrated significantly higher scores on each of the three scales than adults in class 2, with the average differences ranging from 35 points on the prose scale to 37 points on the document scale and 47 points on the numeracy scale. In turn, adults in class 2 outscored adults in class 1, on average, by 25 points on prose literacy, 35 points on document literacy, and 33 points on numeracy. In total, in the ALL population, adults in class 3 outperformed those in class 1 by 60 points or more on each of the three scales.

As noted previously, participants in adult education programs were very unlikely to report incomes from dividends, interest, capital gains, or other investments, the distinguishing characteristic of class 3. Thus, there were not enough adult learners to establish this latent class among adult education participants. In addition, there were no significant differences in the average scores for either the prose or document literacy scales between adult education participants identified as belonging to class 1 and those identified as being in class 2. Numeracy—for which adults in class 2 showed higher average scores (14 points) than those in class 1—was the only scale where there was a significant difference among adult education participants.

Table 6.6
Percent of Learners and Average Scores Overall and by Labor Force Status among AEPS Participants and the ALL General Household Population by Latent Class Analysis on Sources of Income

	Class 1				Class 2				Class 3			
	Percent in class	Average score			Percent in class	Average score			Percent in class	Average score		
		Prose	Document	Numeracy		Prose	Document	Numeracy		Prose	Document	Numeracy
AEPS												
Overall	15.2 (1.2)	214 (4.3)	222 (4.1)	191 (4.1)	84.8 (1.2)	220 (2.1)	229 (1.9)	206 (2.1)	n/a	n/a	n/a	n/a
Employment status												
Employed	7.9 (0.9)	206 (5.9)	218 (5.1)	188 (5.4)	92.1 (0.9)	217 (3.2)	228 (2.8)	206 (2.7)	n/a	n/a	n/a	n/a
Unemployed	21.9 (2.3)	222 (4.7)	226 (4.7)	192.6 (4.7)	78.1 (2.3)	227 (2.6)	233 (2.4)	205 (2.8)	n/a	n/a	n/a	n/a
Not in labor force	23.6 (3.2)	210 (9.3)	217 (7.6)	192.3 (8.1)	76.4 (3.2)	219 (5.5)	226 (5.2)	206 (4.3)	n/a	n/a	n/a	n/a
ALL												
Overall	9.4 (0.6)	237 (4.1)	229 (4.0)	219 (3.9)	65.3 (1.0)	262 (1.6)	264 (1.6)	252 (1.9)	25.2 (1.0)	297 (2.2)	301 (2.2)	299 (2.0)
Employment status												
Employed	2.5 (0.3)	253 (5.2)	251 (4.5)	239 (6.8)	65.4 (1.3)	265 (1.9)	266 (2.0)	255 (2.0)	32.1 (1.3)	298 (2.2)	302 (2.2)	300 (2.0)
Unemployed	16.9 (1.6)	221 (6.6)	216 (6.6)	200 (6.6)	73.6 (2.1)	247 (3.6)	251 (3.8)	231 (4.0)	9.5 (1.9)	281 (9.0)	291 (8.6)	284 (10.1)
Not in labor force	29.4 (2.1)	236 (5.1)	227 (5.2)	218 (4.8)	57.8 (1.8)	268 (3.0)	270 (3.1)	260 (4.1)	12.8 (1.4)	299 (5.4)	299 (5.3)	297 (5.5)

RESULTS BY LEVEL OF EDUCATION

The AEPS data on educational attainment are reported in six categories: no education, up to 8th grade, between 9th and 11th grades, completed high school, received GED certification or equivalent, and attained or completed some education beyond high school (ranging from two-year programs to bachelor's, master's, and PhD programs). These data were collapsed into a single category due to low cell frequencies for each of the individual categories associated with postsecondary education. Overall, results from the Learner Survey revealed the expected relationship between level of education and performance. As shown in table 6.7, those with higher levels of education demonstrated higher proficiencies on all three scales.

The relationship between education and proficiency is less clear for nonnative learners. In part, this is due to the relative impact of their education outside the United States. As shown in table 6.8, some 24 percent of nonnative participants reported they had completed up to 8th grade and 39 percent had some secondary education (i.e., between nine years of school and the completion of high school) outside the United States. An additional 28 percent reported they had had education beyond the secondary level in their native countries, of which 13 percent reported they had completed a bachelor's degree, a level of educational attainment that is higher than that of native adult education participants in the similar category for the native population who reported that they completed a bachelor's degree and most likely reflects the fact that these non-native learners are attending adult education programs to improve their English language skills as well as their English literacy skills. Only about 4 percent of non-native learners reported not completing any schooling before coming to the United States. However, as shown in table 6.8, their average scores are, for the most part, higher than those of non-native learners who reported completing as much as secondary education outside the United States. Given the relatively high average scores of this group, which represents 4 percent of the non-native learners, it is likely these individuals received at least some education after coming to the United States. Thus the relationship between educational attainment and skills for the adult learner population goes beyond levels of schooling and is affected by issues related to nativity and country of education.

RESULTS BY LANGUAGE AND NATIVITY

The U.S. population is becoming older and more diverse, and immigration has had a significant impact on both the general population and the workforce. During the 1980s, immigration accounted for about 21 percent of our nation's population growth, and that contribution rose to 31 percent during the 1990s.

Table 6.7
Percent and Average Score of Adult Education Participants by Years of Schooling Completed in the United States

	Educational attainment in the United States					
	No schooling in the United States	Up to 8th grade	9th to 11th grade	12th grade to completion of high school	GED equivalent	Some education after high school
Percent	33.5 (0.9)	8.8 (0.8)	41.3 (1.8)	8.2 (1.4)	3.1 (0.5)	4.1 (0.8)
Mean score						
Prose	177 (2.8)	225 (5.1)	242 (1.6)	247 (7.5)	257 (6.3)	257 (10.6)
Document	194 (2.3)	230 (5.0)	247 (1.7)	252 (7.6)	257 (5.7)	260 (9.8)
Numeracy	184 (2.5)	203 (4.0)	211 (2.0)	219 (9.0)	246 (7.1)	240 (10.5)

Table 6.8
Percent and Average Scores of Non-native Adult Education Participants by Years of Schooling Completed Prior to Coming to the United States

	No schooling prior to coming to the United States	Educational attainment prior to coming to the United States				
		Up to 8th grade	9th to 11th grade	12th grade to completion of high school	GED equivalent	Some education after high school
Percent	4.3 (0.8)	23.8 (1.9)	16.6 (1.3)	22.2 (1.6)	N/A	28.4 (1.4)
Mean score						
Prose	204 (10.8)	155 (4.5)	185 (5.3)	180 (3.1)	N/A	206 (3.6)
Document	209 (8.8)	177 (3.7)	196 (3.7)	195 (2.9)	N/A	218 (3.2)
Numeracy	182 (9.6)	164 (4.6)	184 (4.2)	183 (3.5)	N/A	208 (3.8)

The U.S. Census Bureau projects that between 2000 and 2015 immigration will account for some 50 percent of our population's growth and significantly more of the growth in our labor force. Fueled by both immigration and higher birth rates, the Hispanic share of the population is expected to rise from 14 percent in 2005 to just over 20 percent by 2030. More importantly, according to data from the American Community Survey, in 2004, some 57 percent of the Hispanic population between 16 and 64 in the United States was foreign born and more than half of this immigrant population lacked a high school diploma (Kirsch, Braun, Yamamoto, & Sum, 2007).

Given the demographic patterns we are seeing in the general population, it is not too surprising that close to half of all participants in adult education programs reported that English was not their native language. As shown in table 6.9, 29 percent of adult education participants reported they learned Spanish as their mother tongue, 7 percent learned an Asian language, 2 percent learned a European language, and 6 percent learned some other language.

As would be expected, English, as the testing language for the AEPS, played a role in overall performance. In all domains, learners with a mother tongue of English performed better than learners reporting other languages as their mother tongue. The differences in performance between those whose mother tongue was English and those whose mother tongue was Spanish averaged 26 points in numeracy, 47 points for document literacy, and 54 points for prose literacy (see Table 6.9). The impact of mother tongue was even more evident when the prose performance of those whose mother tongue was English was compared with those whose mother tongue was a language other than Spanish. Then, the average performance differences in favor of English speakers were only 21 points in numeracy and 51 points in document literacy but 70 points on the prose literacy scale, no doubt reflecting the distinct linguistic differences between English and these other languages.

Table 6.9
Mother Tongue and Skills on the Prose Literacy, Document Literacy, and Numeracy Scales

			Performance					
	Percentage		Prose literacy		Document literacy		Numeracy	
Mother tongue	%	SE	Mean	SE	Mean	SE	Mean	SE
English	55.5	(0.8)	246	(2.6)	250	(2.8)	216	(3.3)
Spanish	29.3	(0.5)	192	(2.9)	203	(2.3)	190	(2.4)
European[1]	1.8	(0.4)	198	(7.4)	212	(5.6)	193	(7.5)
Asian[2]	6.9	(0.9)	176	(8.3)	199	(7.3)	195	(7.6)
Others	6.4	(0.7)	167	(5.5)	184	(4.7)	167	(4.7)

[1]French, German, Greek, Italian, Polish, and Portuguese
[2]Chinese, Japanese, Korean, Tagalog, and Vietnamese

Immigrants were highly represented in the population of adult learners: 43 percent reported that they were born outside the United States. The data in table 6.10 show that proficiency, particularly on the prose and document scales, was related to nativity. Among native learners, there is a 9 point difference between mean performance on both the prose and document scales for those whose mother tongue was English versus those who spoke Spanish. Comparison of those same two language groups among non-native learners reveals much larger differences—39 points on the prose scale and 28 on the document scale. Comparison of learners with the same language backgrounds demonstrates that nativity has a major impact on performance. Native learners whose mother tongue was English scored, on average, 21 and 23 points higher than non-native learners on the prose and document scales, respectively. Native learners whose mother tongue was Spanish scored 51 and 42 points higher than non-native learners.

Nativity also showed an impact on performance differences among ethnic groups. One group of particular interest is Hispanics, as some 35 percent of participants in adult education programs are Hispanic. Data collected regarding nativity showed that 63 percent of the Hispanic participants in adult education, compared to 36 percent of the non-Hispanic population, reported that they were non-native. The data showed that there was a 30-point difference between the performance of Hispanic and non-Hispanic adult learners on

Table 6.10
Mother Tongue and Skills, by Birth Place

	Percentage		Performance					
			Prose literacy		Document literacy		Numeracy	
Mother tongue	%	SE	Mean	SE	Mean	SE	Mean	SE
Native learners								
English	94.7	(0.9)	247	(2.6)	251	(2.8)	217	(3.3)
Spanish	4.5	(0.7)	238	(7.3)	242	(8.0)	211	(7.6)
European[1]	0.3	(0.2)	c	c	c	c	c	c
Asian[2]	0.1	(0.1)	c	c	c	c	c	c
Others	0.2	(0.1)	c	c	c	c	c	c
Non-native learners								
English	3.0	(0.8)	226	(14.5)	228	(12.8)	197	(15.2)
Spanish	62.6	(0.9)	187	(2.9)	200	(2.3)	188	(2.5)
European[1]	3.8	(1.0)	198	(7.6)	211	(6.4)	192	(8.2)
Asian[2]	15.8	(2.1)	176	(8.2)	199	(7.3)	195	(7.6)
Others	14.7	(1.7)	166	(5.3)	183	(4.6)	166	(4.5)

[1]French, German, Greek, Italian, Polish, and Portuguese
[2]Chinese, Japanese, Korean, Tagalog, and Vietnamese

the prose scale (see table 6.11). However, this difference disappears when we look at place of birth within these two groups. For example, average performance on the prose scale was similar for native Hispanics and native non-Hispanics (246 compared to 247 points). Similar performance levels were also found between non-native Hispanics and non-native non-Hispanics (186 as opposed to 180 points) in prose literacy.

This same pattern held for the document and numeracy scales as can be seen in figure 6.1, which illustrates that, in general, the performance pattern is more similar in regard to nativity than ethnicity. The lines showing the performance of Hispanic natives and non-Hispanic natives are essentially identical. Those for Hispanic non-natives and non-Hispanic non-natives are identical for document literacy and numeracy. The variation in mean scores on prose literacy for Hispanic and non-Hispanic non-natives is most likely due to the fact that the non-Hispanic non-native group includes speakers of languages that are markedly different from English, which has a significant negative impact on their English-language prose proficiency.

Of course, nativity, language, and ethnicity do not operate in isolation but instead interact, influencing proficiency in prose and document literacy in particular. The varying backgrounds, languages, and life experiences of individuals within those groups naturally affect the skills and knowledge they bring to the types of literacy and numeracy tasks represented in the Learner Survey.

IMPACT OF TESTING LANGUAGE

One assumption that might be made non-native learners are tested is that assessing them in a language other than their native tongue would put them at a significant disadvantage and not allow them to fully demonstrate their literacy skills. The AEPS addressed this issue by randomly assigning a group of Hispanic learners to either an English or Spanish version of the prose and document literacy items from the Learner Survey.

As expected, results showed that a representative sample of Hispanic learners demonstrated significantly higher average literacy skills in Spanish than a random equivalent sample of Hispanic learners who took the test in English. On the prose scale, those tested in Spanish had mean scores that were 29 points higher than those tested in English (see table 6.12). On the document scale, those tested in Spanish had scores that were 12 points higher.

These data also demonstrate that allowing for language differences did not eradicate differences in literacy performance. The largest percentage of Hispanic learners, whether they were tested in English or Spanish, performed at level 1. The average performance of the Spanish-tested Hispanic adult learners was, in fact, significantly lower than the average performance of adults in the general population (i.e., ALL), and not statistically different from the

Table 6.11
Ethnicity, Nativity, and Skills on the Prose Literacy, Document Literacy, and Numeracy Scales

	Ethnicity					
	Hispanic			Non-Hispanic		
	Overall	Native	Non-native	Overall	Native	Non-native
Overall						
Percentage	35.0 (0.1)	13.9 (0.8)	63.3 (0.9)	63.6 (0.6)	84.2 (1.2)	36.3 (0.9)
Prose literacy						
Mean scores	200 (2.6)	246 (3.6)	186 (3.0)	230 (2.5)	247 (2.6)	180 (4.3)
Percentage by skill level						
Level 1	64.1 (1.4)	32.5 (2.9)	73.3 (1.7)	40.1 (1.7)	28.9 (1.9)	74.3 (2.4)
Level 2	26.0 (1.2)	45.6 (2.5)	20.3 (1.2)	40.8 (1.4)	48.3 (1.7)	17.7 (1.7)
Level 3	8.9 (1.1)	18.8 (3.0)	6.0 (1.1)	17.5 (1.9)	20.9 (2.4)	7.1 (1.30)
Levels 4/5	1.0 (0.3)	3.1 (1.3)	0.4 (0.1)	1.6 (0.4)	1.9 (0.6)	0.9 (0.3)
Document literacy						
Mean scores	210 (2.1)	249 (4.0)	199 (2.3)	238 (2.6)	251 (2.9)	199 (3.7)
Percentage by skill level						
Level 1	60.8 (1.7)	26.2 (3.8)	70.9 (2.0)	35.0 (1.9)	24.8 (2.2)	66.5 (2.1)
Level 2	29.3 (1.5)	50.0 (3.2)	23.2 (1.4)	42.0 (1.4)	48.2 (1.8)	23.1 (1.4)
Level 3	9.4 (1.0)	21.7 (3.4)	5.9 (1.1)	20.8 (1.8)	24.5 (2.2)	9.5 (1.5)
Levels 4/5	0.5 (0.2)	2.1 (1.0)	0.0 (0.0)	2.1 (0.6)	2.5 (0.9)	0.9 (0.2)
Numeracy						
Mean scores	194 (2.2)	216 (3.5)	187 (2.5)	209 (2.8)	217 (3.5)	186 (4.0)
Percentage by skill levels						
Level 1	73.1 (2.2)	60.5 (3.5)	76.8 (1.8)	62.5 (2.4)	58.7 (3.1)	74.4 (2.2)
Level 2	23.2 (1.4)	34.0 (3.3)	20.0 (1.4)	26.4 (1.1)	29.9 (1.4)	15.9 (1.2)
Level 3	3.4 (0.6)	4.5 (1.4)	3.1 (0.6)	10.1 (1.7)	10.6 (2.2)	8.5 (1.4)
Levels 4/5	0.3 (0.2)	1.0 (0.6)	0.1 (0.1)	0.9 (0.2)	0.9 (0.3)	1.2 (0.2)

Figure 6.1
Mean Prose Literacy, Document Literacy, and Numeracy Scores by Ethnicity and Nativity

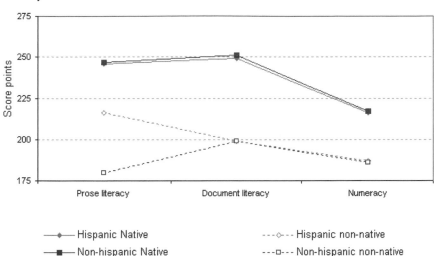

average performance of participants in adult education programs (i.e., AEPS). The average performance of the English-tested Hispanic adult learners on the prose literacy scale was also significantly lower than the average performance of the other groups of adults and adult learners.

These results suggest that while the testing language played a role in the average performance of Hispanic learners, they have not acquired basic literacy skills, either in English or in their native language. This is not surprising, given that they are participating in adult education programs. However, it is important to keep in mind that, on average, these adults have both a language and a literacy challenge.

CURRENT AND FUTURE CHALLENGES

As this chapter shows, participants in federally funded adult education programs have a range of challenges to meet in order to develop the literacy and numeracy skills needed in the twenty-first century. The AEPS data show that, across all three domains measured, the largest proportion of adult learners performed at level 1. While one would anticipate that those participating in adult literacy programs would have lower-level skills than adults in the general population, the finding that their demonstrated skills are concentrated at the most restricted literacy and numeracy level has implications for the intensity and duration of the educational interventions required for them to develop the skills needed to participate successfully in today's society.

Table 6.12
Skills in Prose Literacy and Document Literacy among Spanish-Speaking Learners Tested in English and Spanish

| Hispanic populations | Mean | | | | | | | | | | Distribution by proficiency levels | | | | | |
| | | | | Level 1 | | Level 2 | | Level 3 | | Level 4 | | Level 5 | |
	Score	SE	SD	%	SE	%	SE	%	SE	%	SE	%	SE
Prose literacy scale													
English tested	200	(2.6)	62.2	64.1	(1.4)	26.0	(1.2)	8.9	(1.1)	0.7	(0.2)	0.3	(0.2)
Spanish tested	229	(8.9)	62.4	43.1	(3.7)	34.1	(2.3)	19.7	(2.1)	2.7	(0.5)	0.4	(0.4)
Document literacy scale													
English tested	210	(2.0)	50.5	60.9	(1.7)	29.2	(1.5)	9.4	(1.0)	0.5	(0.2)	0.0	(0.0)
Spanish tested	222	(6.1)	48.6	50.2	(3.2)	37.6	(2.0)	11.6	(2.1)	0.5	(0.2)	0.0	(0.0)

Skill levels, however, are not the only challenge that adult learners face. Changes in the workplace, in large measure driven by globalization and technological innovations, have increased the demand for workers with higher-level skills and more years of schooling. In fact, some two-thirds of the job growth between 1984 and 2000 occurred in professional, management, technical, and high-level sales occupations. Projections by the Bureau of Labor Statistics suggest that these same occupations will generate about 46 percent of all job growth between 2004 and 2014 (Kirsch et al., 2007). And, the ALL data showed that the workers in these job categories were much more likely to have access to employer-sponsored training programs, which, in a kind of rich-get-richer scenario, allows them to keep abreast of changing technologies and continue to improve their skills. One consequence of this shift in the composition of jobs has been the economic return to education and skills, resulting in the widening of the average income gaps between those with 16 years or more of schooling and those with a high school education or less. The challenge for the future will not be finding a job; it will more likely be finding a well-paying job with employer-supervised training, or one that offers opportunities for further training (Kirsch et al., 2007). Without the skills to compete for such jobs, those with restricted literacy and numeracy skills are likely to continue to fall behind.

The AEPS findings highlight the challenges faced by adults in ESL programs. Comparisons between the English and Spanish literacy of native Hispanics provide evidence that many ESL learners have the same literacy needs as the general adult education population. Therefore their challenge is not solely to acquire English language skills and map those on to some core set of literacy skills they possess in their native language. Rather, they need to acquire both English language and English literacy skills.

The implications of these findings are particularly important given that the number of adults who will need to develop this joint set of literacy and English language skills is growing at unprecedented rates. Over the period 2000–2015, the U.S. Census Bureau projects that net international immigration will continue to increase in both absolute terms and as a percent of the nation's overall population growth. In fact, immigration is projected to account for more than half of the nation's population growth during that period (Kirsch et al., 2007).

If we combine the existing skills distributions found in the general household population with the expected shifts in our demographics, it appears that the pool of human capital in the United States, as measured by these literacy domains, will decrease with a concomitant increase in inequality. For example, if we compare the percentage of adults at level 1 on the prose scale, as reported by the NALS, with the percentage that is projected by Kirsch, et al., for the year 2030, the percentage of 16- to 65-year-olds in the general population with the most limited set of English literacy skills is expected to grow from 17 to

27 percent (2007). This means that the increase in the number of adults in the United States at level 1 is expected to grow by more than the total number of adults currently participating in federally sponsored adult education programs.

Given such challenges, how can the adult education system best serve the needs of both current and future populations of adult learners? Are learners spending enough time in adult education programs to bring about the needed improvements in their literacy and numeracy skills? Are the instructional services they receive organized and delivered in a way that maximizes the learning opportunities of these learners? Is technology being used effectively to teach the information and communication technology skills that are becoming increasingly integrated with all aspects of our lives? The data from the Adult Education Program Survey, in combination with the economic and social trends outlined in this chapter, should cause us to question whether we as a nation are providing the resources that adult learners need to meet current and future challenges.

REFERENCES

Baldwin, J., Kirsch, I., Rock, D., & Yamamoto, K. (1995). *The literacy proficiencies of GED examinees: Results from the GED-NALS comparison study.* Washington, DC: American Council on Education and Educational Testing Service.

Becker, G. (2002) The age of human capital. In E. P. Lazear (Ed.), *Education in the twenty-first century.* (p. 3) Stanford, CaA: Hoover Institution Press.

Comings, J. P., Sum, A., & Uvin, J. (2000). *New skill for a new economy: Adult education's role in sustaining economic growth and expanding opportunity.* Boston: Institute for a New Commonwealth.

Freeman, C. E. (2004). *Trends in educational equity of girls and women: 2004* (NCES Report No. 2005–016). Washington, DC: U.S. Department of Education, National Center for Education Statistics.

Friedman, B. M. (2005). Meltdown: A case study. *Atlantic Monthly, 296*(1), 66–68.

Kirsch, I., Braun, H., Yamamoto, K, & Sum, A. (2007) *America's perfect storm: Three forces changing America's future.* Princeton, NJ: Policy Information Center, Educational Testing Service.

Kirsch, I., Jungeblut, A., Jenkins, L., & Kolstad, A. (1993). *Adult literacy in America.* Washington, DC: National Center for Education Statistics.

Lazarsfeld, P. F., & Henry, N. W. (1968). *Latent structure analysis.* Boston: Houghton Mifflin.

National Reporting System for Adult Education.. (2001). *Measures and methods for the National Reporting System for Adult Education: Implementation guidelines.* Washington, DC: U.S. Department of Education, Division of Adult Education and Literacy, Office of Vocational and Adult Education.

National Reporting System for Adult Education. (n.d.). *Fast facts.* Retrieved from http://www.nrsweb.org

OECD. (2001). *The well-being of nations: The role of human and social capital.* Paris: Author.

OECD. (2004). *Learning for tomorrow's world: First results from PISA 2003.* Paris: Author.

OECD & Statistics Canada. (2005). *Learning a living: First result of the Adult Literacy and Life Skills Survey.* Paris, France and Ottawa, Ontario, Canada: OECD & Statistics Canada.

Patterson, B., Dayton, C. M., & Graubard, B. (2002). Latent class analysis of complex survey data: Application to dietary data. *Journal of the American Statistical Association, 97,* 721–729.

Sticht, T. (1998, September). *Beyond 2000: Future directions for adult education.* Washington, DC: U.S. Department of Education, Division of Adult Education and Literacy. Retrieved August 14, 2006, from http://www.nald.ca/fulltext/beyond/cover.htm

Strucker, J., Yamamoto, K., & Kirsch, I. (2006). *The relationship of the component skills of reading to the IALS performance Tipping points and five classes of adult literacy learners.* Boston: NCSALL/World Education.

Sum, A., Kirsch, I., & Taggart, R. (2002). *The twin challenges of mediocrity and inequality: Literacy in the U.S. from an international perspective.* Princeton, NJ: Policy Information Center, Educational Testing Service.

Sum, A., Kirsch, I., & Yamamoto, K. (2004). *Pathways to labor market success: The literacy proficiency of U.S. adults.* Princeton, NJ: Policy Information Center, Educational Testing Service.

Tamassia, C., Lennon, M., Yamamoto, K., & Kirsch, I. (2007). *Adult education program study: Final report on the program and learner surveys.* Princeton, NJ: Educational Testing Service.

Part Three

ADULT LITERACY BEYOND THE CLASSROOM

Chapter Seven

FAMILY LITERACY AND COMMUNITY LITERACY

Victoria Purcell-Gates

Family literacy is born within communities of practice. Practice is defined not as the repetitive doing of a skill but refers to the things that one does in one's world. Practice is defined as the beliefs, values, styles, and roles that make sense in the world. If reading and writing are things that make sense and that people do in their world and as part of their lives, then literacy (more specifically, print literacy) practiced within families is family literacy. Thus, family literacy refers to all the ways that people read and write, including what they read and write and why they do so, within family groups.

A PEEK AT THE PAST

Why are educators interested in family literacy? Educators first became aware of the term "family literacy" with the publication of Denny Taylor's 1985 book of the same name. In this book, Taylor presents the results of a study of five different families and the ways that the reading and writing of print were woven throughout their daily lives. Taylor observed the families, visiting them in their homes, accompanying them on daily errands, and so on, documenting all instances of the use of print in their home environments. The focus of the study was actually the children in the homes, and Taylor's underlying assumption about literacy in the home is captured in the title of the book: *Family Literacy: Children Learning to Read and Write*. Taylor was, in essence, documenting what it was that children were learning about reading and writing through their experiences using print in their home and out-of-school lives, as well as through observing and participating in their parents' literacy activities.

Taylor's book helped to coin the term "family literacy," but she was not the only one who was interested in the roots of literacy development in the home, especially during the preschool years. During this time, a new field of literacy research on what is usually referred to as emergent literacy was growing. Today, the term "early literacy" is used as well for this developmental period. Emergent literacy researchers were interested in how young children begin to develop the awareness of, concepts for, and knowledge of literacy that are needed to learn to read and write. Although most agreed that children become readers and writers within the context of formal school instruction, the goal of the emergent literacy researchers was to explore children's early experiences with print use in their homes and communities before beginning school and during the early years of schooling. This was a clear statement by literacy researchers that formal instruction was not the only avenue for literacy learning. Rather, the belief was that literacy learning depended on, or was influenced by, out-of-school experiences with print, and that the things that young children learned from these experiences provided the basis for making sense of beginning literacy instruction in school.

Between 1985 and 2000, a great deal of research fleshing out this notion of emergent literacy was completed. Researchers documented the role of environmental print on children's early print knowledge (Goodman, 1984), the ways in which knowledge of letter-sound correspondences began in self-directed invented writing and spelling (Read, 1971), parent-child storybook reading routines (Harkness & Miller, 1982), and what the children learned about written language structure and vocabulary from these activities (Purcell-Gates, 1988). The researchers studied the development of spelling/writing abilities (Clay, 1975), the emergence of text comprehension abilities (Snow & Ninio, 1986), and the beginnings of motivations to read and write as the result of growing up with people who read and write for many different reasons (Cochrane-Smith, 1984).

In the midst of all this research centered around the homes of young children, some professionals and legislators were taking note of a fairly obvious but simplistic set of statistics. They highlighted the documented relationships between children's success in school (i.e., scores on reading achievement tests, grades, and teacher reports) and the degree to which parents involved themselves with their children's learning through such activities as monitoring and helping with homework and involvement with their children's schools. This, in combination with the belief (not that well documented) that children whose parents read to them do better in school, particularly with learning to read, led them to propose policy that called for the development of family literacy programs in which parents could learn how to become more involved with their children's education and support their children with their learning in school. Thus, the term "family literacy" was appropriated, but with an altered meaning. It was changed from literacy that happens in families to programs that teach parents how to support their children's school success and engage in activities like storybook reading.

It is undoubtedly clear that I view the area of family literacy from the original perspective: literacy that happens in the lives of people outside a formal learning situation (i.e., school). In this way, I think of family literacy, and of literacy in general, as cultural practice. I will devote the rest of this chapter to exploring this perspective. I will present evidence to support my conviction that understanding family literacy practices is crucial to understanding and helping to facilitate children's literacy learning in school. I will then provide suggestions for families and for teachers of ways that they can build on the literacy practices that occur in children's homes. Many of these suggestions have been found to be effective in raising children's reading and writing scores on tests of literacy achievement and in increasing literacy practice in homes in ways that have been shown to be significantly related to early literacy success in schools for young children. By the end of this chapter, it will be obvious to the reader why I consider the transformed definition of family literacy (i.e., family literacy seen as ways to support children's learning in school), while certainly laudable, to be a simplistic and incomplete understanding of the relationships between the literacy worlds of children and the literacy instruction they receive and rely upon in school.

FAMILY LITERACY IS CULTURAL PRACTICE

What's cultural about the practice of literacy? First, please note the word "practice" in the previous sentence. Family literacy is about the practice of literacy, not about types of literacy or levels of literacy. The practice of literacy is just that—reading and writing events. These reading and writing events are behaviors, or actions, and they always are shaped by situations, or contexts.

Let me introduce the example of a working mother whom I will call Marge. Marge has three children, ages three, four, and eight, and she packs a lot of actions, or behaviors, into her day. She begins her day by rising early, showering, waking the children, and helping them get ready for school and day care. She feeds them and herself breakfast, listens to the news and the weather on TV while eating, and delivers the kids to school and day care. She then drives to work, where she spends eight hours as a claims adjustor for an insurance company. At five o'clock, she packs some files into her briefcase; drives her car to the day-care center, where her children await her; drives home; fixes dinner; helps the children with their homework; helps them take baths and prepare for school the next day; reads each child a story; and then settles down with the files she brought home from work. She logs on to her computer, reads her e-mail and responds to friends and family members, and pays several household bills. Exhausted, she goes to bed at 11 o'clock after glancing at the newspaper and going through her mail.

Throughout this action-packed day, Marge read and wrote many different types of texts. These literacy events were always shaped by Marge's life as a mother who works as a claims adjustor and holds beliefs and values that shape her parenting, her choice of work and choice to work, her daily routines, her interests, and so on. On a broader scale, Marge's life is shaped by the North American culture and lifestyle in which it is situated. She has access to such things as a car, a computer, day-care options, libraries, televisions, and so on. Within society and her personal lifestyle, she read such texts as notes for teachers, day-care schedules, print about the weather on TV, road signs, claims forms, directions on frozen food containers, children's homework assignments and texts, electronic bank account statements, directions on shampoo bottles, and newspapers. She wrote such texts as notes to teachers, memos to herself, reports for work, checks to pay for child care, and letters to her family. Thus, the texts that Marge read and wrote and her purposes for doing so were embedded in social practices that were culturally shaped.

Doesn't everybody read and write these everyday kinds of texts? No. In some homes, moms chat on the phone with friends and family, never thinking to get the news from a newspaper. Mom may work not as a claims adjustor but as a nurse. The texts that are work related for this mom do not include claims forms, but perhaps hospital intake forms, doctors' instructions for patients, and drug dosage instructions. Before bedtime, Mom and Dad settle the children into bed and let them watch TV with the lights out for a half hour before it's time to sleep. This is a practice that carries over from their own lives when they were children.

In Central America, depending on the country and its political and economic realities, Moms may be seen reading community news from handwritten public placards, writing notes to families and sending them by personal couriers, or joining community members on the streets to watch soccer games and related scores and advertisements on giant TV screens mounted on the backs of flatbed trucks. There are infinite patterns of living in homes and communities around the world and within these different patterns there are the literacy practices that are shaped by them—literacy practices that mediate people's cultural and social patterns. In this way, literacy in families (as well as literacy writ large) is cultural practice.

Those of us who study literacy as situated within cultural and social contexts operate within a theoretical frame for literacy that reflects some or all of the following assumptions and beliefs:

- Literacy is best understood as a set of social practices; these can be inferred from events that are mediated by written texts.
- There are different literacies associated with different domains of life.
- Literacy practices are patterned by social institutions and power relationships, and some literacies become more dominant, visible, and influential than others.
- Literacy practices are purposeful and embedded in broader social goals and cultural practices.
- Literacy is historically situated.
- Literacy practices change, and new ones are frequently acquired through processes of informal learning and sense making (Barton & Hamilton, 1998, p. 7; Street, 1984).

It is important to note that within this framework, culture is seen as multiple and fluid. Culture refers to contexts for human activity that are shaped by social structures, languages, conventions, history, and goals. It even reflects considerations of geographical location, as in the statement "The culture of New England is different from that of Arizona." In fact, because I think about this in the plural, culture in relation to literacy practice is always cultures, and cultures are constructed as multiple in that people usually participate in multiple cultural contexts. These contexts are fluid and shifting over time and life circumstances, overlapping, blending, and separating. These contexts can be thought of as nested in the sense, for example, that an immigrant from Guatemala might be a woman who is highly educated and participates within the legal system of the new country as a judge. Thus, she reflects the nested cultural realities of geographical location (Central America, Guatemala), legal status (immigrant), gender (women), education (graduate degree), and profession (judge). All these contexts, or cultures, transact to shape her life and her literacy practices. She moves across them fluidly as one or the other takes precedence for her at given moments in time.

THE PROBLEM WITH PROGRAMS FOR FAMILY LITERACY

Family literacy is born within communities of practice. In working within this framework for literacy, it is clear how this statement can be made. Thus, when one is thinking of the different types of family literacies that abound within different communities of literacy practice, it is crucial to keep the social and cultural communities of practice in the framework. Family literacy should not be thought of as a set of activities that can be taught or that can be transferred from one cultural community into another. Transferring a set of literacy activities that are shaped by and embedded within one sociocultural community to another is, in effect, trying to transfer one cultural practice into another culture. That simply doesn't work because cultural beliefs and behavior patterns shape cultural practices.

Cultural patterns and cultural practices, including literacy practices, constitute integrated organisms. Just as the human body will not accept a foreign transplant without massive doses of anti-rejection drugs, cultural communities of literacy practice do not accept foreign literacy practices. That is, they won't accept new other-culture literacy practices without changing those practices in significant ways. They must be changed, or shaped, to fit into the cultural organism that is the receiver community. I will elaborate on this point toward the end of this chapter with the example of the cultural practice of parent-child storybook reading.

The Greenhouse for Literacy Development

The ecological environment of literacy practice provides the conditions for literacy development of the children who grow within it. In this way, the literacy practices of families within communities can be thought of as constituting individual greenhouses for literacy development. What constitutes this environment?

To explore this, I will look at how children learn to speak and interact orally with others. Educators know that oral language development takes place within a context of oral language use. That is, from the moment of birth (and some claim this process starts before birth!), children find themselves in the midst of linguistic interaction with others. This interaction consists of gestures, routines, actions, and talk. Sometimes, the talk is directed to a baby, and other times not. From birth, a baby enters into this world of talk, participating as a language user. Over the first five years of life, within this environment of oral language practice, children acquire the ability to interact orally with people in their world. They learn the syntax of the language around them. They learn the words and meanings that are used in their language environments. They learn the phonological (sounds) systems of people who speak in their worlds. They also learn the pragmatics of the language that they participate in, such as when to say "thank you" and to whom, when to be quiet and when to speak, what to talk about at the dinner table, and what to talk about with their best friends. By age five they are competent language users of the language with which they are surrounded and in which they interact and communicate with loved ones in their homes and members of their social communities.

The same process occurs with written language development. Children begin to learn about reading and writing from the first instance of someone using print—reading and writing—in their worlds. While for virtually all children, the process of learning to talk begins at birth, this is not so for learning to read and write. There are far fewer literate people in the world than there are people who speak. If a child is born into a family that cannot or does not read and write, then there is nothing in that environment that the child can use to learn about reading and writing.

Before the research on emergent literacy began, it was believed that children learned their oral language at home before beginning school and began to learn to read and write in school at the average age of six and a half. Educators now know that many children begin to learn to read and write before they enter formal schooling. What do these children learn about literacy in these early years?

To begin with, I want to introduce the greenhouse, or ecology, metaphor for written language development and think of an environment of literacy practice. Literacy practice can be thought of in several ways. In my research, I tend to approach literacy practice from the perspective of texts. In other words, I look at and document all the different texts that people read and write in the course of their daily lives. Here is a partial list of texts that I documented for one study that I did in a community of migrant farm workers in the United States: accident reports, Bible, bills, information books on pregnancy, calendar, catechism texts, checkbook, checks, church announcements, comic books, commercial driver's license manual, cookbooks, documents, flyers, food labels, forms, household products, informational texts on child development, informational texts on diet, personal letters, children's magazines, other magazines, maps, medical records, medicine directions, messages on refrigerator magnets, newspapers, notes from school, notes to family, novellas, savings account books, schedules, shopping lists, signs as labels (e.g., on bathrooms), regulatory signs (e.g., "No running in the hall"), songbooks, storybooks, tabloids, video labels, work logs, community announcements, and medical forms. Another cultural community would have a different array of texts that people read and write, for reasons that I have discussed above.

While texts are a key aspect of a literacy environment, they do not alone constitute the environmental greenhouse needed by young children to begin to learn about reading and writing. For children to learn about reading and writing within this literacy practice greenhouse, texts need to be read or written by people who are close to the child—family members, neighbors, members of activity groups like church or preschool sports teams, and others. These two aspects of literacy practice—texts and people reading and writing them for different culturally related purposes—constitute the center of an environment of textual practice that is essential for the formation of crucial fundamental concepts and skills needed to learn to read and write.

What Do Early Literacy Learners Learn from Cultural Practices of Literacy?

What do preschool or other young children learn about literacy within different textual practice environments in family homes and communities? What happens with children who are not taught to read individual words by their parents or who are not among the relatively few children who are seemingly self-taught (Durkin, 1966)? Few children, irrespective of social class, income, and opportunity, learn to read and write to the point that they can independently read or write printed texts that they have never before seen (a commonly accepted benchmark for having learned to read and/or write). So, what do most children learn about reading and writing within their own individual literacy practice greenhouses?

Values, Beliefs, Texts, and Purposes for Reading and Writing

One can think about the answer to this question by visualizing a set of nested concentric circles, each representing a domain of literacy knowledge or understanding. The outside domain of the knowledge circle contains the values, beliefs, and practices that children experience and learn in their homes and communities. Within this context, children learn what literacy is, how it is used, who reads or writes which texts, and how essential or nonessential literacy is to life. In other words, children's definitions of literacy itself is a reflection of the definitions of literacy held by their parents, their relatives, their siblings, and other people with whom they interact. This notion of literacy is complete and makes sense to each child. While different definitions or conceptions of literacy exist due to differing sociocultural contexts, none of these are deficient or underdeveloped. They are simply different.

Natures and Forms of Texts Present in Their Lives

Constrained by those conceptions of literacy of their communities, children learn the natures of the written texts in use in their communities and the features of those texts (e.g., grocery lists, personal letters, written stories). This domain of knowledge, or learning, constitutes the middle circle.

What does this mean to learn the natures of different texts and their features? While I do not have space to explore this fully, I will address this through what is known in some academic circles as *genre theory*. Essentially, this theory asserts that language in use is made up of different forms. In written language, some examples of different forms, or text types, are grocery lists, personal letters, news stories, and fiction stories. We have documented hundreds of different textural forms, or genres, in the Cultural Practices of Literacy Study at the University of British Columbia. Genre theory holds that language forms such as these are sociocultural constructions (Reid, 1987). That is, these forms are constructed by social groups to meet their communicative needs. Different written language forms are not prescribed by rules, teachers, or by "language police." Rather, people construct forms of written language and use them and/or change them as needed. The social contexts within which written language forms are used shape both the needs and purposes for the forms, and the forms that different texts take are guided by their communicative functions.

Some simple examples will help here. Take the grocery list. The sociocultural context of this textual form includes the following:

- An economic system that calls for commerce
- An economic context that includes stores that sell food (after all, grocery lists do not exist in the little rural communities in El Salvador, where the daily staples are only beans, corn, coffee, and sometimes rice, and these are usually homegrown)
- An economic context that provides enough money for people to buy more than a few items at a time

When these factors are present, it becomes necessary at times to find a way to remember all the items that an individual needs to buy during the next trip to the store. Because items need to be remembered, one feature of grocery lists is the presence of individual items (rather than a paragraph or two in which the writer writes about the need to buy these items). Since the language that people use to write a grocery list is composed of separate items, it is usually constructed as a list of items to make it easier to read and use during shopping. All this taken together represents a socially constructed literacy practice— values, beliefs, historical and economic contexts, text, and function. The form of the text is shaped by its function for the people who use it.

Other examples can be similarly deconstructed to reveal the relationships between textual functions and textual forms: letters to Grandma function to maintain family ties and to communicate and solicit personal information. The body of the letter contains information about recent events, declarations of love, questions about the well-being of Grandma, and so on. The letter is written in connected discourse in a familiar manner (compared to the discourse one finds in formal business letters), much like a personal conversation. Letters to Grandma usually open with a salutation and close with a sign-off. Different sociocultural groups form the salutations and sign-offs differently, reflecting cultural norms—for example, compare a typical North American salutation and sign-off to this Latin American salutation *Hola Victoria, le deseo lo mejor para este año* (I wish you the best for this year) and sign-off *Que el Señor la llene de muchas bendiciones, signature* (May God give you many blessings). Children learn the different textual forms and their features for the texts that are used in their homes and communities.

Another aspect of many types of written language is its decontextualized nature. This means that texts such as stories, notes, and personal and formal letters must be written, or shaped, to convey meaning without such oral language features as gesture, intonation, and interaction. This is true for most written texts, except perhaps for signs, comic books, advertisements, and subtitles in movies or on the television. This need for clarity within the text itself results in longer and more integrated sentences and more attention to making clear who is being referred to and what is being talked about (without relying on a reader who can say something like, "What do you mean?" or "Who stole the dog?"). Again, children learn about this central aspect of written texts by experiencing the reading and writing of them in their homes and communities. Several significant emergent literacy studies focusing on different textual genres such as storybooks (Purcell-Gates, 1988), personal letters, and grocery lists (Harste, Woodward, & Burke, 1984) have documented this.

Nature of Print-Speech Match

As children are read to and helped to read and write the texts that are present in their lives, they begin to learn print concepts and the nature of the print-speech mapping that is used for these texts. This knowledge/skill dimension constitutes the innermost circle of the model for emergent literacy learning. Depending on the orthography of the language, they learn how print captures language, or speech, and the rules for doing so. For an alphabetic language like English, Spanish, French, or German, this knowledge includes the emerging insight that individual letters map onto individual phonemes (sounds) and that there is a system to this. They begin to learn that letters have invariant shapes (a *W* is no longer a *W* if it is turned upside down). They learn that numbers are different from letters and that number words are words but numbers are numbers. They learn that people read the words, not the pictures. They learn that reading takes place from the top left of the page to the right and then sweeping back to begin again at the left side of the line underneath, and so on. Of course, children whose family literacy practices involve other orthographies (such as Hebrew, Arabic, Mandarin, and so on) learn the print-speech mapping for those. For example, young children in Israel have been shown to "pretend write" a story beginning at what in America is the back page and from right to left.

Thus, when they begin formal instruction, children, or beginning learners of any age, take to school knowledge of the texts that exist in their home worlds; the values and beliefs about literacy practice that involve these texts; the understanding of how different texts from their worlds function; linguistic knowledge of the natures, forms, and features of these texts; and the way that these texts are formed through writing and reading of that writing. The textual practice worlds of children constitute family literacy, and family literacy shapes the understandings about literacy practice with which children begin formal literacy instruction in school. Different literacy worlds mean different types of knowledge brought to the school door. I will illustrate this with brief descriptions of some of the children with whom I have worked and studied:

- Five-year-old Megan knew that her mother got letters from her boyfriend and would read them aloud with her friends on the front porch of their house in South Boston. She knew the genre of letters—personal letters—how they sounded, and what kinds of words were in them. She also knew about texts like food container texts, store signs, and labels (Purcell-Gates, 1996).

- Seven-year-old Donny knew that his name could be written and read. He did not know anything else about print. No one could read or write in his family except to sign their names. He also knew that reading and writing were hard to learn and not worth the effort. His life was full without it, whatever *it* was. It had no value in his world (Purcell-Gates, 1995).

- The young children in the farm fields of southern Michigan travel between the United States and Mexico, and between Texas, Florida, and Michigan, with their parents, who are migrant farm workers. They know that print is on important documents that must be kept safe in a box and hidden in the room behind the blanket. Their ability to cross the border depends on these documents. These documents need to be shown to officials so that they can get into Head Start. They are needed in order to see the doctor. Perhaps most important, this type of print is needed in order to get food from the store. The children also know from the letters that go back and forth to families in Mexico, greeting cards, banners, and words on cakes for birthdays and weddings and other celebrations that print is sometimes part of family togetherness (Purcell-Gates et al., n.d.).

- Celia knew that print was a part of communicating with members of her family who had immigrated to the United States from El Salvador to avoid the death squads. She also knew that the Bible was written and read and knew much of the content. She knew that testimonials regarding the oppression and torture of her people were written to be read and shared. She knew that participation in the communal governance of her postwar community meant written agendas, minutes, and resolutions for the *asambleas*. Finally, since her mother was the proprietor of a small store in her community, she knew a few food labels as sight words (Purcell-Gates & Waterman, 2000).

- Five-year-old Laura knew that storybooks contain stories that can be read out loud and listened to. Each time a story is read, it sounds the same. It always has the same words in it and the same pictures. The words are storybook words. When asked to pretend to read from a book with pictures but no words, she can sound like a storybook. She can make up language that says: "There once was a brave knight and a beautiful lady. They went on a trip. A *dangerous* trip. They saw a little castle in the distance. A mean, mean, mean hunter was following them through the bushes at the entrance of the little castle" (Purcell-Gates, 1988, p. 158).

Relationships between Early Literacy Knowledge and School Success

What do the data show of the relationship between early literacy knowledge acquired in family literacy contexts and success in school? Two of my studies used a battery of early/emergent literacy assessments. The tasks assess an array of concepts and knowledges that are essential to learning to read and write, and that research has indicated are learned or emerge over time as part of the emergent literacy period. These tasks include (1) intentionality or the understanding that print says something and is functional in people's lives; (2) written register, or knowledge of the syntax (grammar), vocabulary, and decontextualized nature of written language; (3) concepts of writing or the understanding that writing is the formation of letters and words that capture language; (4) concepts of print or Clay's (1979) array of print convention understandings, like "What is a letter? What is a word?" (5) directionality (read left to right); and (6) the alphabetic principle, or the understanding that print maps onto speech at the phoneme level. I used a series of play-like tasks to assess the degree to which children hold these concepts.

One study explored the ways that children make sense out of their beginning literacy instruction and if those different ways of making sense are related to how successful they are in learning to read and write (Purcell-Gates & Dahl, 1991). We nested this study purely within a low-income population because we wished to deconstruct the relationship of socioeconomic status to low reading achievement.

The sample for this study consisted of one classroom from each of three inner-city schools in the midwestern region of the United States. My colleagues and I selected 12 students from each classroom (6 boys and 6 girls) for assessment. We also chose two boys and two girls from these 12 for close observation over two years. We measured the children's entering literacy knowledge at the beginning of kindergarten, followed the four focal children and the classroom instruction for kindergarten and first grade, and used norm-referenced assessments at the end of kindergarten and first grade, as well as teacher assessments, to document their levels of success.

After following the same group of children for two years of schooling and administering pre- and post-tests of achievement, we found that the score for intentionality—the knowledge that print "says" something and that it functions in different ways in people's lives—was the best predictor of the level of end-of-first-grade success in reading and writing. The other early literacy concepts were also related to success in learning to read, with the exception of knowledge of written register.

How Can Parents Enhance Early Literacy Knowledge?

What is it that happens in homes that allows children to acquire early literacy knowledge? We know that knowledge of written language grows in the greenhouse of literacy practice, but how does this happen? What do parents do to foster literacy? Which textual practices are helpful for which types of early literacy knowledge? To explore the answers to these questions, I collected data from the homes of low-socioeconomic children to relate to the results of the study described above. This subsequent study, which I refer to as the 20-home study (Purcell-Gates, 1996), had 20 volunteer families in the sample, each with at least one child between ages four and six, and 24 children in the sample. The families were of varied ethnicities, so I matched research assistants to homes by ethnicity. The research assistants collected an aggregated week's worth of observations in the homes (from the time the focal children got up in the mornings to when they went to bed). They noted all reading and writing events and indications of reading and writing events (like a letter waiting to be mailed). At the end of the data collection, we gave each focal child the same array of early literacy assessments used in the prior study. We also documented any school curricula for literacy for each child. I then conducted a series of analyses.

The results added complexity and depth to the picture of emergent literacy learning in the homes. First, the children's grasp of what I now called the big picture (measured with the intentionality task, which best predicted end-of-first-grade success in the K–1 study) was significantly related to the frequency of literacy events and the frequency of mother-child interactions around print in the home. The following recommendations for parents to foster early literacy development emerged from these studies:

#1: Read and Write a Lot

The most effective way to prepare children for school success in literacy is to read and write a lot for your own purposes in the presence of your children. Read different types of texts, such as recipes for cooking, newspapers for the news, magazines for enjoyment, and information articles for health tips. Write different types of texts, such as notes to touch base with family members, letters to complain about a service, lists for shopping, and diaries for reflection. The more you read and write, regardless of what you read and write, the more your child will learn that print is meaningful and functional and that it is possible and desirable to be able to read and write it.

#2: Involve Your Children in Literacy Events

This suggestion is actually a part of the one above and, together with #1, is documented as being the most effective way to prepare children for school success with literacy. While you are reading and writing for many different real-life purposes, involve your children. When you stop the car at a stop sign, point out to them that the word on the sign says "Stop" and explain that the sign is why you stopped. When grocery shopping, point out the different food products and the brands and information on the boxes. Talk aloud about what you are reading or read the text aloud. For example, you might say something like, "I need to buy Cheerios. Where is it? Oh, here it is, see? It says Cheerios here [pointing to the word]. Let's see how much sugar is in a serving. Here it is; it says that one cup has 35 grams of carbohydrates [pointing to the print];

that's sugar. Okay, I guess that's okay" (or not, depending on your nutritional beliefs). Answer all the questions your children have about print of the "What does that say?" nature. Simply telling them what it says is usually preferable to making a reading lesson out of your answer.

The second major finding of the 20-home study was that children's knowledge of the forms and natures of written language (measured by the written register task of pretend reading, the concepts of writing task, and the concepts of print task) was greater in homes where parents and others read and wrote more complex texts—like children's books, newspapers, magazines, books, and impersonal letters. The degree to which parents read these more complex texts was not related to their levels of education. Some parents with postsecondary degrees did very little reading and what they did was of simple texts, such as on food labels, lottery tickets, and coupons. Others without high school degrees read more texts like newspapers, reports, and the Bible, in addition to less complex texts such as those above.

Written language in longer, more complex texts is syntactically more varied and integrated and includes more different types of vocabulary words. It is also more clearly decontextualized. Knowledge of these aspects of written language puts young children at a distinct advantage when they enter school. Vocabulary knowledge alone has been found to be highly related to school success. When children begin writing on their own, if they have a feel for the syntactic possibilities for written text and for how it must contain within it all of the meaning (i.e., decontextualized), they will be more fluent and effective than those children for whom written language is almost like a second language. The basic concepts of print, which are related to reading and writing more complex texts in the home, are critical to being able to take from beginning literacy instruction. Without a sense of what letters and words are, or the understanding that the beginning of a word is the first letter on the left of the word, and so on, children often become confused and stray down nonproductive paths as they try to learn to read and write in school.

#3: Add More Complex Texts to Your Literacy Practices

People can often think of more complex texts that are functional within their existing literacy practices. For example, if you are interested in sports, in addition to following the games on television, purchase a newspaper and read the stories and statistics in the sports section. If a question comes up at the dinner table about Aunt Edna's diabetes, and you wonder what kinds of foods she can and cannot eat, you can go the Internet and surf the health sites, reading aloud for the others or printing out the relevant information. If your child asks you why the dinosaurs became extinct, tell your child that you will go to the library and get some books or articles that discuss this. Then read these with your child as you both explore the answer.

The Case of Storybook Reading

As promised, I now return to the cultural practice of reading to children as a routine. The final major result of the 20-home study was that written register—children's knowledge of the syntax or grammar, vocabulary, and decontextualized nature of many written texts—was related to the frequency with which parents read to their children. The results of the K–1 study also revealed, however, that there was no relation between this knowledge and success at reading and writing at the end of 1st grade. The effect of this practice may not show up until about 4th grade (Chall & Snow, 1988), when children are past the learning-to-read stage.

Other research and research reviews reveal other noteworthy findings about school and home literacy. Some research has shown that children learn about the structure of written language in kindergarten and 1st grade if their teachers read a lot to them as part of the daily routine (Purcell-Gates, McIntyre, & Freppon, 1995). There is no evidence that importing storybook reading into homes that would normally not include it for the purpose of preparing their children for literacy success is effective. Further, there is much anecdotal evidence that parents who are told to read to their children by well-meaning educators actually do so. Clearly, more research is needed on the effect of exporting storybook reading to homes where it is a foreign practice, given the common and absolute belief that all parents need to read to their children if they are to succeed in school.

All the suggestions for parents provided above are meant to take advantage of existing literacy practice cultures in the home. The take-home message is that parents can help their children acquire important early literacy concepts by using existing practices and do not have to incorporate foreign routines of reading and writing. Family literacy is naturally occurring literacy in families, and it is within those literacy practice greenhouses that young children begin to grow and develop as readers and writers.

REFERENCES

Barton, D., & Hamilton, M. (1998). *Local literacies: Reading and writing in one community*. London: Routledge.

Chall, J., & Snow, C. (1988). School influences on the reading development of low-income children. *Harvard Education Letter, 4*, 1–4.

Clay, M. M. (1975). *What did I write?* Portsmouth, NH: Heinemann.

Clay, M. M. (1979). *Reading: Patterning of complex behavior* (2nd ed.). Auckland, New Zealand: Heineman.

Cochrane-Smith, M. (1984). *The making of a reader*. Norwood, NJ: Ablex.

Durkin, D. (1966). *Children who read early*. New York: Teachers College Press.

Goodman, Y. (1984). The development of initial literacy. In H. Goelman, A. Oberg, & F. Smith (Eds.), *Awakening to literacy* (pp. 102–109). Exeter, NH: Heinemann.

Harkness, F., & Miller, L. (1982). *A description of the interaction among mother, child, and books in a bedtime reading situation.* Paper presented at the seventh annual Boston University Conference on Language Development.

Harste, J., Woodward, V., & Burke, C. (1984). *Language stories and literacy lessons.* Exeter, NH: Heinemann.

Martin, J. R., Christie, F., & Rothery, J. (1987). Social processes in education: A reply to Sawyer and Watson (and others). In I. Reid (Ed.), *The place of genre in learning: Current debates* (pp. 58–82). Geelong, Australia: Deakin University, Centre for Studies in Literacy Education.

Purcell-Gates, V. (1988). Lexical and syntactic knowledge of written narrative held by well-read-to kindergartners and second graders. *Research in the Teaching of English, 22*(2), 128–160.

Purcell-Gates, V. (1995). *Other peoples' words": The cycle of low literacy.* Cambridge, MA: Harvard University Press.

Purcell-Gates, V. (1996). Stories, coupons, and the TV guide: Relationships between home literacy experiences and emergent literacy knowledge. *Reading Research Quarterly, 31,* 406–428.

Purcell-Gates, V., & Dahl, K. (1991). Low-SES children's success and failure at early literacy learning in skills-based classrooms. *JRB: A Journal of Literacy, 23,* 1–34.

Purcell-Gates, V., McIntyre, E., & Freppon, P. (1995). Learning written storybook language in school: A comparison of low-SES children in skill-based and whole language classrooms. *American Educational Research Journal, 30,* 659–685.

Purcell-Gates, V., & Waterman, R. (2000). *Now we read, we see, we speak: Portrait of literacy development in a Freirean-based adult class.* Mahwah, NJ: Lawrence Erlbaum.

Purcell-Gates, V., et al. (n.d.) Literary practices of U.S. migrant workers with young children in Head Start. *Cultural Practice of Literary Studies Ongoing Projects.* Retrieved January 10, 2007, from http://educ.ubc.ca/research/cpls/content/ongoing_migrant.html

Read, C. (1971). Preschool children's knowledge of English phonology. *Harvard Educational Review, 41,* 1–34.

Reid, I. (1987). *The place of genre in learning: Current debates.* Geelong, VIC, Australia: Deakin University Press.

Snow, C., & Ninio, A. (1986). The contribution of reading books with children in their linguistic and cognitive development. In W. Teale & E. Sulzby (Eds.), *Emergent literacy: Writing and reading.* (pp. 116–137). Norwood, NJ: Ablex.

Street, B. V. (1984). *Literacy in theory and practice.* Cambridge: Cambridge University Press.

Taylor, D. (1985). *Family literacy: Children learning to read and write.* Exeter, NH: Heinemann.

Chapter Eight

WORKPLACE LITERACY

Larry Mikulecky

The most commonly accepted definition of "workplace literacy" comes from the National Literacy Act of 1991: "an individual's ability to read, write, and speak in English, and compute and solve problems at levels of proficiency necessary to function on the job." In the 1990s, this term was often used synonymously with such terms as "basic skills" and "employee basic skills" to avoid the negative connotations associated with the word "illiteracy" and in recognition of the fact that workplace reading and writing are often integrated with the use of oral language, computation, and computers, and knowledge of workplace procedures. This definition also recognizes that one is not either literate or illiterate.

Workplace literacy is concerned with having skills sufficient for the tasks at hand. Workplace literacy is also a broad label that has been used to describe several quite different sorts of education related to the workplace (e.g., special programs focusing upon specific workplace-related literacy skills, basic skills and high school diploma/GED preparation programs offered in workplace settings, off-site welfare-to-work programs, and school-to-work transition programs that teach general workplace literacy skills). The label also has been used to describe particular literacy strategies, functions, tasks, and materials used in workplaces.

Who attends and what one observes in workplace literacy programs have shifted to reflect changes in the literacy abilities and levels of workers and the literacy demands of jobs. These changes have been particularly dramatic in the area of job demands but have also been apparent in workers' changing literacy abilities.

These factors are connected. As workers increase their literacy abilities, their use of literacy to complete their job tasks also tends to increase.

Changes in Literacy Abilities and Demands

In 1890, the International Ladies' Garment Workers Union established the Cloak Maker's Social Educational Club in New York to teach members of the Cloak Makers' Union how to read and write English and how to become citizens (Cook, 1977). The workplace literacy demands of the cloak makers were not particularly strong, but the massive influx of Eastern European immigrants in the late 1800s presented the country with millions of workers with little mastery of English and even less mastery of literacy. Literacy demands were low, but literacy skills were even lower. In addition, union organizers knew that their members needed to be able to read and properly mark election ballots in order to develop more control over their working conditions.

By the early twentieth century, testimony by the director of the Bureau of Mines before U.S. congressional committees had begun to cite the many miners who were ill equipped to read safety warnings as a partial rationale for funding adult literacy programs (Cook, 1977). In 1910, so-called moonlight schools were established in rural Kentucky. These schools used the local newspaper to teach literacy skills to coal miners and other adults on nights when it was possible to use moonlight to walk to the Rowan County schoolhouse. Reading lessons were extremely simple; for example, the first lesson used only eleven different words (Cook, 1977).

Concerns about Literacy in the Military

Demands on workers' literacy for military work increased as both civilian and military jobs changed to require more literacy skills. During World War I, thousands of recruits needed help in writing letters home and needed to depend on officers or other soldiers for important job-related information presented in print. Thomas Sticht, in *The Military Experience and Workplace Literacy* (1995), reports that during the Civil War over 90 percent of enlisted men were involved in combat-related activities that called for little or no literacy, while craftsmen and clerical or technical personnel made up less than 10 percent of the force. Whereas 90 percent of the troops had been used as combat troops in the 1860s, less than half the force was used as combat troops 50 years later during World War I. The other half completed job tasks that made increasing demands on their literacy skills and abilities.

The decline in the percentage of general combat troops and increase in white-collar and blue-collar military jobs continued into World War II, when there were about equal proportions of each type. During World War II, the

U.S. military took the lead in teaching job-related reading skills to adults by using *Private Pete* and *Sailor Sam,* special reading materials produced by the military. Thomas Sticht (1997) reports that the stories in the books told the tale of a new recruit leaving home, going to a recruiter, riding a train to camp, being assigned a barracks, and so forth. Topics and vocabulary taken from barracks life, semaphore use, firefighting, elementary navigation, and seamanship were used to teach navy recruits to read. The materials reinforced and extended rudimentary basic reading skills while allowing learners to develop new vocabulary and concepts about military life.

By the late 1980s and early 1990s, the literacy level of the U.S. population had increased considerably, and so had the literacy demands for most jobs. In the military, the percentage of purely combat troops had declined to about 15 percent, and even those troops were expected to have a relatively high degree of literacy. The U.S. Department of Labor had convened the Secretary's Commission on Achieving Necessary Skills to work with employers, unions, and researchers to develop an outline of workplace competencies (including literacy) necessary for the twenty-first century (U.S. Department of Labor, 1992). The competencies identified by the commission helped shape the curricula of many workplace literacy programs through the end of the twentieth century. The commission concluded that successful workplace performance integrated written and oral communication with the following workplace competencies:

1. Resources: allocating time, money, materials, space, and staff
2. Interpersonal skills: working on teams, teaching others, serving customers, leading, negotiating, and working well with people from diverse cultural backgrounds.
3. Information: acquiring and evaluating data, organizing and maintaining files, interpreting information, and using computers to process information
4. Systems: understanding social, organizational, and technological systems; monitoring and correcting performance; and designing or improving systems
5. Technology: selecting equipment and tools, applying technology to specific tasks, and maintaining and troubleshooting technologies

It wasn't just for high-tech jobs that workers reported having to use literacy on a regular basis. In the mid-1990s the National Adult Literacy Survey reported results of a national survey of over 26,000 representative adults. Employed adults also reported their literacy use on the job. In all job categories, including that of laborer, the majority of workers reported literacy use on at least a weekly basis, and most reported needing literacy on the job much more often. Frequent literacy use ranged from 98 percent for managers to 56 percent for farming, forestry, and fishing workers (Mikulecky, 2001).

Few studies before the National Adult Literacy Survey had gathered detailed information on the type and frequency of workers writing on the job. The

National Adult Literacy Survey provided some detail on the extent to which Americans wrote frequently on the job. Surprisingly high percentages of workers reported that they frequently wrote on the job (at least once a week). More than half of workers (54%) reported frequently writing reports, while 45 percent reported frequently filling out forms, and 40 percent frequently writing memos. In only two occupations—farming and manual labor—did less than 30 percent of workers report frequently writing reports. Three-fourths of managers reported writing memos regularly, as one might expect, but so did 58 percent of clerical workers, 51 percent of salespeople, and 40 percent of transportation operatives.

The presence of workplace literacy demands permeates even low-level part-time jobs. Tannock (2001) describes literacy demands encountered by youths applying for part-time jobs, such as bagging groceries or working in fast-food restaurants. Many applicants now must fill out extensive job application forms and must take multiple-choice tests such as personality, customer service, and food handler tests before being employed. After employment, they must fill in daily and sometimes hourly forms on job duties and read and use service scripts to ask customers if they wish to purchase additional food or products. Tannock goes on to point out that successful youths must also be sophisticated enough to know how to read, manipulate, and negotiate all these literacy tasks to maintain personal integrity while keeping their jobs. In the twenty-first century, literacy demands are present at all levels of employment.

The need to use literacy related to computers and the Internet to do one's job expanded rapidly beginning in the late 1990s. The U.S. Department of Commerce reported that as of "September 2001, about 65 million of the 115 million adults who are employed and age 25 and over use a computer at work" (National Telecommunications and Information Administration, 2002, p. 57). In the 13 months between August 2000 and September 2001, the percentage of adults using the Internet at work increased from 26.1 percent to 41.7 percent. By 2003, the Department of Labor reported that 77 million Americans, or 55 percent of employees, were using computers as part of their jobs (Bureau of Labor Statistics, 2005).

An important part of many jobs included the ability to participate in continuing training, often using computers. In 2000, the U.S. military surveyed combat medics to determine their readiness to receive training and access job-related medical information on the Internet. Nearly 80 percent of combat medics indicated they already had the ability to use e-mail, word processing, and the Internet for communicating and accessing information (Stein, Mays, Abbott, & Wojcik, 2000). Since the vast majority of workers have expanded literacy abilities and experiences, more use of these abilities is often added to job demands. The 20 percent of combat medics without computer literacy abilities are likely to soon find e-mail, word processing, and Internet literacies are new workplace literacy demands. The same is true of individuals with below-average literacy abilities in other jobs in which the average literacy ability of workers is rising.

INFLUENCE OF IMMIGRATION, NEW CERTIFICATION PROGRAMS, AND RETRAINING

During the later twentieth century and early twenty-first century, the United States experienced an immigration surge reminiscent of the immigration surge of the late nineteenth and early twentieth centuries. Between 1980 and 2000, the number of people in the United States who spoke languages other than English at home more than doubled to one in five individuals; this figure is projected to double again by 2025 (U.S. Census Bureau, 2001). Close to one half of the students in adult literacy classes reported that they were also there to learn English as a new language. In the early twenty-first century, Department of Labor initiatives included funding for several million dollars in grants to special workplace language training programs focused on Spanish speakers and other language groups, as well as policy guidelines to emphasize ESL training as part of other broad departmental initiatives (U.S. Department of Labor, 2006). The Employment Training Administration through the High Growth Job Training Initiative funded several grantees in the biotechnology, health-care, hospitality, energy, retail, and advanced manufacturing industries to develop training curriculum and related products that could be used by workers who are learning English. In the hotel industry, project HERE was funded to deliver occupational English training to 2,000 new citizens and immigrant workers for entry-level hospitality positions through a partnership of employers, educators, and government. Occupational English proficiency training was offered on site to 450 incumbent workers at 10 major area hotels. Other projects focused on community organizations, health and safety training, and developing digital literacy materials (U.S. Department of Labor, 2006).

Other influences on workplace literacy in the twenty-first century were occupational certification programs and transitions to community college training programs. Moderate and higher-paying jobs in many occupation areas became associated with official certifications that required written tests of knowledge. For example, truck drivers who wished to haul particular loads or work for higher-paying companies were required to pass the commercial driver's license examination. Study materials and the written examination called for literacy well beyond basic levels. In the moving and storage industry, written examinations and certification programs were developed for becoming a certified moving consultant or a registered international mover. These and many other certifications provide individuals and companies with competitive edges. Workplace literacy programs are sometimes needed to help individuals prepare for these examinations for certification, and these programs often operate in conjunction with training sponsored by industry.

To be competitive in the global economy, employers in manufacturing and service industries (or subcontractors to such employers) found it important to receive certification from the International Organization for Standardization (ISO) as part of the ISO 9000 certification process. This certification essentially involves documenting each stage of production or service in order to make sure all employees are able to follow the documentation, and using quality assurance processes that involve employees in data collection and record keeping, as well as a variety of other activities related to literacy and mathematics. To gain and maintain certification, audits are done to determine that what has been described and documented is actually occurring. This certification process has increased the literacy demands for many workers, as employers that are not ISO certified have tended to disappear or decrease in size, while ISO-certified employers have grown in size and number. For more detail, see Jo Anne Kleifgen's (2005) detailed documentation of the increased and new literacy demands brought about by the ISO standards for "a small company competing in a capitalist economy and feeling the pressure to adopt the official litearcies of a high competitive market" (p. 467).

Workers displaced by technology or job outsourcing also often must acquire retraining and further education if they hope to maintain their standard of living. New occupations offering remuneration comparable to that paid in workers' previous jobs often require extended training at a technical or community college. Although displaced workers may have graduated from high school, the literacy skills of many are not sufficient for succeeding in vocational and community college classes. Many students must take workplace literacy programs before or as they receive community college training; many of these programs are offered by community colleges. These workplace literacy programs often involve learning new vocabulary, new technologies, study skills, and academic strategies that go far beyond the eleven words learned by adults in the first classes of the Kentucky moonlight schools of the early twentieth century.

Workplace Literacy Examples

Analysis of workplace literacy tasks usually reveals that tasks rarely lend themselves to isolated examples of just reading and writing. Tasks labeled as involving workplace literacy often involve a mixture of listening, speaking in a professional manner, taking notes, using a variety of reading and skimming strategies while reading from paper and computer screens, doing arithmetic to calculate needed information, and responding in both oral and written form. Take, for example, a typical customer service representative task. The customer service representative might start by answering a telephone inquiry from someone requesting late payment of a bill. While using a headset to speak to the customer, the customer service representative asks for the customer's name and other relevant information, calls up the customer record on a computer screen, and checks the payment history. This requires rapid reading of print organized in blocks on screen. The customer service representative needs to decide how reliable the customer is and if any extension of time can be given. Written policy guidelines are accessed via a help screen. These guidelines include job aids with rules concerning the length of an extension and whether some percentage of the bill must be paid immediately. After calculating the effect of the rules (in this case using another function of the computer), the customer service representative tells the customer the result and probably initiates a discussion on the possibility of the customer paying as required. If the customer service representative is unable to answer the customer's questions during the brief time the customer is on the phone, a letter will need to be sent. A word-processing program with several dozen form letters will be called up on the screen. The customer service representative will be expected to select an appropriate form letter from menus, modify the address and body of the form letter, and print a letter and envelope to be mailed to the customer. These jobs in the rapidly growing service sector are not high-paying jobs, but they do call for skills that challenge the bottom half of high school graduates who compete for them.

Canadian researchers have produced the most detailed listing of workplace literacy skills for a wide range of jobs. Human Resources and Skills Development Canada, as part of its Essential Skills and Workplace Literacy Initiative (2006), produced nearly 200 worker task profiles based on more than 3,000 interviews. The profile for each occupation describes several dozen job tasks categorized by the initiative's nine essential skill areas (i.e., reading text, document use, numeracy, writing, oral communication, working with others, continuous learning, thinking skills, and computer use). Tasks are categorized by five levels of complexity ranging from 1 (basic tasks) to 5 (advanced tasks). The classification for typical writing tasks for bricklayers, for example, is level 2 because the job involves less complex writing tasks, such as the revision of work orders, writing estimate sheets on the cost of materials or labor, and filling out simple forms (e.g., incident reports).

Some sense of the workplace literacy demands of typical occupations can be gathered through a review of the reading demands of three occupations with salaries that range from 25 percent below average to 10 percent above average. Higher-paying jobs requiring a higher level of skill tend to have considerably greater workplace literacy demands.

Receptionists and Switchboard Operators

Receptionists and switchboard operators greet people arriving at offices, hospitals, and other establishments; direct visitors to the appropriate person or service; answer and forward telephone calls; take messages; schedule appointments; and perform other clerical duties. They are employed by hospitals, medical and dental offices, and other offices throughout the public and private sectors. This is a relatively low-paying job with an income about 25 percent below average, according to the Essential Skills and Workplace Literacy Initiative (2006).

Some examples of reading tasks, with their corresponding level of complexity ratings, are:

- Reading phone messages and passing them along to the appropriate individual (1)
- Reading memos regarding policy, procedures, security, personnel changes, and daily events (1)
- Reading mail and forwarding it to the appropriate individual, along with any necessary forms (1)
- Reading forms related to the office, such as insurance forms and hospital admitting forms (2)
- Reading notes from supervisors explaining job tasks or giving instructions (2)
- Reading operating manuals for computer systems and software to fix equipment when it breaks down or learn new software functions (3)
- Reading client files to answer client questions and to prepare the physician or dentist for appointments (3)

Automotive Service Technician

Automotive service technicians inspect, diagnose, repair, and service mechanical, electrical, and electronic systems/components of cars, buses, and light/commercial trucks. This job pays about 5 percent below average, according to the Essential Skills and Workplace Literacy Initiative (2006).

Reading tasks in this occupation, along with their corresponding complexity levels, include:

- Reading e-mail, notes from other colleagues, and short descriptors on parts (1)
- Reading comments from service representatives and customers on work orders to get subjective accounts of problems and understand work scheduled for customers' vehicles (2)
- Reading instructions and safety warnings on product labels and notes on assembly diagrams (2)
- Reading instructions and safety warnings on product labels and notes on assembly diagrams (2)
- Reading articles about service and repair innovations in automotive periodicals and magazines to broaden their knowledge of the automobile service industry (2)
- Reading bulletins and incident reports received from automobile manufacturers that describe recall details and recurring faults with particular models (2)
- Reading repair manuals to find technical information for each model in order to diagnose and repair mechanical faults (3)
- Scanning the labels on automotive parts for part numbers, serial numbers, sizes, colors, and other information in order to confirm that parts are the ones specified on work orders and repair manuals before they are used (2)

- Filling out job estimates as well as problem, defective parts identification, and warranty forms as well as motor vehicle inspection forms and fleet maintenance forms in order to highlight any deficiencies and to establish that regular maintenance has been performed, and accident and insurance forms to give professional opinions about of the causes of accidents and the extent of resulting damage (2)

- Obtaining information about vehicles to be serviced by looking at work orders and scanning for details such as car make, model, and year; service operations required; and the time for pick-up, as well as reading short descriptions of problems provided by the customers or service advisors (3)

- Entering repair and service data onto work orders or into electronic billing and database systems, including the time spent, parts used, steps taken to repair each car, and comments to explain unusual repairs or additional parts used (3)

- Finding out about electrical, hydraulic, coolant and other systems by studying schematic diagrams (e.g., a technician might locate the devices and connections in the accessory circuit as the preliminary step in repairing a faulty radio) (3)

Paramedic

Paramedics administer pre-hospital emergency medical care to patients and transport them to hospitals or other medical facilities for further medical care. As in many of the growth occupations in health care, to be certified, an individual usually needs to complete a college, hospital-based, or other recognized program in emergency medical technology or courses in emergency health care and supervised practical training. Success in these programs requires a moderately high degree of academic literacy skill. This occupation pays about 10 percent above average, according to the Essential Skills and Workplace Literacy Initiative (2006).

Reading tasks in this occupation, along with complexity levels, include:

- Reading notes, medical files, and patient charts to become aware of the condition of the patient, to initiate a treatment plan as per medical direction and/or protocol, and to make a working diagnosis and initiate a treatment plan (2)

- Reading do-not-resuscitate orders to be aware of what is to be done for a patient who is subject to these orders in order to apply directives, using medical discretion in regard to pain relief and palliative measures (3)

- Reading memos from management, coworkers, and other medical professionals in order to gain an understanding of new procedures and to interpret, evaluate, and apply the that information (3)

- Reading specialized material (e.g., *The Compendium of Pharmaceutical Specialties*) to obtain one or two pieces of very specific information, such as the names of medications, to integrate and synthesize information with information gleaned from other sources in order to expand understanding of the care to be applied; and to do an in-depth analysis in order to develop and contribute to protocols to bring about changes and improvements in procedures (4–5)

- Reading a variety of trade magazines, journals, and other professional literature to be aware of current practices (3)

These examples, plus hundreds of others and samples of workplace materials, are available on the Essential Skills Web site (2006). What is striking about these examples is the pervasiveness of literacy in daily work and how different these materials and tasks are from what most students experience in school classes.

Issues Associated with Workplace Literacy

Scholarship on workplace literacy has focused upon several issues related to how programs are organized, who should pay for programs, and the gaps between rhetoric used to describe and justify workplace literacy programs and what actually occurs in the workplace.

Program Organization

Most workplace literacy classes meet only a few hours a week and then for a limited number of weeks. Mikulecky, Lloyd, Horwitz, Masker, and Siemantel (1996) found that though some programs might offer as much as 200 hours of instruction, typically programs offer less than 50 hours of instruction. This is the equivalent of less than two weeks of instruction that a child would receive during the school year. Even though (or perhaps because) there is little instructional time, there has been a good deal of discussion and contention around what workplace literacy instruction should focus upon and how to most effectively use the limited time.

According to Jurmo (2004), the types of workplace literacy programs can be classified as those that

1) Focus primarily on the specific litearcies used for the job (sometimes called functional context education) since past research has shown that there is only a little transfer from short-term general literacy instruction to being able to read and write on the job
2) Focus primarily on general skills or possibly on a goal, like receiving the equivalent of a high school diploma, since job skills and even employers may change
3) Have a balance of job-related and learner-centered goals and activities, often developed through collaboration with employers, unions, and educators

There are arguments for and against each of these ways to organize workplace literacy programs, but all the arguments are overshadowed by the severe limitations placed upon a program providing fewer than 50 hours of instruction. Not much can be accomplished in so short a time, no matter what approach is used. Mary Ellen Boyle (2001), a critic of workplace literacy programs, has observed that "concern about the nature of the curriculum serves to obfuscate the minimal impact such programs can have, notwithstanding the employer focus or curriculum designs" (p. 85).

Some programs have tried to address the problem of limited time by encouraging students to attend a series of classes and by offering a menu of classes on several topics. Other programs have encouraged workers to extend their training from workplace literacy classes to other technical classes available through community colleges.

Employers often lean toward programs focusing heavily on specific workplace skills of immediate, use while employees and unions tend to favor more general and learner-centered programs. Indeed, some employers have expressed concern that they might lose employees to other employers or occupations if they provide too much general education. A survey of 121 workplace literacy programs revealed that about 45 percent focused almost completely on workplace skills, another 45 percent used a combination of workplace and learner-center approaches, and only 10 percent limited themselves to just general skills (Mikulecky et al., 1996).

Who Should Pay for Programs?

The type of workplace literacy program offered is heavily influenced by who pays, and nearly everyone would like someone else to pay. Some employers argue that the government should pay since all of society benefits from an educated workforce and business has already paid once for public education through taxes. Acknowledging the public benefit of an educated workforce, but also pointing out the immediate benefits to employers, government often calls for joint government/employer support. Government funding has usually been limited to one to three years of full or partial funding, with the expectation that business would eventually pay for ongoing support of programs. Workers and unions argue that unless a program is offered during work hours, when an employee is being paid, the employee is also being asked to pay with his or her time. It is argued that when employees are paying in this fashion, they should have more voice in the goals of workplace literacy programs. Some programs have experimented with offering classes that take up one hour of worker time and one hour at the beginning or end of a shift.

Nelson (2004) examined the question of whether jointly funded government/employer workplace literacy programs should continue once government funding ends. She examined 50 workplace programs funded in Massachusetts between 1988 and 2000 and found that 48 percent continued for at least one year after government funding was discontinued. This finding is somewhat deceptive, however, since the results differed so much by employer size. Ninety-three percent of large firms (i.e., 14 of the 15 programs employing 500 or more workers) continued their workplace literacy programs, while only 23 percent of midsized firms (i.e.. 100–500 employees) continued their programs. There were only two small employers (i.e., fewer than 100 employees) in the study, and both continued their programs. After size was controlled for, neither industry type nor union involvement was a significant factor in explaining results. Reasons given for continuing or discontinuing workplace literacy programs were diverse but tended to cluster around recognized multiple benefits to both employers and employees, continuing/discontinuing leadership of the company or workplace literacy program, and in a few cases the sense that the government-funded program was able to resolve literacy problems after three years.

Gaps between Rhetoric and Reality

Workplace literacy has long been entwined with the political rhetoric of national competitiveness and safety. As early as the beginning of the twentieth century, some advocates of workplace literacy programs characterized these programs as solutions to the problem of deficient, illiterate workers, who were blamed for causing a host of safety and productivity problems. Illiterate mine workers were linked to the problem of mine safety (a dubious proposition at best), and employers who offered literacy classes were seen as taking the high moral ground and possibly deflecting some criticism about mine safety.

In the 1980s and 1990s, some literacy scholars began to critically examine this rhetoric and contrast it with what they observed in workplaces and workplace literacy programs. Their studies and analyses addressed the oversimplification and dangers of this blame-the-worker rhetoric. (One such oversimplification was the belief that if the worker had more literacy skills, problems of safety and competitiveness would disappear.)

Sarmiento (1989) presents analyses from labor union perspectives that decried and argued against the tendency to blame workers' literacy levels for labor/management problems that were much more complex than a lack of simple reading and writing abilities among employees. Others described the efforts made over several decades by employees through their unions to secure both broad-based and specific education and training with sufficient scope to make a difference (see, e.g., Hensley, 1993).

Several extensive studies challenged an overly simplified view of solving complex problems by just hiring literacy instructors or by just teaching literacy skills directly related to a job (i.e., functional context approach). These studies challenged the blame-the-worker rhetoric by documenting the broader context of the workplace and workplace literacy programs and by focusing upon the complexities of what actually occurred in the workplace and in workplace literacy programs. Researchers such as Gowen and Hull have identified a number of flaws and outright dangers in taking an overly simplified functional context approach. Gowen's (1992) study of a workplace literacy program in a hospital describes attempts to construct written manuals, guidelines, and directions for workplace tasks based on official job descriptions and official guidelines for how entry-level hospital workers were to do their jobs. In one case, guidelines for how janitors were to retrieve used needles from trash cans might have endangered the workers if the guidelines had actually been followed. In addition, Gowen's observations and interviews reveal that many workers sought literacy support for goals outside the workplace and reacted negatively to only being offered literacy training for jobs they wished to move beyond. Hull and her colleagues did a series of studies of workplaces and workplace literacy programs that tried to capture the complete work context and counter the belief that workplace literacy programs were really preparing employees for actual workplace literacy demands. In a 1993 study of a community college program designed to prepare learners for banking occupations, Hull found that there was little correspondence between the approaches used in classes and what was called for in actual jobs. In a later study, Hull, Jury, Ziva, and Katz (1996) found a large range of literacy tasks in electronics jobs. Some tasks were ones that workers needed to do individually, but others were collaborative and allowed workers to help and teach each other. This evidence was offered as a counter to rhetoric claiming that downsizing of the workplace was forcing employers to seek or retain only employees with literacy levels sufficient for independent functioning on the job.

Some of the rhetoric associated with workplace literacy programs suggested that workplace literacy classes increased workers' abilities to democratically participate in workplace decision making and gave them access to promotion and higher standards of living. Hull and her colleagues (1996) performed a series of studies in the electronics industry and found that most of the complex literacy activities involved workers monitoring themselves with little decision-making power and that literacy skills needed to perform jobs did not seem to transfer to the skills needed for promotion to more desirable supervisory positions.

Boyle (2001) conducted interviews with human resource managers who offered workplace literacy programs and her own critical analysis to address why, if workplace literacy programs do not teach much literacy, they continue to exist. She posited several possible explanations in answer to this question, including that workplace literacy programs are (1) of symbolic value since literacy is seen as a good in and of itself, (2) less expensive than restructuring wages and benefits more equitably, (3) a way to assimilate immigrants and socialize workers into the team and group processes of the new workplace, and (4) a way for those in power to occupy the moral high ground by offering hope (perhaps false hope) of worker advancement through education.

Predicting the Future of Workplace Literacy

Workplace literacy in the future is likely to be influenced by at least three trends. These are the continued literacy growth and education of the adult population, new sorts of literacy emerging from new technologies, and technological aids that replace literacy tasks for some workers and create new ones for other workers.

Education and Workplace Literacy Demands

A clear trend over at least the last 150 years has been for demands on workers' literacy in many occupations to increase as the average literacy level of workers in those occupations increased. It is very likely that this trend will, to some degree, continue as employers seek ways to more effectively, efficiently, and profitably provide goods and services. The example of the increased electronic literacy of combat medics making possible more use of electronic communication and tools illustrates this trend of increased literacy demand both following and leading increased literacy skills among workers.

New Electronic Literacies

As new forms of electronic literacy have emerged (e.g., e-mail, the Internet, electronic spreadsheets, and electronic presentation media), these forms have been incorporated into the workplace. This is very likely to continue as the cost of handheld devices decreases while memory and programming complexity increases. Information is increasingly presented on screen or other visual displays in a mix of print and three-dimensional visuals that can be controlled by the user. This, too, is likely to continue. These new mixed literacies call for the user to search and navigate through higher levels of visual and print detail, requiring new or at least modified interpretation, search, and decision-making skills. In the military, pilots already activate information in Heads-Up displays through trained-eye focus. It seems likely that the literate worker of the near future will need to learn still more tools. In addition to being able to simply activate new literacy tools, workers will be expected to compose intelligent questions while using search engines and expert systems efficiently in real time on the job.

Electronic Performance Support Systems and Expert Systems

Many current workers interact with computer screens and enhanced help systems to do the jobs previously performed by dozens of others. Knowing how to use support systems allows people with moderate education and training to perform at higher levels. Employees using computer programs can identify potential drug interactions in prescriptions, diagnose automobile problems, answer thousands of customer service questions, and even provide lifesaving second opinions to rookie emergency room physicians. In some cases, the expert systems support the employee, and in others they replace him or her by allowing others (including customers) to do what was formerly someone's job.

Many low-level and lower-midlevel jobs disappear when customers pump and electronically pay for their own gasoline, schedule their travel online, and check themselves in at the airport. These trends increase the number of more complex computer programming and computer maintenance jobs. This phenomenon of electronic job support and replacement will expand as cheap computer memory and speed make it possible to develop job supports and expert systems for more and more job tasks. Many low-level and lower-midlevel jobs already involve simply moving from one computer-supported job task to another.

In a sense, the resources to develop and maintain electronic support systems are available because the workers using these systems can be paid at very low levels (i.e., very low pay because nearly anyone can now do the job and the job could disappear entirely with the next wave of new technology). On the positive side, such "dumbed down" jobs can temporarily support people who have gained little from our education system. On the negative side, very little learned in such jobs is likely to be of much use in moving up to jobs at the middle skill level, and some (perhaps many) people will be trapped in jobs well below their ability levels.

These support systems tend to widen the gaps between job levels and social classes. It is nearly impossible, without extensive training and additional education, for workers to move from low-level jobs (sometimes supported and dumbed down by computers) to higher-paid and midlevel jobs that require search skills, critical judgment, and additional training. What one learns by following step-by-step directions on a computer screen and selecting yes/no options does little to prepare one for promotion. One can rarely learn enough to be promoted while doing such jobs.

Midlevel jobs are characterized by to the use of support systems, which employees must be able to operate with a good deal of facility to perform at levels well beyond their own personal knowledge and expertise (i.e., not knowing the answer, but being able to find it quickly). In addition to enhanced search skills, middle-level workers must know enough about an occupation to determine when the computer-generated advice and information seem inappropriate. Ranges of skill and expertise within these midlevel jobs is and will continue to be fairly wide and call for entry-level skills at or beyond what is currently expected of average high school and two-year postsecondary graduates. Being prepared to keep up with new knowledge and tools is a requirement of these jobs.

Lucrative top-level jobs will call for the ability of workers to go beyond what is programmed into information systems for doing traditional daily work. These jobs will require workers to deal with atypical situations and problems, use multiple literacies to invent or extend systems to solve problems, and create new knowledge. Such jobs will call for continued mastery of one or more knowledge bases plus skills in using many different information systems.

The gap between low- and midlevel jobs is likely to grow, as will the gap between mid- and top-level jobs. Crossing the gaps will require higher literacy levels, broader skill sets, and the access and ability to benefit from more extensive formal education. These gaps between employment levels will tend to stratify social classes and make class boundaries less permeable.

CHALLENGES FOR INDIVIDUALS, EDUCATORS, AND SOCIETY

Workplace literacy challenges will continue to require many types of learning. Some of these challenges will involve learning to keep up with new technologies and job tasks created by changing job descriptions. Simply doing one's job will increasingly require communicating electronically with many displays of print and learning how to quickly locate and use accurate information and to make judgments about when the electronic support systems are wrong. In addition, it is also highly likely that cyclical formal education for new employment will be required as workers' jobs disappear or are outsourced to less expensive locations and employees.

For educators, workplace literacy changes bring several challenges. Larger percentages of the population will need to be educated to achieve higher skill levels than has ever been accomplished before. Ways to increase the knowledge and skills of adults who have not sufficiently benefited from the traditional education they once had or for whom high-quality traditional education was not available must be found. In addition to broadening formal education to include more complex knowledge and skills, educators will be challenged to find ways to continue educating adults using new venues and learning formats. It seems clear that the increased demands for education will create a problem of access if the only access is through an instructor and classroom with limited availability. More time for learning and guided instruction must be woven across the day and not limited by the administrative convenience of educators.

For society, the main challenges created by changes in workplace literacy have to do with social class. As the gaps between job levels and social classes widen and as it becomes more difficult to bridge these gaps, we will all be faced with choices. Can we find ways to make the boundaries between social classes more permeable? If we cannot or choose not to do this, can we tolerate the changes to lifestyle (i.e., increased violence and limited freedom) that always occur when inequities are glaringly apparent and there is little hope for many of gaining a higher quality of life for oneself and one's family? These are questions that not only involve workplace literacy but are part of larger issues related to political vision and will.

REFERENCES

Boyle, M. E. (2001). *The new schoolhouse: Literacy, managers and belief.* Portsmouth, NH: Praeger.
Bureau of Labor Statistics. (2005, August 3). Computer use at work in 2003. *Monthly Labor Review Editor's Desk.* Retrieved October 1, 2006, from http://www.bls.gov/opub/ted/2005/aug/wk1/art03.htm

Cook, W. D. (1977). *Adult literacy education in the United States.* Newark, DE: International Reading Association.

Essential Skills and Workplace Literacy Initiative. (2006). Retrieved September 12, 2006, from http://srv600.hrdcdrhc.gc.ca/esrp/english/general/home_e.shtml

Gowen, S. G. (1992). *The politics of workplace literacy.* New York: Teachers College Press.

Hensley, S. M. (1993). Union roles in workplace literacy. *Community Services Catalyst, 23*(2), 1–3.

Hull, G. A. (1993). Critical literacy and beyond: Lessons learned from students and workers in a vocational program and on the job. *Anthropology and Education Quarterly, 24,* 373–396.

Hull, G. A., Jury, M., Ziva, O., & Katz, M. (1996). *Changing work, changing literacy? A study of skill requirements and development in a traditional and restructured workplace: Final Report.* Berkeley, CA: National Center for the Study of Writing and Literacy. (ERIC Document Reproduction Service No. ED 397423)

Jurmo, P. (2004). Workplace literacy education: Definitions, purposes and approaches. *Focus on Basics, 7*(B), 22–26.

Kleifgen, J. A. (2005). ISO 9002 as literacy practice: Coping with quality-control documents in a high-tech company. *Reading Research Quarterly, 40*(4), 450–468.

Mikulecky, L. (2001). Education for the workplace. In C. Kaestle, A. Campbell, J. Finn, S. Johnson, & L. Mikulecky (Eds.), *Adult literacy and education in America: Four studies based on the National Adult Literacy Survey.* Washington DC: National Center for Education Statistics.

Mikulecky, L., Lloyd, P., Horwitz, L., Masker, S., & Siemantel, P. (1996). *A review of recent workplace literacy programs and a projection for future changes* (Technical Report TR 96-4). Philadelphia: National Center on Adult Literacy.

National Literacy Act of 1991. P.L. 102-73. H.R. 751, 102nd Cong. (1991).

National Telecommunications and Information Administration. (2002). *A nation online: How Americans are expanding their use of the Internet.* Retrieved September 12, 2006, from http://www.ntia.doc.gov/ntiahome/dn/index.html

Nelson, C. (2004). After the grant is over. *Focus on Basics, 7*(B), 1–5.

Sarmiento, A. (Ed.). (1989). *Workplace literacy and workplace politics.* Washington, DC: Work America.

Stein, C. R., Mays, M., Abbott, C. A., & Wojcik, B. (2000). *Medic training 2000 (MT2K): Surveys regarding computer literacy.* Fort Sam Houston, TX: Center for Healthcare Education and Studies.

Sticht, T. G. (1995). *The military experience and workplace literacy: A review and synthesis of policy and practice* (Technical Report No. TR94-01). Philadelphia: National Center on Adult Literacy.

Sticht, T. G. (1997). The theory behind content-based instruction. *Focus on Basics, 1*(D), 6–13.

Tannock, S. (2001). The literacies of youth and youth workplaces. *Journal of Adult and Adolescent Literacy, 45*(2), 40–43.

U.S. Census Bureau. (2001). *Census 2000.* Washington, DC: Author.

U.S. Department of Labor. (1992). *Learning a living: A blueprint for high performance.* Washington, DC: Secretary's Commission on Achieving Necessary Skills.

U.S. Department of Labor. (2006). *Accomplishments report: U.S. secretary of labor Elaine L. Chao reaches out to Hispanic workforce.* Retrieved July 9, 2007, from http://www.dol.gov/21cw/hispanicworkforce.htm

Chapter Nine

LITERACY IN LATER LIFE

Anne DiPardo

Stereotypical images of the elderly, born of our own hopes and anxieties concerning who we might become if we're fortunate enough to attain old age, are as pervasive as they are taken for granted. Whether kindly, crusty, or wry, the older adults we meet on television and in films are generally a little out of step, perhaps touchingly quaint. Ask adolescents what first comes to mind when they think of senior citizens, and the litany will likely include wheelchairs, walkers, a propensity for staring peacefully at the horizon, and a certain misty-eyed preoccupation with the past. It's a little hard to reconcile these images with those of still-glamorous 55 plus movie stars that crowd the pages of the American Association of Retired Persons' glossy publications alongside advice on such matters as online dating, political lobbying, and adventure travel.

With regard to literacy practices, elders are commonly imagined composing memoirs, writing to distant loved ones, thumbing through the yellowing pages of keepsake books, or reading to a young child nestled in rapt attention. Granted, these are among the more benign images in this age-phobic society of ours, and they'll likely be with us for some time to come. To contemplate changing conceptions of later life, however, is to realize that today's elders are expanding our sense of what is possible, both by living longer and by having much to say and do. It's a safe bet that baby boomers won't rest until they make us see that elders are perfectly capable of mastering newer literacies—Blogging, instant messaging, and Web surfing along with their grandchildren—and using literacy to explore, question, and cross boundaries, and make their voices heard.

Often, only our own aging brings the full realization that diversity, struggle, and psychological complexity stay with us throughout the human life span. As we honor the intricacies of a particular group of people endeavoring to negotiate their later years in whatever ways they find meaningful and satisfying, generalizations tend to give way to questions, and recommendations to fresh ways of thinking about the roles that literacy can play in the lives of twenty-first-century elders. The scant research on older adults' literacy practices tells us little more than what we might already have assumed—that reading habits established at an early age tend to carry over, for instance, or that elders read for a range of purposes (Smith, 1993). It seems that few of us—creatures of habit that we are—suddenly take up regular literacy activities just because we've time on our hands in retirement, though those of us who have always relied on reading and writing to communicate, express ourselves, and connect are likely to embrace the written word with redoubled enthusiasm.

Where older people crave such activities, the available opportunities have important consequences in terms of the social interaction they provide, the larger social purposes they serve, and the effects they ultimately have on participants' minds and spirits. Programs and services for older adults are profoundly influenced by a society's conception of the roles and identities of its older members—and, in the case of programs involving literacy, also by conceptions of what it is to read and write in engaging and meaningful ways. As conceptions of both literacy and aging are provoking considerable debate these days, such programs are necessarily in a period of flux and change, an instability soon to be further complicated by the approach of a population of older adults unprecedented not only in terms of its size, but also its penchant for activism.

To explore older adults' literacy practices, then, is to contemplate changes in the field of gerontology, our nation's demographics, available reading and writing venues, and also expanding opportunities to use literacy to connect across generational and social boundaries. The discussion that follows will take up several dominant themes in scholarly and community-based work with elders. I turn first to the implications of the successful aging movement for our thinking about literacy in later life then address two common foci in literacy programs for older adults—reading and writing groups devoted to life-history review and efforts to engage older adults in intergenerational service activities. In closing, I address the larger implications of new perspectives on literacy and aging and consider the challenges and opportunities that lie ahead.

GERONTOLOGICAL PERSPECTIVES ON LITERACY

Until recently, gerontologists interested in older adults' literacy practices have focused primarily on the relationships between literacy and the losses of memory, mobility, and motivation that can come with old age. (Of particular note is research on diminished eyesight due to such age-related maladies as glaucoma or macular degeneration, leading to medical and technological innovations intended to slow the process of aging and make the most of remaining vision.) Meanwhile, this focus on the physiological and cognitive decline has attracted its share of critics. In recent years, the so-called successful-aging movement (Rowe & Kahn, 1998) has called into question the inevitability of old-age pathology, arguing that there is much we can do to remain fit, happy, and active. If we eat well, exercise wisely, and remain vigorously engaged in the world around us, goes the argument, we need not devolve into frail old people teetering around nursing homes—rather, we can become stereotype-busting, vital members of society, enjoying life and making important contributions to the greater good.

In some respects, the successful aging movement harkens back to what has long been known in the gerontological literature as continuity theory, which argues that well-being in later life is contingent on an ability to draw on healthy roles, habits, and identities forged across a lifetime of introspection and civic engagement (Atchley, 1989). This perspective suggests that literacy activities that provide meaning and satisfaction earlier in life can and should be carried over to our later years, continuing to play a significant part in how we manage our health and finances, stay connected to family and friends, and find entertainment and relaxation. Literacy can be regarded as part and parcel of a successful old age, especially where it promotes intellectual stimulation, a sense of personal efficacy, and social connection.

As appealing as all this is, the successful-aging movement has not been without its thoughtful skeptics. Cultural historian Thomas Cole (1992) traces the successful-aging conception of virtuous self-preservation back to the Victorian belief that just as surely as bad living leads to decrepitude, virtue and impeccable hygiene can ensure a high-quality later life. He argues that the truth is never quite as simple as this—that while we can indeed do much to take care of ourselves, old age is inevitably marked by uncertainty and vulnerability to the whims of fate. Our final years are a time of paradox, Cole maintains—perhaps not as terrible as the medicalizing, pathologizing discourse would have it, but seldom quite the transcendent, self-determined experience that the successful-aging literature describes. In this complicated time of life, it's a fair bet that literacy practices vary both across populations and particular individuals, assuming multiple forms and functions, and shifting and evolving over time. Just as literacy can impart satisfaction, meaning, and a sense of agency at any time of life, so too can it inform later life in ways that are as significant as they are diverse.

In response to traditional gerontology's emphasis on scientific data and approaches to ameliorating the pathologies of old age, scholars in the humanities have recently argued the need to understand the historical and cultural influences on our images of elders in society, as well as the "moral, aesthetic, and spiritual issues" that can attend the aging process (Cole & Ray, 2000, p. xi). Known collectively as humanistic gerontologists, these critics call for greater attention to issues of meaning, value, and representation—such as how prevalent images of the elderly in popular books, magazines, and films are serving to reify stereotypical views of elders and to perpetuate their unduly narrow social roles (Wyatt-Brown, 2000). As the title of literary scholar Margaret Morganroth Gullette's book *Declining to Decline* (1997) suggests, humanistic gerontologists share the successful-aging movement's desire for more positive late-life years that provide opportunities to offer one's insights and services to the wider society.

While much of the research on literacy in old age has focused on dealing with illness and cognitive deterioration, this new interest in the cultural, political, and historical contexts of aging raises a host of provocative questions. We've much to learn, for instance, about how elders themselves describe the differences between the way their generation is depicted in print and their own self-perceptions. Beyond probing *what* and *why* older adults read and write, we might come to deeper understandings of how our perspectives change over time—for example, by asking older adults to reflect on their writing then and now, or to consider how their responses to favorite novels have shifted upon rereadings at different times of life.

Clearly change is in the air as both academics and the general public ponder what it means to grow old in today's world, endeavoring to reach beyond the medicalized, problem-focused perspectives of traditional gerontology to new possibilities and avenues of inquiry. As we will see next, these new perspectives on aging have also shaped two particularly strong currents in contemporary literacy programming for older adults—writing groups focusing on life review, and innovative volunteer efforts that forge connections across generations.

LITERACY TO LOOK BACK AND WITHIN: THE PERSONAL MEMOIR

Over the past several decades, efforts to encourage, support, and understand elders' life-history narratives have been guided by psychologist Robert Butler's (1963) concept of life review. Arguing that a tendency to reminisce is a natural part of old age, Butler took exception with the traditional belief that looking back is somehow pathological or an early indication of encroaching senility. Gerontologists have drawn on Butler's work in arguing that memoir writing offers a host of benefits, including an enhanced ability to cope with the challenges of old age, as well as a sense of dignity and satisfaction. Across the social sciences and humanities, many scholars have come to regard such narratives as both expressing and creating personal identities. If we understand the stories we tell about our lives as constructed rather than discovered whole, then it makes sense to pay attention to the different stories we might create and their consequences for the quality of our lives and for our understandings of who we are or might become (Sarbin, 1986). To tell satisfying stories about one's life experiences is to hold a rich perspective on one's past, present, and future. The construction of such narratives in old age can be especially meaningful as moral, aesthetic, and emotional concerns often assume center stage (Myerhoff & Ruby, 1992). Along with concern for crafting graceful and engaging stories, elder writers may have a particular interest in pondering questions of value and worth (Did I do the best I could? How do I feel about these events now?).

The urge to reminisce about one's life and to reflect on the vicissitudes of old age is reflected in an abundance of memoirs by the elderly, including such notable examples as books by former president Jimmy Carter (1998), writer Doris Grumbach (1993), and psychotherapist Florida Scott-Maxwell (1968). The tendency to reminisce is also evidenced by the many memoir-writing groups springing up at senior centers around the country. (For practical advice on creating and guiding such groups, see Birren & Deutchman, 1991.) Writing teacher and humanistic gerontologist Ruth Ray (2000) finds that memoir writing can bring up elders' multiple and sometimes conflicting identities by provoking a critical process of dialogue with oneself and others and, on occasion, conflict and struggle.

In addition to traditional self-narratives—written individually, though inevitably informed by conversation both in and beyond a given support group—efforts to facilitate elders' memoir writing have encompassed a range of related approaches and texts. Guided autobiography, for instance, begins with group exploration of particular themes in human development, followed by individual writing, and then group sharing and discussion (Birren & Deutchman, 1991). Daybooks or diaries can become important avenues for reflecting on the experiences of later life, whether they remain privately held or are publicly circulated and made available to inform others' meditations on their own life trajectories. Examples of published daybooks include May Sarton's late-life diaries (1996) and Carl Klaus's accounts of retirement (1999) and life as a widow (2006).

Often such notebooks register the emotional complexity of the social, cultural, and biological experiences of aging, providing an outlet, as Florida Scott-Maxwell (1968) puts it, for those who "wave away crossword puzzles, painting, petit point, and knitting" (p. 65), preferring to record their confessional and sometimes blunt thoughts in the "only safe place" (p. 20). Echoing Thomas Cole's (1992) discussion of paradox and uncertainty in old age, Scott-Maxwell (1968) savors the private opportunity to make grand pronouncements and shift moods and topics at will:

What fun it is to generalize in the privacy of a note book. It is as I imagine waltz-ing on ice might be. A great delicious sweep in one direction, taking you your full strength, and then with no trouble at all, an equally delicious sweep in the opposite direction. My note book does not help me think, but it eases my crabbed heart. (p. 15)

The pervasiveness of this urge to ruminate and reflect notwithstanding, phi-losopher and social essayist Simone de Beauvoir (1972) urged the elderly to avoid a preoccupation with reminiscing, arguing that "in old age we should wish still to have passions strong enough to prevent us turning in upon our-selves" (p. 540). We must, she emphasized, "go on pursuing ends that give our existence meaning—devotion to individuals, to groups or to causes, social, political, intellectual or creative work" (p. 3). I turn next to an array of inno-vative programs that reflect this interest in forging vital connections, with a particular eye to helping, understanding, and connecting across generations.

LITERACY TO REACH OUT: LITERACY AND INTERGENERATIONAL ENGAGEMENT

A promising new range of literacy-related programs for older adults are endeavoring to connect elders to children and adolescents through shared read-ing and writing activities. Such programs bring to mind the influential argument of psychologist Erik Erickson and his colleagues, who found that older adults often feel a profound desire to promote the well-being of future generations—an attitude that they termed "grand generativity" (Erikson, Erikson, & Kivnic, 1986, p. 74). This altruistic desire is reflected in a number of popular books, including Mitch Albom's (1997) best-selling account of his visits with a dying professor named Morrie, quadriplegic psychotherapist Daniel Gottlieb's let-ters to his autistic grandson (2006), and psychologists Kenneth Lakritz and Thomas Knoblauch's interviews with compassionate elders (1999).

While many of us have seen this spirit in action in our own communi-ties and families, it is admittedly far from automatic or guaranteed. Freed of the responsibilities and burdens of raising their own children, older adults often assume a more relaxed attentiveness toward grandchildren and other youngsters. Alternatively, elders' lack of contact with the very young can lead to mutual stereotyping and disdain. As older adults represent a powerful vot-ing bloc, it is imperative that the decisions they make at the polling booth be informed by keen understandings of the needs, interests, and promise of the young, including those with cultural, linguistic, or socioeconomic backgrounds that are different from their own.

Perhaps most prominent among such intergenerational literacy efforts are the variety of tutoring programs, which may be locally based or affiliated with such umbrella organizations as the Retired and Senior Volunteer Program, a branch of the national volunteer network known as Senior Corps. Such high-quality programs provide systematic preparation and guidelines, often offering special preparation in working with culturally diverse young people (Blake, 2000). In partnership with teachers and schools, such programs tap into an often underused segment of the population to ensure that students are receiving the individual help they need to bolster their reading and writing skills.

In addition to face-to-face tutoring, literacy outreach programs offer a number of related opportunities. One local program, for instance, engaged senior-citizen volunteers and 8th-grade students in joint readings of young-adult novels and weekly correspondence in shared response journals (DiPardo & Schnack, 2004). As young people and elders read books together about the Holocaust, elder partners wrote about their memories of the Second World War, offering the perspectives of those left behind on the home front as well as those who experienced warfare firsthand. In addition to fostering more thoughtful reading, such correspondences or pen-pal exchanges also offer incentives for young people to work on their writing, as the chance to address an interested real-world audience can foster increased interest in clarity, correctness, and rhetorical effectiveness. In many instances, such exchanges can foster reciprocal learning, as young people share their lives, interests, and expertise with elders—as in one innovative program in which teens teach older adults how to surf the Internet and send e-mail (Haynes, 2002).

A number of programs engage elders in literacy-related activities with the very young as well. Often such programs invite older adults to read aloud to small children, whether as Senior Corps "foster grandparents" or as classroom volunteers who provide early literacy experiences imbued with emotional warmth and caring attention. Innovative preschool programs located adjacent to senior housing offer opportunities for old and young to interact around literacy-related activities, such as reading and listening to stories. For example, One Generation, a Los Angeles-based organization, provides day care for frail older adults that are coordinated with parallel programs for young children between six months and six years old. Innovative efforts such as these provide noncoercive yet structured opportunities for the old and young to interact, filling an important gap both for young children who may not enjoy regular contact with grandparents and for elders who lack ready access to grandchildren.

Other opportunities that combine literacy activities and civic engagement are emerging in what has come to be known as the service learning movement in schools and colleges (see Service Learning Clearinghouse, 2007). In an effort to create learning opportunities that connect course objectives to public challenges, educators are inviting students to move beyond classrooms and libraries into a host of community settings, in many instances providing opportunities to interact with older adults around issues of literacy. Students may conduct oral history interviews with elders for courses in history, aging studies, composition, or sociology, for instance, and collaborate with these older adults in developing their course papers. As in programs designed for younger students, these partnerships may involve such activities as joint reading and journaling or exchanges of ideas via e-mail or instant messaging. Through such activities, elders enjoy opportunities to offer their perspectives to young adults, while students are able to connect ideas they are encountering in textbooks and lectures to the actual experiences of living people.

In her book about aging entitled *Another Country*, best-selling author Mary Pipher (1999) laments our society's tendency toward age segregation. "We have street gangs of ten-year-olds, and old-age ghettos in which our elders are more and more cut off from the real world," she writes. "Children play with cyberpets while old women stare out their windows at empty streets" (p. 11). Efforts to engage elders and the young in literacy activities can clearly address emotional as well as academic challenges, satisfying older adults' need for stimulation and a feeling of usefulness as well as young people's need for caring attention. The design of vital and productive programs depends, however, on the still-emerging understanding that older adults can live vibrant later lives, contribute to the greater good, and master the emerging literacies of an electronic age.

LOOKING TO THE FUTURE: NEW LITERACIES AND THE NEW AGING STUDIES

Future efforts to engage older adults in satisfying and productive literacy activities will continue to be influenced by new scholarly perspectives on the aging process, an increasingly activist older population, and a growing recognition of elders as a diverse, powerful, and too-often-underused segment of the population. Such efforts will no doubt be informed as well by rapidly changing conceptions of what it means to be a fully literate person in today's world, with ever-evolving digital technologies and growing capacity to connect across cultural, linguistic, and political boundaries.

Those presently approaching old age likely recall school-based literacy instruction emphasizing discrete skills (e.g., vocabulary lists, sentence diagramming, spelling tests) and reading lists of canonical works (e.g., *Julius Caesar, Silas Marner, The Scarlet Letter*). Traditionally, skilled literacy has primarily meant an ability to comprehend literal meanings in the texts we read and grammatical felicity in the writing we produce—surely abilities that still matter, though they are arguably no longer enough. Elders' posting on the American Association of Retired Persons' issues blogs (n.d.), for instance, engage in dynamic high-stakes discussion of everything from hospice care to wellness strategies, from prescription drug benefits to global aging. These written conversations not only serve multiple purposes—informing, comforting, lobbying, and so on—but also reach out across geographic, cultural, and socioeconomic differences. Using such tools effectively requires not only a capacity to master new technologies, but also the savvy to use literacy to interact around issues of personal, national, and global significance with a wide and diverse community of fellow participants.

Meanwhile, humanistic gerontologists are promoting yet another set of literacy skills—that is, the capacity to critique the stereotypical images of older adults that pervade texts of all kinds (e.g., Featherstone & Wernick, 1995). Books that provide more satisfying portraits of older adults are finding a ready audience among the elderly (see Wyatt-Brown, 2000) and will likely come to inform the age consciousness of younger readers as well. These representations of the elderly may show both their vulnerability and their knowing gaze, such as the frail but insightful elders in Anne Tyler's best-selling novel *A Patchwork Planet* (1998). In an effort to confront old-age stereotypes directly, psychiatrist Allan Chinen (1999) has written a set of "fairy tales for the second half of life" in which elderly protagonists are not only prominently featured, but also shrewd, wise, and triumphant. Much as images of female presidents in film and television may serve a role in preparing the country for an actual woman in the real White House, such tales can change the way we imagine the old, replacing images of the evil crone in the deep woods with elders whose long years on the planet have made them insightful, compassionate, and judicious. As popular images change, so too might a society's view of what older adults have to offer and how they might participate in meeting the challenges facing our society and world.

Those who study conceptions of the human life span have argued that much is amiss in the traditional ascendance-and-decline view of development over many decades of living. In old age, these scholars tell us, some of us manage to achieve actual wisdom, developing enriched understandings of the interdependency of rationality and emotion, mind and body, and self and world (Labouvie-Vief, 1994). While a person could conceivably become wise at any age, these scholars describe a kind of sagacity that generally comes only after years of living and searching. The wise elder is said to move beyond the reductive either/ors that shape so much public discourse these days, deftly balancing reflection and worldly engagement, acknowledging the ambiguity of life's big dilemmas yet maintaining an ability to act, and integrating critical assessment with compassion and intuition (Sternberg, 1997). That is, wise elder tend to take in a big purview, managing to be at once introspective and outward looking, attending to the needs of family, friends, and community, as well as society and the world.

Granted, old age doesn't always bring wisdom any more than active participation in literacy activities necessarily brings satisfaction, empowerment, and social benefits at any stage of life. Nevertheless, as we begin to see beyond the rigid stereotypes that have both constrained who elders can become as well as our collective ability to tap into what they understand and have to offer, we find that older adults' participation in literacy can hold great value in both private and public terms. As today's elders explore new tools and find fresh uses for familiar ones, they are poised to give us more robust conceptions of how literacy activities can not only enrich one's subjective experience of old age but also bring to the wider society deeper understandings of later life and ready access to the wisest among us.

REFERENCES

Albom, M. (1997). *Tuesdays with Morrie: An old man, a young man, and life's greatest lesson.* New York: Doubleday.

American Association of Retired Persons. (n.d.) *Issues blog.* Retrieved August 14, 2006, from http://aarp.typepad.com

Atchley, R. (1989). A continuity theory of normal aging. *The Gerontologist, 29,* 183–190.

Beauvoir, S. de. (1972). *The coming of age.* New York: Putnam.

Birren, J. E., & Deutchman, D. E. (1991). *Guiding autobiography groups for older adults: Exploring the fabric of life.* Baltimore: Johns Hopkins University Press.

Blake, A. (2000, September). *Senior volunteers in literacy programs: A study of design and practice.* Washington, DC: Corporation for National and Community Service.

Butler, R. (1963). The life review: An interpretation of reminiscence in the aged. *Psychiatry: Journal for the Study of Interpersonal Processes, 26,* 65–76.

Carter, J. (1998). *The virtues of aging.* New York: Ballantine.

Chinen, A. B. (1999). *In the ever after: Fairy tales and the second half of life.* Wilmette, IL: Chiron.

Cole, T. R. (1992). *The journey of life: A cultural history of aging in America.* New York: Cambridge University Press.

Cole, T. R., & Ray, R. E. (2000). Introduction. In T. R. Cole, R. Kastenbaum, & R. E. Ray (Eds.), *Handbook of the humanities and aging* (2nd ed., pp. xi–xxii). New York: Springer.

DiPardo & Schnack (2004). Expanding the web of meaning: Thought and emotion in an intergenerational reading and writing program. *Reading Research Quarterly, 39,* 14–37.

Erikson, E., Erikson, J., & Kivnick, H. (1986). *Vital involvement in old age.* New York: W. W. Norton.

Featherstone, M., & Wernick, A. (Eds.). (1995). *Images of aging: Cultural representations of later life.* London: Routledge.

Gottlieb, D. (2006). *Letters to Sam: A grandfather's lessons on love, loss, and the gifts of life.* New York: Sterling.

Grumbach, D. (1993). *Extra innings.* New York: W. W. Norton.

Gullette, M. M. (1997). *Declining to decline: Cultural combat and the politics of the midlife.* Charlottesville: University of Virginia Press.

Haynes, K. (2002, December 23). Teen tutors connect with seniors. *Los Angeles Times,* p. B3.

Klaus, C. (1999). *Taking retirement: A beginner's diary.* Boston: Beacon Press.

Klaus, C. (2006). *Letters to Kate.* Iowa City: University of Iowa Press.

Labouvie-Vief, G. (1994). *Psyche and Eros: Mind and gender in the life course.* New York: Cambridge University Press.

Lakritz, K. R., & Knoblauch, T. M. (1999). *Elders on love.* New York: Parabola.

Myerhoff, B., & Ruby, J. (1992). A crack in the mirror: Reflexive perspectives in anthropology. In B. Myerhoff & M. Kaminsky (Eds.), *Remembered lives: The work of ritual, storytelling, and growing older* (pp. 307–340). Ann Arbor: University of Michigan Press.

Pipher, M. (1999). *Another country: Navigating the emotional terrain of our elders.* New York: Riverhead.

Ray, R. (2000). *Beyond nostalgia: Aging and life-story writing.* Charlottesville: University of Virginia Press.

Rowe, J. W., & Kahn, R. L. (1998). *Successful aging.* New York: Dell.

Sarbin, T. (1986). *Narrative psychology: The storied nature of human conduct.* New York: Praeger.

Sarton, M. (1996). *At eighty-two: A journal.* New York: W. W. Norton.

Scott-Maxwell, F. (1968). *The measure of my days.* New York: Penguin.

Service Learning Clearinghouse. (2007). Intergenerational. Retrieved June 25, 2007, from http://search.servicelearning.org/index.php?q=intergenerational

Smith, M. C. (1993). The reading abilities and practices of older adults. *Educational Gerontology, 19,* 417–432.

Sternberg, R. J. (1997). *Successful intelligence.* New York: Plume.

Tyler, A. (1998). *A patchwork planet.* New York: Knopf.

Wyatt-Brown, A. M. (2000). The future of literary gerontology. In T. R. Cole, R. Kastenbaum, & R. E. Ray (Eds.), *Handbook of the humanities and aging* (2nd ed., pp. 41–61). New York: Springer.

Chapter Ten

INTEGRATING TECHNOLOGY AND ADULT LITERACY EDUCATION

David J. Rosen

This chapter addresses the incorporation of technology in adult literacy education, how technology is used in the classroom and computer lab by teachers and learners, and how it is used by adults learning at home, at work, and in other places with access to the World Wide Web.

WHAT IS ADULT LITERACY EDUCATION?

Throughout this chapter, adult literacy education refers to a range of programs offered by paid professionals and volunteers in community-based organizations, public schools, colleges, workplaces, libraries, and other organizations. It includes basic literacy, adult basic education, adult secondary education, and preparation for college. It includes numeracy as well as literacy and English for speakers of other languages.

WHAT IS TECHNOLOGY?

Information and communications technology, or simply technology, refers here primarily to computers and the Internet but may also include computer peripherals, such as printers, and other electronic devices, such as cameras, portable digital audio players, televisions, and videocassette recorders used for teaching and learning.

ACCESS TO COMPUTERS AND THE INTERNET: AT SCHOOL, HOME, AND WORK

According to the Pew Internet and American Life Project (2006), which collects data on Americans' use of the home computer and the Internet, 73 percent of American adults—consisting of nearly equal numbers of women and men—now use the Internet. This is a dramatic change since the 1995 Rand Corporation Study on the use of the Internet, which coined the term "digital divide" (Anderson, Bikson, Law, & Mitchell, 1995). That study documented a huge chasm between the better-educated, more affluent, and younger Americans who used e-mail and other Internet services and everyone else who didn't. The Rand Corporation study urged universal access to e-mail so that by 2005 nearly everyone in America would have an e-mail address. At the time, it was hard to imagine that nearly all Americans would have an e-mail address; yet a decade later, we were well along that path. Throughout the country, the majority of adults now have e-mail. In Boston, for example, even many homeless adults have e-mail, and there is a free downtown storefront computing center where they can check their e-mail and use the Web.

The Pew Internet and American Life Project (2006) reports that 88 percent of individuals between 18 and 29 years old and 84 percent of those between 30 and 40 use the Internet. While only 32 percent of those 65 and older use the Internet, that figure is higher than many expected, and it is growing. There is still a digital gap based on color (white, non-Hispanic 73%; black, non-Hispanic 61%). That gap has also narrowed, however, as has the gap between urban and suburban (75%) and rural access (63%). The biggest gaps are related to household income (of those earning at least $75,000 per year, 91% or more have access, while of those earning less than $30,000 per year, only 53% have access) and educational attainment (91% of those who attended college have access, while only 40% of those with less than a high school education have access).

Most Americans now have the Internet at home, and 62 percent of those also have high-speed access. People who do not have a computer and access to the Internet at home may use one at work or have access to one at a local public library or a community computing center. The digital divide, however, has not been bridged for all Americans. Many poor and undereducated Americans, the people served by adult literacy education programs—particularly those who live in rural areas or who are African American—do not have access at home.

In many cases, even those who do have home access may not actually use it. Adult literacy educators have found that some learners, especially women, who live in homes where there is Internet access may not have sufficient computer comfort and competence to take advantage of this access. They may be discouraged from getting basic computer skills by family members who prefer not to share the computer. At the end of this chapter, we will look at the digital divide problem again to see what is being done, and what more can be done to bridge the digital divide for low-literate Americans.

COMPUTER LITERACY

In a class discussion about using technology that I observed a few years ago during a visit to a community-based adult literacy program in Boston, an instructor used the term "computer literacy." A student near me turned to another and said, tongue in cheek, "I told you. They want to teach everyone here to read, even the computers." Of course, computer literacy is a metaphor referring to the basic skills one needs to use a computer. It refers to competence and comfort in using computers; the ability to easily and fluently word process, save, and find files; send and receive e-mail; navigate Web pages; and search the Internet for information. The definition of computer literacy changes frequently, however, as new applications are created. For example, some people might now regard sending instant messages, blogging (writing Web logs), and uploading digital videos to public Web sites as basic computer skills.

Is computer literacy important for those enrolled in adult literacy education programs? If so, why? In a society where adults are increasingly expected to use a computer at work, to complete daily living tasks such as applying for a driver's license, ordering movie tickets, and finding driving directions online, students in adult literacy education classes need to learn these skills too. Some useful instruction is available by computer. For example, instructional software provides students with additional practice as they learn how to decode words or can help English language learners acquire better listening and pronunciation skills. Computer software offers useful tools for improving basic skills. For example, as Antonia Stone (1996), founder of the Community Technology Centers Network, has demonstrated, word processing can be used for improving writing for learners at all levels, including basic literacy. Using most of these computer-assisted instruction programs and tools, however, requires basic computer competence and comfort.

Some recent research suggests that situations where students must have to drop out of classes—often for reasons out of their control—could be changed if students were offered online learning options for periods when they could not attend class (Comings, 2000; Reder & Strawn, 2006). This, of course, would require comfort and competence in using a computer and the Web. In some adult literacy education programs, programs in colleges, community-based organizations, schools, and libraries, students learn to use computers soon after enrolling, even as they are learning basic reading and writing skills. In these programs, computers are nearly as common as pencils, and computer literacy begins immediately and is infused with learning in reading, writing, numeracy, and other studies.

WHAT DO ADULT LEARNERS NEED TO KNOW ABOUT COMPUTERS?

Many adult literacy education programs, and some states, have defined what students need to know and to do in order to achieve above-basic competence in computer use. Arizona and Maryland, for example, have created lists of adult education computer use standards (Arizona Department of Education, 2005; Maryland State Department of Education, 2004). These include using input devices such as keyboards and mice; navigating various software applications; saving and finding files; printing documents; solving routine software and hardware problems; using productivity tools; using computer-assisted instruction; managing personal information; using online resources to communicate, collaborate, and find information; critically evaluating information found on the web; organizing results of research; creating presentations; understanding, describing and practicing responsible uses of technology; knowing how to properly care for, maintain, and upgrade hardware and software; and demonstrating healthy computer ergonomics such as appropriate posture and hand/wrist positions. Not stated explicitly in these competencies, but underlying them all, is a fearless attitude toward using technology. Technology educator Marc Prensky (2001) refers to adults over 30 as "digital immigrants," because they must acquire basic technology skills. It is hard for "digital natives," those born in the 1980s, who have grown up with computers, and for whom operating computer games and using instant messaging are second nature, to understand a generation that might find these machines intimidating.

WHAT DO TEACHERS NEED TO KNOW?

Teachers are often the gateway to their adult students' attainment of technology literacy. Yet when teachers themselves are not comfortable and competent, the gate is closed. Unfortunately, this contributes to the digital divide. Older adult literacy education teachers, who are more often digital immigrants than digital natives, have had few opportunities to learn and use these skills. If teachers do not have regular daily access to a computer with high-bandwidth access to the Internet at work and at home, and if they do not have opportunities to be exposed to new applications, to practice them, and to apply and evaluate them with students, they do not get over the computer literacy barrier and do not feel comfortable, competent, and willing to take risks in using technology in the classroom.

What are these risks? Integrating technology has many challenges. For example, if a teacher plans a lesson that depends on access to the Web, that access could disappear just when it is needed; if the teacher needs to print something, the printer could malfunction; if every student needs to go to the same Web page at the same time, that number of simultaneous users will slow access to some Web sites a crawl or cause a crash; if there is one Web site that it is critical to the lesson, it may malfunction the day the teacher needs it. Sometimes even the best plans go awry. At a technology conference in a hotel in Austin, Texas, a few years ago, just as I was ready to do a Web-based presentation, the hotel's Internet service went down. Always prepared with a backup plan, I had saved the critical pages to my laptop, but I hadn't realized that someone had changed the settings on my laptop the day before, and I couldn't get it to work. These glitches are so common that a group of adult literacy education and technology advocates has created a Web page of them that also offers some solutions (www.TechGlitches.com).

Underlying these risks is the possibility of a teacher looking foolish before a group of students who know more than the teacher does about technology. The teaching paradigm in most adult literacy education classes is what some refer to as "sage on the stage" or in some cases "guide by the side." Neither of these is successful, however, for integrating technology in a classroom. A new paradigm that acknowledges that the teacher is a learner too, that there may be students who have more technology expertise than the teacher, and that everyone needs to help each other learn is needed. I would call this paradigm "We're All In This Together." This shift requires courage and practice. For some teachers, it is not easy; yet it may be the most important change to bring about real integration of technology. Digital natives know that to learn technology, you must dive in, swim around, and use whatever knowledge you—and those around you—have to solve whatever problems you face. You may recognize this as a strategy set for playing computer games, the hatchery of the digital native.

Some states have defined teacher competencies for integrating technology with adult students. The U.S. Department of Education-funded AdultEd Online project, sponsored by the University of Michigan's Project IDEAL and the Sacramento County, California, Office of Education, has defined competencies for teachers' technology integration. AdultEd Online (2006) has also developed an assessment instrument, a professional development planning process, and online resources to enable teachers to attain competency in using technology.

WHAT DOES IT MEAN TO INTEGRATE TECHNOLOGY IN ADULT LITERACY EDUCATION?

One of the most widespread applications of computer technology in adult literacy education is computer-assisted instruction, or computer-assisted language learning. Nevertheless, little research is available on its effectiveness in adult literacy education. Computer-assisted instruction is used for drill and practice, direct instruction, and in some cases managing instruction. Early computer-assisted instruction was text based with a questions-and-answer format. Then, drill and practice was increasingly followed by game formats. Now, software often incorporates simulations, graphics, audio, and video. Some adult literacy education computer-assisted instruction is entirely simulation. A learner may solve problems in an office, solve a mystery, or measure objects on a shop floor. In one of these simulations, "The Office," learners use interactive online tools, such as simulated computers with e-mail, and reference books to look up information. In another, a numeracy simulation for learning statistical process control, learners use an interactive micrometer to measure "widgets" (LexIcon Interactive Media Solutions, n.d.). Drill and practice may be effective in helping students memorize numerical facts, improve spelling, or improve decoding skills; however, the strategic use of computer-assisted instruction requires an experienced teacher and close monitoring so that students use the software effectively. Too often, when computer-assisted instruction is not carefully planned, students find it repetitive and boring, or they become frustrated when they get stuck and can't get past a technical obstacle. When planned well and monitored carefully, however, computer-assisted instruction can accelerate learning, provide more and different kinds of explanations, offer more opportunities to practice at one's own pace, and give regular, systematic feedback on learning attained. Some students find some kinds of computer-assisted instruction, especially simulations, very engaging.

Computer-assisted instruction comes in small packages designed to do one, or just a few things. For example, beginning-level English listening skills, numerical fact drill and practice, spelling of lists of common words, or English grammar may be the focus of computer-assisted instruction. These software programs are relatively inexpensive, and they vary in quality. Computer-assisted learning also comes in much larger packages called integrated learning systems. These address much more, such as all levels of English language learning, or all levels of basic skills. An integrated learning system is more expensive and almost always includes an objectives-based learning management system to help teachers assign lessons and track students' progress. Some common examples of these include PLATO, ELLIS, Skills Bank/Skills Tutor, and Aztec Learning Systems. A useful list of integrated learning systems and other commercial and free software can be found at Newsome Associates (n.d.).

Over the past several years, many teachers and some curriculum developers have developed free education software, much of which is on the Web. Some teachers have created their own classroom Web sites, or class online learning groups, by using Yahoo groups, Trackstar, or Quia, for example. Teachers in states such as Arizona have indexed online instruction to the state English language learning standards for adults. These will be found at the Splendid ESOL Web (Pima College Adult Education, n.d.). I have created Web-based lists of free adult literacy education Web-based learning resources that can be found at Newsome Associates (n.d.).

With the enormous amount of commercial and free instructional software now available, how does a teacher, and how do students working on their own, choose the best software to meet instructional and learning objectives? There are many strategies, ranging from casually asking colleagues to formally evaluating software and testing it out with students. Most teachers who use instructional software ask for software recommendations from colleagues in their school or program, at workshops and conferences, and in online discussions about software, for example on the National Institute for Literacy Technology electronic discussion list. Some consult lists of software, such as those found in the software reviews section of "The Literacy List" (Newsome Associates, n.d.). Some, who may also use these as initial strategies to narrow down what software products to review, will also review the software against a set of criteria and test it out with their students. *Software Buyers' Guide* by the Northwest Regional Literacy Resource Center (n.d.) has a quick and simple set of criteria for software review. The Adult Literacy Resource Institute (1999) in Boston several years ago brought together a group of teachers, reviewed several software review instruments, and developed one comprehensive instrument called the Software Evaluation Worksheet. The key questions in all these software review instruments involve suitability for the intended users based on what their learning needs and objectives are, how easy the software is to navigate, whether or not the software is engaging, and ultimately whether or not it enables the intended population to accomplish their learning objectives efficiently.

Computer-assisted instruction, particularly in its early years, was sometimes disparaged by teachers who found its cookie-cutter workbook approach did not add much value to learning, especially in light of the additional expense, training, and time required to use it effectively. Although some teachers still do not like using computer-assisted instruction, many more have found it helpful as a supplement to learning when students use it under the guidance of a skilled teacher.

CONSTRUCTIVIST APPROACHES TO ADULT LEARNING WITH TECHNOLOGY

A different approach to learning, sometimes called project-based learning, or constructivism, does not employ technology to deliver instruction but instead looks at ways that students can use electronic technology as a set of project organization or presentation tools to accomplish learning-related purposes. Constructivism is a theory of cognitive growth in which learning is thought to be an active process, one in which a person constructs new ideas or concepts while transforming existing knowledge. Meaning is made from one's experiences and from a cognitive structure based on those experiences. A learner constructs knowledge by actively connecting and absorbing new information or experience into his or her existing knowledge structure. The new knowledge or ideas become useful and integrated as the learner sees relationships among existing concepts and knowledge and the new ideas. The learner selects and interprets information, constructs hypotheses, and makes decisions by relying on a cognitive structure of schema, or mental models. Constructivism is often regarded as an approach that is participatory, engaged, and learner centered.

Electronic technology offers many basic skills opportunities to learners whose teachers use constructivist approaches. Adult learners, like other adults, want to use computers for communication, finding information, shopping, and entertainment. Some of the tools needed for these personal uses are the same as those needed for educational uses and meet a range of learners' high-priority needs. These may include e-mail, finding information through online search engines, word processing, or finding and watching video files. Other tools include reading or contributing to electronic discussion lists (Listservs); making graphics; publishing articles, flyers, and Web pages; searching or creating databases; and using spreadsheets.

Those who want to learn to write, or to improve their writing skills, find that word processing makes learning to write easier, especially when they learn word-processing skills at the same time that they are learning writing skills such as spelling, sentence building, and paragraph construction. Adding to, erasing, and moving text are all easier with word processing than writing by hand. Built-in spell-checking programs are handy, especially for adults who are new writers. The process of writing, getting corrections, and editing is much easier electronically. Many adults appreciate that after extensive editing, their final writing product, printed out, looks good and is not blemished by erasure marks or smudges or marked with edits. For certain kinds of writing, and for other reasons, adults need to search for and verify information. Library research is still useful but with online search engines, online encyclopedias, specialized electronic discussion lists, Web pages that can be easily and quickly edited by readers (wikis), and subject-matter indices (portals), adult learners may search from home, work, or school. Learning to use these research tools to improve one's writing has the added value that conducting research may be applied to other areas of learning.

A constructivist approach begins not with a curriculum and a set of intended learning outcomes, but rather with a question, problem, decision, topic, presentation, or product of interest to students. For example, learners may be interested in improving access to health information in their community, and the project might be producing brochures or slide presentations for community education meetings on asthma, nutrition, smoking, cholesterol, or other health concerns. Adult learners may want to improve voter turnout in their community and, to do so, may research the rules for voter registration and produce a multilingual community digital slide presentation on how to vote, and why. They may want to start small businesses and may want to research and present information on how to write a business plan and how to secure a business loan. In the process of doing research and making presentations, students acquire reading, writing, speaking, and listening skills. They may also acquire numeracy skills or specific content knowledge that will help them in daily living and/or on tests. They use CD-ROM or online encyclopedias, dictionaries, and other electronic research tools to search for answers to their questions; they use computers to do word processing and publish the results of their projects; and they use presentation software to show their projects in class and in the community. Depending on the project, they may also create tables, charts, graphs, spreadsheets, and databases.

Some teachers and students make Web pages to present their learning. For over a decade, Susan Gaer, a community college instructor at Santa Ana College in Southern California, has worked with English language teachers of adults and children across the world to do projects that result in student Web presentations. Learners submit recipes in English for an international cookbook. They research the cost of common food items in their neighborhoods, such as pizza, and then compare prices and the cost of living in different communities. They write about cultural or ethnic home remedies. They do intergenerational cultural projects in which they interview family members. They match up with classes in other parts of the world for international "community virtual visits" (Gaer, n.d.). Another project, developed by the Literacy Telecommunications Collaborative in Boston, has students create virtual visits for computer stores, home-buying agencies, museums, libraries, and state capitals (Rosen & Macdonald, 2004). In each case, a group of students actually visits the site and conducts interviews, takes digital photos, makes audio files, and then creates a virtual visit of the actual visit for those who may be interested in learning about the organization but cannot visit in person.

ASSISTIVE TECHNOLOGY AND UNIVERSAL DESIGN.

Technology offers adult learners with disabilities—those who are blind or sight impaired, those who are deaf or hearing impaired, or those who have learning disabilities or specific reading disabilities—an opportunity to participate in classes and make progress in learning. Assistive technology, such as a browser that reads Web pages out loud, a speech recognition program that allows someone to write through dictation, special devices for typing or executing commands for those who can't use a keyboard, provides special access. Universal design is an approach to creating learning environments that provide a full range of access tools for everyone, including those with disabilities. For example, a sidewalk curb cut benefits those in wheelchairs, but the majority of those who use them are bicyclists, roller skaters, and people pushing strollers; this benefits them as well. Handicapped-accessible bathroom stalls that accommodate wheelchairs also benefit able-bodied people who need more room. Useful universal design-learning features for those with disabilities, now standard issue in many computers, include the capacity to easily enlarge text and voice recognition programs, and other features, such as some text readers, can be installed for free. Florida TechNet (n.d.) provides a list of good resources for adults with learning disabilities, including assistive technology resources.

NEW USES OF TECHNOLOGY FOR LEARNING

New digital technologies are being developed every year. Some are potentially useful to teachers and adult learners; some are not. To determine if they are useful, new technologies must be tried, evaluated, and discussed. If they appear to add value to teaching and learning, then their authors' claims should be researched and proved. As of May 2007, there are at least four new technologies that appear to have potential for adult literacy education: wikis, podcasts, m-learning, and learning portals.

Wikis

Wiki-wiki is a Hawaiian word that means "very, very quickly." A wiki is a Web page where anyone can quickly add or change text. Wikis, where people come together to learn and add to knowledge, are used for a variety of purposes. The best-known wiki application is a free worldwide encyclopedia called Wikipedia. Other free and useful wikis include the Adult Literacy Education Wiki; wikiHow, a collection of ever-increasing articles and sets of instructions on how to make or do things; and Wikimapia, a detailed worldwide map onto which one can add information.

The Adult Literacy Education Wiki (http://wiki.literacytent.org) is designed for practitioners, researchers, and learners to pose and answer important questions in the practice of adult literacy education. It is intended to help teachers, tutors, administrators, and other practitioners easily find professional wisdom and research regarding specific questions about practice. It is a practitioner's professional development site, a community of practice. The Adult Literacy Education Wiki covers topics ranging from basic reading and writing for adults and adult basic education to adult secondary education and English language learning. There are, as of this writing, 30 topic areas, including adult literacy professional development, assessment, basic literacy, curriculum development, English for speakers of other languages, family literacy, learning disabilities, numeracy, project-based learning, reading, and technology. In some topic areas, in addition to discussion, there is a summary, glossary, and a list of further resources. These resources are often links to research.

WikiHow (http://www.wikihow.com) describes itself as "the How-To Manual that anyone can write or edit." This is an excellent resource for those who teach writing. Students can pick something they believe they know how to do well, such as cooking, a sport or hobby, a kind of home repair, pet care or training, or a home health remedy. The teacher can introduce a format, such as that used on wikiHow—title, introduction, steps, tips, and things you'll need—and then ask each student to write a wikiHow article using the format. These articles can then be edited in pairs, in small groups, by the class as a whole, or by the teacher. The editing process enables the writer to see how others might misunderstand the writing and to understand how to write more clearly and completely. The articles can then be posted on wikiHow. Once posted, there is a good chance that they will be revised again. The site has a group of friendly editors who look at each new article, usually within a few hours. Because wikis have an accessible history of the changes to each page, the writer can see each person's edits and learn how the article has been improved. The writer also has the pleasure of having an article published for the world to read!

Wikimapia (http://wikimapia.org) is useful for learning map-reading skills, but because it is a wiki and an individual can put boxes on the map with text and links to Web pages, it is also useful for students who want to improve their reading and writing skills. A group of students who live in the same area, for example, can zoom in on a map of their neighborhood, often to the rooftop level, and can label the structures or geographical features that are important to them. This could be a useful activity for two classes to share in a classroom virtual visit project.

Podcasts

Podcasts are digital audio files that can be listened to on a computer or a handheld digital listening device known as an MP3 player. (One example of an MP3 player is an iPod.) Through a protocol known as an RSS (really simple syndication) feed, a person can automatically have these files downloaded and saved on a computer and then they can be synched with a portable MP3 player. Learners can download audio presentations, language learning audio files, and other audio files and listen to them while commuting or waiting for appointments—anywhere and anytime. English language learners might find these useful for improving listening skills. Students who have difficulty reading and want to learn certain kinds of content (for example for the GED social studies test) could get the content from articles downloaded in audio files.

M-learning

Mobile learning (m-learning) is text-based audio, or visual instruction delivered through a mobile phone or Web-accessible PDA (portable data assistant). While digital immigrants complain that the screen or keyboard is too small and cumbersome for this to be useful, digital natives are already using mobile phones to access information and to get and read directions and maps, and in some countries (the United Kingdom, Australia, and South Africa, for example), they are being used for adult learning. Web-accessible PDAs often have a larger screen and an attachable full-size keyboard. For some video MP3 players there are high-quality goggles through which to view the images and text. It is likely that as technologies merge there will a variety of kinds of reasonably sized, lightweight, Web-accessible, affordable portable devices. These could be portable learning assistants for adult literacy education students.

Learning Portals

Some teachers object to using the World Wide Web with their students because it is so easy for them to get lost or distracted. Learning portals may be the answer to this problem. A learning portal is a Web site that selects and organizes learning resources and often displays them in its own browser, so it is very easy for a Web neophyte to find his or her way. A particularly useful example of this is a free plain-English portal developed by the Westchester County Public Library in New York called Firstfind.info. Designed for low-literate library patrons who want to use the Web to answer questions in areas that are of interest to adults, such as education, family, government, health, jobs and job training, housing, technology, Firstfind.info is also used by some adult literacy education teachers to find suitable information at a reading level their students can handle.

TECHNOLOGY PLANNING

A few states (Arizona, California, Hawaii, Vermont, and Massachusetts, for example) have state adult literacy and technology plans. In these states, and others, schools and programs often have technology plans as well. Technology planning usually involves administrators, teachers, adult learners, a technology coordinator, and others coming together to prepare for technology to be integrated in teaching practice and be made widely available to students. The planning process increases understanding, commitment, and ultimately the resources to implement the plan. A particularly useful tool, developed by the Outreach and Technical Assistance Network in California (n.d.), is an online technology plan form for adult literacy education programs. The process includes forming a planning team, determining the scope of the plan, creating a vision statement, assessing the current state of technology integration in the program, establishing goals and objectives, addressing funding issues, creating a staff development plan, and a creating a strategy for evaluating and revising the plan over time.

WHAT DO WE NEED TO DO TO BRIDGE THE DIGITAL DIVIDE?

In 1995, one of the conclusions of the Rand study was that individuals' accessibility to e-mail is hampered by low income, low levels of education, and racial gaps in the availability of computers and access to network services. The authors recommended looking at "creative ways to make terminals cheaper; to have them recycled; to provide access in libraries, community centers, and other public venues; and to provide e-mail 'vouchers' or support other forms of cross-subsidies" (Anderson et al., 1995, p. 15). Most of these recommendations have been implemented, and they have made a difference. Many more Americans have computers at home and access at work and elsewhere. Access is not the same as regular use, however. Many low-literate or limited-English-proficient adults who are not comfortable and competent using computers live in homes with high-bandwidth access to the Web. In addition to continuing to make sure all families have access, we must now redouble our efforts through adult literacy education programs and in other ways to ensure that immigrant and low-literate adults can comfortably use technology at home. This means that basic computer skills, like reading, writing, and numeracy, must be a mainstay of every adult literacy program. It means that adult education teachers must have these competencies themselves. To acquire these skills, states need to make a considerably greater investment in paid professional development so that teachers have the training and the time to try out, evaluate, and integrate new technologies in their practice.

REFERENCES

AdultEd Online. (2006). *Technology integration competencies for adult educators.* Retrieved December 10, 2006, from http://www.adultedonline.org/TechIntegCompetencies.pdf

Adult Literacy Resource Institute. (1999, October 4). *Software evaluation worksheet.* Retrieved December 10, 2006, from http://alri.org/softreview/swworksht.html

Anderson, R., Bikson, T., Law, S. Mitchell, B, (1995). *Universal access to e-mail feasibility and societal implications.* Rand Corporation. Santa Monica, CA . Retrieved December 10, 2006, from http://www.rand.org/pubs/monograph_reports/MR650/index.html

Arizona Department of Education. (July, 2005). *Arizona adult education technology standards.* Retrieved December 10, 2006, from http://www.ade.az.gov/adulted/Documents/AEStandards/Technology_Standards.pdf

Comings, John. (2000, March). Helping adults persist: Four supports. *Focus on Basics, 4*(A). Retrieved December 10, 2006, from http://www.ncsall.net/?id = 332

Florida TechNet. (n.d.). *Resources for adults with learning disabilities.* Retrieved December 1, 2006, from http://www.floridatechnet.org/bridges/resources.html

Gaer, S. (n.d.). *Email projects home page.* Retrieved December 1, 2006, from http://www.otan.dni.us/webfarm/emailproject/email.htm

LexIcon Interactive Media Solutions. (n.d.). *Basic skills.* Retrieved December 1, 2006, from http://www.workingsimulations.com/main_site/basicskillHome.html

Maryland State Department of Education. (2004). *Maryland adult education technology standards.* Retrieved December 10, 2006, from http://www.umbc.edu/alrc/Standards/Texts/TechnologyStandards.pdf

Newsome Associates. (n.d.). Retrieved December 1, 2006, from http://www.newsomeassociates.com

Northwest Regional Literacy Resource Center. (n.d.). *Software buyers' guide: 2001–2002 edition.* Retrieved December 10, 2006, from http://www.nwlincs.org/softreview/rev.htm

Outreach and Technical Assistance Network. (n.d.). *California technology plan development tool.* Retrieved December 1, 2006, from http://www.otan.us/Techplans/public/login.cfm?fuseaction = login

Pew Internet and American Life Project. (2006, April). *Demographics of Internet users.* Retrieved December 10, 2006, from http://www.pewinternet.org/trends/User_Demo_4.26.06.htm

Pima College Adult Education. (n.d.). *The splendid ESOL Web.* Retrieved December 10, 2006, http://cc.pima.edu/~slundquist/index.htm

Prensky, M. (2001). Digital natives, digital immigrants. *On the Horizon, 9*(5). Retrieved December 9, 2006, from http://www.marcprensky.com/writing/Prensky%20-%20Digital%20Natives,%20Digital%20Immigrants%20-%20Part1.pdf

Reder, S., & Strawn, C. (2006, November). Self-study: Broadening the concepts of participation and program support. *Focus on Basics, 8*(C). Retrieved December 10, 2006, from http://www.ncsall.net/?id = 1150

Rosen, D. J., & Macdonald, T. (2004, April 13). *Virtual visits.* Retrieved December 10, 2006, from http://alri.org/visits/vv.html

Stone, A. (1996). *Keystrokes to literacy: Using the computer as a learning tool for adult beginning readers.* Chicago: National Textbook Company.

Chapter Eleven

RESOURCES FOR ADULT LITERACY

Jackie Taylor

Adult literacy education is an emerging profession that has positive effects on the lives of learners and the practitioners who teach them. Adult learners often report important outcomes resulting from improved literacy skills. Teachers often report entering the profession not on purpose but quite by accident because they stumbled into the profession and fell in love with it. As Quigley (2006) reminds us, the earliest definitions of "profession" were not about "competence, or knowledge, or working full-time, or career aspirations, or having a framed diploma on the wall" but about "professing one's personal commitment to a vocation—to a calling" (p. 11). A married couple who had earned their GEDs and moved on to college once told me about how adult literacy education helped them break intergenerational cycles of poverty:

> Our kids were growin' up to be like us.... We found we had to do these things [go back to school] in order to create a new life with our kids. And now they're on the same page we are. My daughter continually says she can't wait to graduate high school so she can go to college. It's great to hear that. Our older boys—when we first got together, they didn't want to go to school; they didn't care nothin' about goin' to school because that's the way we were. When we changed that scenario, certain mentalities were broken.

Adult literacy is more than reading and writing; it involves instructional areas like basic computer skills, getting health information, family or intergenerational literacy, English language learning and civics education for immigrants, workplace basic skills, and basic skills for the homeless and the incarcerated. Adult learners come to programs for the most part voluntarily (though there are exceptions)—unlike the mandated K–12 system. They choose to strengthen their literacy skills for a variety of purposes despite the constraints of daily responsibilities. They bring a wealth of personal experience and expertise to the adult literacy education classroom. Staff in such programs most often reflect the diversity of the community and perform their responsibilities in ways that even some certified professionals may be unable to accomplish. What other emerging profession has thousands of volunteers and thousands more part-time professionals? What do they know about adult literacy education that is not apparent to the public at large? Even the term "adult literacy," which might refer to reading and writing, has broader meanings that embrace a range of literacy skills used for multiple purposes that are essential for adults to carry out their roles and responsibilities within the family, workplace, and community. This chapter is especially for those who are considering careers in adult literacy education. As an adult educator, I will guide you along some pathways in my field, shedding light on resources that I hope you find valuable in your journey.

ADULT LITERACY'S HISTORY

To understand why adult literacy is an emerging profession, it is useful to look at the field's history. A valuable resource in doing that is *The Rise of the Adult Education and Literacy System in the United States: 1600–2000* by Tom Sticht (2002). Sticht recounts the rich history of adult literacy and its roots in social change, including the moonlight schools that were started in 1911 by Cora Wilson Stewart. The struggles and successes of advocates to advance the profession of adult literacy education resulted in the establishment of the Adult Education and Literacy System by Congress in 1966 with the passage of the Adult Education Act. This system of government-funded education programs allocates funds for the hiring of a greater number of full-time and part-time teacher professionals. Now under Title II of the Workforce Investment Act, more than 4,000 state, local, and community-based organizations annually receive federal funds for adult education.

WHAT RESOURCES ARE AVAILABLE FOR UNDERSTANDING THE ISSUES IN ADULT LITERACY?

In December 2005, the National Assessment of Adult Literacy (NAAL), released by the National Center for Education Statistics, reported that 93 million adults (45% of the adult population) have basic skills deficiencies in reading, writing, or math; 30 million of them have very limited skills; and 11 million of them cannot communicate in English. Yet only 3 percent of the

93 million undereducated adult Americans have access to adult education and family literacy services, which is primarily due to limited funding (McLendon, 2006). The National Institute for Literacy hosted a series of Webcasts on the NAAL that describe and present the assessment results; these can be found on the institute's Web site. Another useful source of information on the NAAL is the Web site of the U.S. Department of Education's National Center for Education Statistics in the Institute of Education Sciences. The National Council of State Directors of Adult Education has also produced a series of resources on the NAAL that provide useful information for discussing the assessment results with stakeholders in the community and the media, including fact sheets, talking points, frequently asked questions, and an archive of newspaper articles.

Another way to learn about the need for adult literacy services is to examine the U.S. Census Bureau data. The Office of Vocational and Adult Education in the U.S. Department of Education has created both state and regional profiles from the 2000 census that present the census data by number of years of school completed, age, gender, poverty level, and other critical descriptors.

A valuable resource for understanding the current state of the adult literacy field is *Four Lay-of-the-Land Papers on the Federal Role in Adult Literacy,* the first informal publication produced by the National Commission on Adult Literacy (2006). This independent, blue-ribbon national commission was founded on October 9, 2006, by the Council for Advancement of Adult Literacy and the Dollar General Corporation to chart a course for the future of adult literacy. Over the next two years, we can expect the National Commission on Adult Literacy to continue to make background papers developed for the commission available to the general public.

WHAT IS THE NATURE OF THE ADULT LITERACY TEACHING PROFESSION?

While systems of government-funded education programs provide greater numbers of full-time and part-time teachers, the adult literacy education workforce is still an emerging profession. Eighty percent of instructors are part time, and thousands are volunteers. Yet while many adult educators have training in teaching primary or secondary education, few, when they begin teaching adults, have the knowledge and skills necessary to teach adults and to address the unique needs of learners who seek adult literacy services. The types of resources available in the field (or the lack thereof) reflect the current state of affairs in the professionalization of the field, the availability of funds, and resources helpful in leveraging and advocating for funds.

HOW CAN YOU LEARN MORE ABOUT THE FIELD OF ADULT LITERACY?

Strategies

• Research the impact of adult literacy on learners' lives. Start by talking with adult learners. If you do not have access to anyone who may be participating in an adult literacy program, then view the online video *Stories of Lives Changed*. Produced by the University of Tennessee (2001), this video shares the stories of adult learners whose lives were changed by their participation in adult literacy in welfare reform programs.

• Investigate what your town or community is doing to address adult literacy issues. Talk to adult literacy providers. Seek out adult literacy programs affiliated with libraries, public schools, and community colleges; inquire with basic education programs offered by religious organizations, workplaces, and union halls. Start locally, but if you need assistance finding local, adult literacy providers, see the section below titled "Finding Programs and Job Opportunities."

• Talk to teachers online. Subscribe to any of the National Institute for Literacy's (n.d.b) national discussion lists for adult literacy, which are helpful for those who want to learn more about the adult literacy field. Information posted on electronic discussion lists (Listservs) often leads to other useful sites on the Internet. The institute's discussion lists have a searchable database of list postings. Moderators often summarize discussions with guest speakers, and they are archived. Professional associations such as Teachers of English to Speakers of Other Languages and the Association of Adult Literacy Professional Developers and some state professional development centers also sponsor their own discussion lists. Several associations are listed in the resources section of this chapter. Check with the ones that interest you to learn how to subscribe.

• If you are entering the field, investigate your options for professional development and take advantage of them (see section titled "Adult Literacy Professional Development").

• Talk with people in organizations, agencies, and social services that seem peripherally connected to adult literacy (e.g., prison ministries, VISTA, missions, American Indian reservations, cultural centers).

• Read books and watch movies recommended by adult learners or adult educators for learning about the unique experiences of adult learners (see, e.g., Adult Literacy Education Wiki, n.d.b).

• Always ask questions. Find out from adult learners and adult educators what works where they are, what doesn't work, and why they think this is so. Identify promising practices and adapt them to your situation.

CAREER PATHWAYS IN ADULT LITERACY

Adult educators come from diverse backgrounds and fields of study and follow career pathways through adult literacy that are equally varied: pathways leading from positions as volunteer tutors to program and state directors, adult learners to program managers, and part-time teachers to professional development staff or university researchers. They come from fields like art and architecture, social change movements, the Peace Corps, and K–12 teaching, among others. Adult educators often happen upon adult education and then never wish to leave. But where is the front door to adult literacy? Does the field need one? Would having a front door such as a teacher certification requirement limit the diversity among staff that the field now enjoys—and must have? Can the field support enough full-time positions and provide adequate working conditions to recruit committed, compassionate, high-quality adult educators and keep them? These questions and others have generated a debate in the adult literacy field about program quality, of which career pathways are a part. What questions are central for you in this debate?

A variety of inspiring stories that describe how people entered adult literacy education can be found in the 2002 special summer issue of *Field Notes,* a newsletter funded by the Massachusetts Department of Education and produced by the System for Adult Basic Education Support (Balliro, 2002). More stories can also be found in the Adult Literacy Professional Development area of the Adult Literacy Education Wiki (n.d.a).

While the passage of the Adult Education Act in 1966 created new opportunities for a paid adult literacy workforce, in general, the workforce is not a stable one. Factors such as varied soft-money funding streams that have created insecure positions, inadequate federal and state funding that do not enable full-time positions, and poor working conditions make it challenging—though not impossible—for adult educators to build a stable career. This lack of stability may contribute to higher attrition rates than those seen in elementary and secondary education. Where this is true, the field of adult literacy is faced with a very serious barrier to improving program quality. Organizations like the Association of Adult Literacy Professional Developers advocate program and state policies to improve working conditions and other support for teacher professional development. Adult Literacy Professional Developers is a national association of adult literacy professional developers that advocates in this area.

Some programs, even small community-based programs, do provide full-time positions and benefits for part-time staff. One example is WAITT House, a small Boston community-based organization that keeps the needs of students and staff at the forefront of all decisions. WAITT House increases salaries as the cost of living rises or, when it cannot do this, provides additional vacation leave; the agency provides health insurance to full- and part-time staff and offers generous vacation leave to keep teachers fresh. The organization believes that these basic benefits have helped them to avoid many management and service delivery problems, such as high staff turnover, training more new staff than necessary, inconsistencies in instruction, and discomfort among students because of a high turnover rate among teachers. WAITT is an acronym for "We Are All In This Together."

Adult educators and program administrators collaborate within the program and community to build career pathways in adult literacy. For a list of strategies used by teachers, program administrators, and others, visit the Adult Literacy Professional Development area of the Adult Literacy Education Wiki (n.d.a).

How does one get started in the field of adult literacy? While most enter the K–12 field through teacher preparation programs, most often the front door in adult literacy is literally at the door of the adult literacy education program.

TEACHER EDUCATION

Do teacher certification, licensing, or endorsement programs adequately prepare teachers to teach? Do K–12 teacher preparation programs leading to certification benefit the adult educators who may be required to participate in them? Some argue that adult literacy is so qualitatively different from other teaching fields that an entirely separate adult education certification should be offered; others argue that intensive in-service training in combination with teaching and performance assessments would better prepare adult educators than an academic program. Others argue that the demands of the job are similar to K–12 and all that is needed is the addition of a separate endorsement. Finally, requiring certification or endorsements would prevent some nontraditional but highly effective educators from teaching because they cannot afford to attend a four-year institution. These debates have led states to handle licensing in different ways, ranging from offering full adult education license preparation programs to only requiring an elementary or secondary school teaching license. To learn more about this debate and the issues surrounding teacher preparation and certification in adult basic education, you may wish to read *Professionalization and Certification for Teachers in Adult Basic Education* (Sabatini, Ginsburg, & Russell, 2002).

Teacher preparation programs that specialize in adult literacy education are not common, although many colleges and universities offer some coursework specific to adult education (Sabatini et al., 2002). Higher education courses and related degree programs benefit adult educators who choose to return to college to develop their careers beyond the adult literacy classroom.

IF YOU WANT TO TEACH IN ADULT LITERACY EDUCATION, WHERE SHOULD YOU BEGIN?

Teacher certification or licensing is usually not required to teach in community-based programs or community colleges, but it is usually required to teach adults in local education agencies (public schools) or state correctional institutions. To determine adult literacy education teaching requirements, begin by inquiring at the program where you would like to teach. To find out the certification requirements for your state, contact your state's Department of Education. See the U.S. Department of Education (n.d.a) for listings of state education agencies.

FINDING PROGRAMS AND JOB OPPORTUNITIES

There are several resources that can help you find adult literacy programs. A searchable database of U.S. literacy programs called *America's Literacy Directory* is available online as a joint service of the National Institute for Literacy, the U.S. Department of Labor, the U.S. Department of Education, and Verizon. The database can also be accessed through the institute's toll-free number (800–228–8813).

Adult learners, volunteers, and aspiring teachers can also find programs through ProLiteracy America. ProLiteracy America, the U.S. division of ProLiteracy Worldwide, has approximately 1,200 member programs in all 50 states and the District of Columbia. Another useful resource for finding family literacy programs is the search engine made available by the National Center for Family Literacy.

Some states maintain state hotlines or online resources dedicated to helping learners find programs. For example, the Massachusetts Adult Literacy Hotline provides program referrals, and callers can receive information regarding a variety of services, including adult basic education, English language learning, GED preparation, and GED testing sites (800–447–8844). Contact the state professional development center in your area to find out whether hotlines exist in your state (see U.S. Department of Education, n.d.b, for a listing of state professional development centers). Organizations post job opportunities on their Web sites and to the National Institute for Literacy's online discussion lists.

ADULT LITERACY PROFESSIONAL DEVELOPMENT

Most states have a professional development resource center or related agency dedicated to addressing adult literacy professional development needs. All their services are available, usually free, to people working in publicly funded programs. Those who work in programs that are not publicly funded may have access to some of the services and/or resources available. Whether you are making a career choice in education or you want to learn more about professional development in adult literacy, this next section will provide an overview of the types of professional development resources available.

Recent Research on Adult Literacy Professional Development

The National Center for Adult Learning and Literacy'Professional Development Study (Smith, Hofer, Gillespie, Solomon, and Rowe, 2003)offers insights about how teachers change as a result of their participation in professional development, and ways programs can support teachers in their professional growth and learning. Professional development is one resource for facilitating professional growth, but it should be offered in an environment supportive of change. Smith, et al. (2003), found that the professional development model used did not matter as much as factors that influenced teacher change due to teachers' participation in professional development. Factors included working more hours in adult education; having a well-supported job (good benefits, adequate paid preparation time, paid professional development release time); having a voice in decision making in the program; having one's first teaching experience in adult education; being relatively new to the field; having access to colleagues; not having an advanced degree (above a bachelor's), and spending more time in professional development. Smith et al. found that teachers and administrators should become advocates for the supports they do not have and should continually strive to obtain the best conditions possible that support professional growth and learning. Teachers—especially highly skilled, knowledgeable, and caring teachers—are the key to helping adult learners achieve their goals. Programs that support teacher professional development should strive to increase access to quality professional development for teachers, allow teachers to participate more in decision making, set expectations that teachers must continue learning through professional development, create well-supported jobs for teachers, and increase opportunities for teachers to share ideas and participate together in professional development. Teachers in adult literacy education should expect high-quality professional development, pinpoint what they want to gain from professional development, use professional development to continually improve their skills, dedicate themselves to learning throughout their careers, strive to increase collegiality and teacher decision making in their program, and collaborate with colleagues to improve teacher working conditions (Smith et al., 2003).

As teachers consider their needs for ongoing professional development, they should recognize that there is a growing expectation from the federal level that all education be based on evidence—the integration of professional wisdom with the most rigorous research available should be utilized in making decisions about how to plan, deliver, support, and evaluate instruction and program management. Teachers are being encouraged to become consumers of research for areas in which it is available—to access it, judge the quality of the research and what it means for their situation, integrate it with their own professional wisdom acquired through experience, and use it where they feel it applies. Professional development is a vital link between research and practice, so in order to integrate research with their own work, it is critical that teachers be able to access professional development and choose what will meet their needs best.

A wide variety of approaches and methods should be used to offer professional development so that there is something for teachers (and other program staff) at all levels, and for all areas of adult literacy education. The Association of Adult Literacy Professional Developers has a useful matrix of approaches and methods on the resource section of their Web site for people who plan professional development. Professional development can be organized into four main kinds of delivery: face-to-face professional development (conferences, workshops, courses), online or hybrid professional development, program-based professional development, and supported individual learning.

Face-to-Face Professional Development

State literacy resource centers or state professional development providers usually offer single-session workshops, though it is better if you create a professional development learning plan that provides opportunities to apply what you have learned, share ideas and obtain feedback from colleagues, make improvements, and measure competence based on performance. Single sessions are helpful for networking, sharing and generating ideas, and sparking interests. But a combination of professional development approaches and methods should be used to strike the right balance. State adult education conferences are held in most states by the state literacy resource center and/or the state professional association. ProLiteracy sponsors an annual conference, as do the American Association for Adult and Continuing Education and the Commission on Adult Basic Education . However, conferences can be expensive to attend. Contact your professional association to find out if it offers scholarships to attend any of these events. For a listing of state, national, and international conferences relevant to adult literacy education, see the Developing Professional Wisdom and Research area of the Adult Literacy Education Wiki (n.d.c).

Online or Hybrid Professional Development

In addition to face-to-face professional development, there are also online courses and hybrid learning. Hybrid, or blended, professional development involves learning opportunities that integrate face-to-face with online components in a sustained learning experience over time. Research from the K–12 field shows that single-session workshops are not effective in sustaining long-term changes in teacher practices. A listing of free or inexpensive online professional development opportunities can be found on the Adult Literacy Education Wiki at Online Professional Development Opportunities for Instructors of Adult Education and Literacy (Rosen, n.d.).

Program-Based Professional Development

Program-based professional development provides practitioners opportunities within an adult school or program to share ideas about teaching. As long as the professional development is of high quality and uses effective principles of professional development, local opportunities offered by the program may support teachers in benefiting from professional development. Program-based professional development may take the form of study circles, practitioner research, peer coaching or mentoring, or project-based learning, among others. The National Center for the Study of Adult Learning and Literacy (n.d.) has developed an exceptional array of study circle guides that can be downloaded for free. These guides help individuals design and facilitate study circles based upon the National Center for the Study of Adult Learning and Literacy's research and offer opportunities for teachers to examine research implications, judge their applicability, and use the research in their classrooms and programs.

Supported Individual Learning

Self-study is also an effective way to engage in professional development, especially for practitioners who enjoy studying on their own or find it difficult to attend professional development courses. For those who are interested in learning about research design, a resource that may prove useful is *Becoming an Educated Consumer of Research: A Quick Look at the Basics of Research Methodologies and Design* (Dimsdale & Kutner, 2004), which offers insights into research methodology and design. Another resource that may be useful for becoming a wise consumer of scientifically based research is a brochure from the National Institute for literacy titled *What Is Scientifically-Based Research? A Guide for Teachers* (Baxter & Reddy, 2005). A listing of adult literacy practitioner and research journals can be found in the Developing Professional Wisdom and Research area of the Adult Literacy Education Wiki (n.c.d).

Finding Professional Development Materials Based on Research and Knowledge Gained by Experience

The National Center for the Study of Adult Learning and Literacy (NCSALL) was, for ten years, the only federally funded research and development center focused solely on adult learning. Although NCSALL no longer exists, its efforts in improving practice in educational programs that serve adults with limited literacy and English language skills have been preserved on its Web site. NCSALL's materials can all be downloaded for free; these materials include teaching and training materials; Web-based videos designed to connect NCSALL research with program practices; research reports, summaries, and briefs; and *Focus on Basics,* a quarterly journal designed for adult literacy practitioners.

The National Institute for Literacy, a federal agency that provides leadership on literacy issues, offers some valuable resources for connecting research and practice. Once solely focused on adult learning, the institute now addresses literacy across the life span. Of particular interest to adult educators is the institute's Literacy Information and Communication System, a dynamic online database of quality resources in adult literacy (National Institute for Literacy, n.d.a). It serves as a single point of access to diverse literacy-related resources and public discussion lists as well as professional development opportunities. New efforts are underway to build upon these resources for the field.

NATIONAL DISCUSSION LISTS

As a part of the Literacy Information and Communication System, the National Institute for Literacy (n.d.b) supports several national discussion lists for individuals interested or working in adult literacy. Established in 1995, the National Institute for Literacy's discussion lists give thousands of literacy stakeholders online opportunities to discuss the literacy field's critical issues; share resources, experiences, and ideas; ask questions of subject experts; and keep up to date on literacy issues. The institute's lists provide a means for free ongoing professional development for practitioners in the following areas: adult literacy professional development, assessment, adult English language learning, family literacy, focus on basics, health and literacy, learning disabilities, poverty, race, women and literacy, technology and literacy, workplace literacy, and other special topics.

Subscribers often report that the lists are instrumental to their practice. In a 2003–2004 evaluation commissioned by the RMC Research Corporation, subscribers reported using the lists to:

- Read research reports and findings in order to keep informed of developments in practice
- Share and access information
- Network and share expertise/experiences
- Gain knowledge about adult learners
- Increase professional knowledge of current news and events
- Acquire information related to classroom instruction and resources
- Strengthen subject knowledge and skills to improve instructional practice
- Learn about and benefit from professional development

- Communicate with experts in the field
- Benefit from aspects of program planning, including assessment and technology
- Learn about professional organizations and agencies

To subscribe to this free resource, go to the institute's Web site and click on "Discussion Lists."

The Adult Literacy Education Wiki is a collaborative online space where practitioners can ask and answer critical questions about adult literacy education practice. It provides practitioners the opportunity to learn about adult literacy, including English language learning, numeracy, and adult basic and secondary education. The purpose of the Adult Literacy Education Wiki is to provide an online forum where practitioners can connect research and practice. It is a community of practice with links to research for practitioners, researchers, learners, and others.

The Association of Adult Literacy Professional Developers (n.d.) updates a list on national professional development initiatives that involve connecting research and practice annually. For more information, visit the publications area of their Web site.

DEGREE PROGRAMS IN ADULT EDUCATION

Graduate programs in adult education are usually targeted at adult literacy practitioners looking to extend their career into other areas of adult literacy, such as professional development, research, administration, or teaching in higher education. In 1999, as a project funded under Pro-Net, Evans and Sherman developed a guide to graduate programs in adult education. This guide was considered a snapshot of graduate programs in adult education that were offered in the United States between 1999 and 2000. An updated listing is currently under development by the National Institute for Literacy.

Further information for learning about the field of adult literacy may be found through the state literacy resource center or professional development provider in your state.

REFERENCES

Adult Literacy Education Wiki. (n.d.a). *Adult literacy professional development.* Retrieved December 29, 2006, from http://wiki.literacytent.org/index.php/Adult_Literacy_Professional_Development

Adult Literacy Education Wiki. (n.d.b). *Books and films which inspire teachers.* Retrieved December 30, 2006, from http://wiki.literacytent.org/index.php/Books_and_Films_which_Inspire_Teachers

Adult Literacy Education Wiki. (n.d.c). *Developing professional wisdom and research.* Retrieved December 30, 2006, from http://wiki.literacytent.org/index.php/Developing_Professional_Wisdom_and_Research

Association of Adult Literacy Professional Developers. (n.d.). *Publications*. Retrieved December 29, 2006, from http://www.aalpd.org/publications.htm

Balliro, L. (Ed.). (2002). How I got into the field of ABE and why I stay there [Special Issue]. *Field Notes, 12*(1). Retrieved December 29, 2006, from http://www.sabes. org/resources/fieldnotes/vol12/fn121.pdf

Baxter, S., & Reddy, L. (2005). *What is scientifically-based research? A guide for teachers*. Retrieved December 30, 2006, from http://www.nifl.gov/partnershipforreading/ publications/science_research.pdf

Dimsdale, T., & Kutner, M. (2004). *Becoming an educated consumer of research: A quick look at the basics of research methodologies and design*. Retrieved December 29, 2006, from http://www.air.org/publications/documents/Becoming%20an%20Educated%20Co nsumer%20of%20Research.pdf

Evans, A., & Sherman, R. (1999). *Guide to ABE in graduate programs*. Retrieved December 30, 2006, from http://www.calpro-online.org/pubs/grad%20guide.pdf

McLendon, L. (2006). Adult education and literacy legislation and its effects on the field. In National Commission on Adult Literacy, *Four lay-of-the-land papers on the federal role in adult literacy*. Retrieved December 26, 2006, from http://www.caalusa.org/ fedlayofland-commission1206.pdf

National Center for the Study of Adult Learning and Literacy. (n.d.). *Training materials: Study circle guides*. Retrieved May 14, 2007, from http://www.ncsall.net/ ?id=25#train

National Commission on Adult Literacy. (2006). *Four lay-of-the-land papers on the federal role in adult literacy*. Retrieved December 28, 2006, from http://www.caalusa.org/ fedlayofland-commission1206.pdf

National Institute for Literacy. (n.d.a). *Literacy information and communication system*. Retrieved December 29, 2006, from http://www.nifl.gov/lincs

National Institute for Literacy. (n.d.b). *National Institute for Literacy online discussion groups*. Retrieved December 28, 2006, from http://www.nifl.gov/lincs/discussions/ discussions.html

National Institute for Literacy. (2005). Comprehensive review and analysis of the literacy information and communication system (LINCS). Retrieved December 29, 2006, from http;//www.nifl.gov/nifl/executive_summary.doc

Rosen, D. (n.d.). *Online professional development opportunities for instructors of adult education and literacy (including English language learning and numeracy)*. Retrieved December 29, 2006, from http://wiki.literacytent.org/index.php/AlePDOnline

Sabatini, J., Ginsburg, L., & Russell, M. (2002). *Professionalization and certification for teachers in adult basic education*. Retrieved December 26, 2006, from http://www. ncsall.net/?id = 572

Smith, C., Hofer, J., Gillespie, M., Solomon, M., & Rowe, K. (2003). *How teachers change: A study of professional development in adult education*. NCSALL Report #25, Boston: National Center for the Study of Adult Learning and Literacy.

Sticht, T. (2002). The rise of the adult education and literacy system in the United Taylor, J., Cora, M., & Greenberg, D. (2006). Professional development from your inbox: Making the most of national discussion lists. Retrieved December 29, 2006, from http;//www.nifl.gov/lincs/discussons/professionaldevelopment/PD_Inbox.ppt.doc

Teachers of English to Speakers of Other Languages. (n.d.). Retrieved December 29, 2006, from http://www.tesol.org

University of Tennessee. (2001). *Stories of lives changed*. Retrieved December 30, 2006, from http://slincs.coe.utk.edu/video_library.html

U.S. Department of Education. (n.d.a). *State education agency (state department of education).* Retrieved May 14, 2007, from http://wdcrobcolp01.ed.gov/Programs/EROD/org_list.cfm?category_ID=SEA

U.S. Department of Education. (n.d.b). *State literacy resource center.* Retrieved December 29, 2006, from http://wdcrobcolp01.ed.gov/Programs/EROD/org_list.cfm?category_ID=LRC

RESOURCES IN ADULT LITERACY: ANNOTATED BIBLIOGRAPHY

Connecting Research, Policy, and Practice

Comings, J. (2003). *Establishing an evidence-based adult education system.* NCSALL Occasional Paper. Boston: National Center for the Study of Adult Learning and Literacy. Retrieved December 28, 2006, from http://www.ncsall.net/fileadmin/resources/research/op_comings3.pdf

Comings describes steps that could lead to the development of an adult education system in which decisions are based on professional wisdom and empirical evidence.

Comings, J., Garner, B., & Smith, C. (Eds.). (2000–2006). *Review of adult learning and literacy* (Vols. 1–3). National Center for the Study of Adult Learning and Literacy. Retrieved January 6, 2006, from http://www.ncsall.net/?id=493

Essential to understanding current issues, latest research, and best practices in adult literacy, *Review of Adult Learning and Literacy* features articles on critical topics, annotated reviews, and current updates in policy and practice.

Comings, J., Reder, S., & Sum, A. (2001). *Building a level playing field: The need to expand and improve the national and state adult education and literacy system.* NCSALL Occasional Paper. Boston: National Center for the Study of Adult Learning and Literacy. Retrieved December 28, 2006, from http://www.ncsall.net/fileadmin/resources/research/op_comings2.pdf

Building a level playing field describes issues in adult literacy and makes the argument for a greater commitment to expanding and improving the adult education and literacy system. The authors argue that if this commitment is not made, then the nation will have two different populations: one that is successful in the new economy, and one whose lack of education prevents them from achieving success and leaves them on the margins of society.

Comings, J., Soricone, L., & Santos, M. (2006). *An evidence-based adult education program model appropriate for research.* NCSALL Occasional Paper, Boston: National Center for the Study of Adult Learning and Literacy. Retrieved January 7, 2007, from http://www.ncsall.net/fileadmin/resources/research/op_comings4.pdf

Comings, Soricone, and Santos synthesize the research, theory, and best practices for adult education and put forward the key elements for organizing and managing a program. The authors use available empirical evidence and professional wisdom to describe a program model useful to practitioners and program administrators for designing programs to help learners achieve their goals.

Focus on Basics. [quarterly journal]. (1997–present). Boston: World Education, National Center for the Study of Adult Learning and Literacy. Retrieved December 30, 2006, from http://www.ncsall.net/index.php?id = 31

A quarterly publication of the National Center for the Study of Adult Learning and Literacy, *Focus on Basics* shares best practices, current adult learning and literacy research, and how research is used in practice. Written for a general audience, the journal makes NCSALL research relevant to those working in adult literacy and is useful to others who are interested in learning about adult literacy. Comprised of 31 issues in eight volumes, *Focus on Basics* is timeless in many ways and should serve as a valuable resource for years to come.

Zachary, E. M., & Comings, J. P. (2006). *How do you teach content in adult education? An annotated bibliography.* NCSALL Occasional Paper. Boston: National Center for the Study of Adult Learning and Literacy. Retrieved January 7, 2007, from http://www.ncsall.net/fileadmin/resources/research/op_content_biblio.pdf

Zachary and Comings list resources that identify research and professional wisdom in reading, writing, math and numeracy, English as a second language, general education development, adult learning theory and adult education instruction, and technology and adult education. The book claims not to be exhaustive, but it is thorough. Useful for any adult educator seeking content-based instructional resources, it includes journals relevant to adult literacy education.

Perspectives in Adult Literacy

Belenky, M. F., Clinchy, B. M., Goldberger, N. R., & Tarule, J. M. (1986). *Women's ways of knowing: The development of self, voice, and mind.* New York: Basic Books.

Based on a study of 135 women's lives, the authors describe five perspectives from which women view the world and draw conclusions about truth, knowledge, and authority. This book is essential for understanding women as learners when they find their voice and use it to gain greater control over their lives.

The Change Agent. [biannual newspaper]. (1994–present). Boston: World Education, New England Literacy Resource Center. Retrieved January 6, 2007, from http://www.nelrc.org/changeagent/index.htm

The Change Agent is a biannual newspaper for adult educators and learners. Originally conceived in 1994 as a tool to educate and mobilize teachers and learners to apply their advocacy skills in response to impending federal funding cutbacks from adult education, it has since promoted social action as an important aspect of adult learning.

Demetrion, G. (2005). *Conflicting paradigms in adult literacy education: In quest of a U.S. democratic politics of literacy.* Mahwah, NJ: Lawrence Erlbaum.

Demetrion provides an historical perspective of adult literacy theory, policy, and practice and research over the last quarter century. The book focuses on Freirean-based participatory literacy movement, the British-based New Literacy Studies, and its focus on literacy practices in various roles of adults' lives, and the U.S. government's focus on workforce readiness.

Freire, P. (2000). *Pedagogy of the oppressed: 30th anniversary edition.* New York: Continuum International.

This book is essential for understanding adult literacy education from a radical teaching perspective. For the politically driven educator, Paulo Freire described his experience and draws inspiration from his struggles to lift up the oppressed in Brazil, his home country. One of his most reader-friendly writings, *Pedagogy of the Oppressed* discusses how traditional pedagogy works to reinforce the status quo, as well as the "banking model" of education. The chapters outline a philosophy of education that can bring about radical change.

Quigley, A. (1997). *Rethinking literacy education.* San Francisco: Jossey-Bass.

Rethinking literacy education critically challenges assumptions and literacy agendas that have formed efforts in education. Quigley discusses myths, rhetoric, and stereotypes about literacy, the view of adult literacy through the eyes of teachers and program administrators, program recruitment and retention issues, and transformative action for effective change. This book urges practitioners to reconsider their current practices.

Quigley, A. B. (2006). *Building professional pride in literacy.* Malabar, FL: Krieger.

Quigley offers a useful way for practitioners to critically examine our field and our own individual practice by providing tools for us to reflect upon our work as adult educators. He includes a chapter on the history of adult literacy, as well as chapters to guide teachers in reflecting on their teaching philosophy, whether it is liberal, progressive, vocational, humanist, or radical. *Building Professional Pride in Literacy* provides tools for teaching adults, as well as tools for practitioners to examine how we create our own knowledge through practitioner inquiry.

Zepezauer, M. (2004). *Take the rich off welfare.* Cambridge, MA: South End Press.

Zepezauer puts welfare reform into sharp perspective. *Take the Rich off Welfare* is helpful for anyone who challenges the belief that it is our poor who place a burden on society, and useful for adult educators teaching in the welfare reform system.

Resources for Programs

National Adult Education Professional Development Consortium. (n.d.). *State resource library.* Retrieved December 22, 2006, from http://www.naepdc.org

While this resource is designed to support state directors of adult education, the state resource library resources are easily adaptable for use in adult literacy programs. This site offers resources in thinking about program planning, marketing and recruitment, curriculum and instruction, distance learning, and more.

Taylor, J., Smith, C., & Bingman, B. (2005). *Program administrators' sourcebook: A resource on NCSALL's research for adult education program administrators.* Cambridge, MA: National Center for the Study of Adult Learning and Literacy. Retrieved May 14, 2007, from http://www.ncsall.net/fileadmin/resources/teach/PASourcebook.pdf

Taylor, Smith, and Bingman presents the findings of all NCSALL research related to key challenges for programs, implications for adult literacy programs, and strategies for implementing change based on these implications. This publication is useful for program administrators and others who want simple access to all the findings from NCSALL research and discussion on how administrators might use research to improve programs. The book ends with a foundational chapter entitled "Advocacy for Program Improvement," which highlights access points for influencing policy, roles of administrators in advocacy, areas for advocacy based on NCSALL research, and resources.

U.S. Department of Education, Office of Vocational and Adult Education. (n.d.). *Community partnerships for adult learning.* Retrieved December 15, 2006, from http://www.c-pal.net

This is an excellent resource for learning about the need for partnerships in adult literacy services. Beginning with a program self-assessment, the site guides users through a toolbox of resources for building communities, considerations for curriculum and instruction, professional development, workforce development, technology, program management, and more.

INDEX

ABOUT THE CONTRIBUTORS

BARBARA J. GUZZETTI is a professor of language and literacy at Arizona State University in the Mary Lou Fulton College of Education. She is also an affiliated faculty member in the College of Liberal Arts and Sciences in the Women and Gender Studies program. Her research interests include gender and literacy, science education and literacy, adolescent literacy, popular culture, and the new literacies, including digital literacies.

HAL BEDER is a professor of adult education at Rutgers University. Hal is the director of the National Center for Adult Learning and Literacy's National Labsite for Adult Literacy Education. His book, *Adult Literacy: Issues for Policy and Practice,* won the Imogene Okes Award for outstanding research in 1991.

ALISA BELZER is an associate professor of adult literacy education at Rutgers University. She began working in adult literacy education in 1987 and has been a program coordinator, tutor trainer, classroom teacher, and tutor. Her research interests include authentic assessment, professional development and teacher research, policy, learner beliefs, and adult reading development.

ANNE DIPARDO is a professor in the Language, Literacy, and Culture program at the University of Iowa, where she teaches graduate and undergraduate courses in literacy studies and teacher education. She has written about elders' literacy practices in collaboration with Pat Schnack, founder of Partners in Reading. Anne currently serves as the coeditor of *Research in the Teaching of English,* a journal of the National Council of Teachers of English.

LAURIE ELISH-PIPER is a professor of reading in the Department of Literacy Education at Northern Illinois University. She also directs the reading clinic and teaches reading courses for undergraduate, graduate, and doctoral students in the areas of adult literacy, literacy assessment, and elementary reading. She currently chairs the International Reading Association Family Literacy Committee and is coeditor of the committee's online journal, *Exploring Adult Literacy.*

IRWIN KIRSCH is a distinguished presidential appointee and director of the Center for Global Assessment at Educational Testing Service. He is an internationally recognized expert in the area of literacy and has served as a consultant for a number of organizations, including the U.S. Department of Education, the National Institutes of Health, the OECD, Statistics Canada, UNESCO, and the World Bank. His research interests include the psychology of literacy, issues of comparability and interpretability in large-scale assessments, and the use of technology to link learning and assessment.

MARYLOU LENNON has worked at the Educational Testing Service on a number of large-scale adult literacy assessments, including the Young Adult Literacy Survey in 1985 and the National Adult Literacy Survey and the Adult Literacy and Life Skills Survey. She also helped develop both paper- and Web-based individualized literacy assessments as well as a multimedia instructional program designed to teach applied literacy skills to adults and at-risk students. In addition to her adult literacy work, her interests include simulation-based assessments of performance in information and communication technology environments.

LARRY MIKULECKY is a professor of education at Indiana University–Bloomington. He has written and done research on adult and workplace literacy for 25 years. Mikulecky has served as a member of the National Academies of Science Panel to set performance standards for the U.S. National Assessment of Adult Literacy and is on research advisory boards for the National Institute for Literacy in the areas of literacy and ESL instruction of adults.

VICTORIA PURCELL-GATES holds a Tier I Canada research chair in early childhood literacy at the University of British Columbia, where she is a professor in the Language and Literacy Department. She studies early literacy development within homes and communities and within formal schooling contexts.

DAVID J. ROSEN has worked in the field of adult literacy education since 1982 and has been the director of the Adult Literacy Resource Institute at the University of Massachusetts, Boston, for over 15 years. He has been a keynote speaker at adult literacy education conferences in Philadelphia, St. Louis, and New York, and in Dublin, Ireland. Rosen has published extensively on adult literacy and technology, including as a National Institute for Literacy national literacy leadership fellow in 1996, one of the first studies on adult learners' and teachers' use of the World Wide Web.

M. CECIL SMITH is a professor of educational psychology at Northern Illinois University. He received his PhD in educational psychology from the University of Wisconsin–Madison in 1988. His research interests pertain to adult literacy, adult development, and adolescent identity and schooling.

RALF ST. CLAIR is a senior lecturer in the Department of Adult and Continuing Education at the University of Glasgow. His research interests include literacy education, educational policy, and program evaluation.

JOHN STRUCKER has for the past 10 years been a research associate at the National Center for the Study of Adult Learning and Literacy and a lecturer in education at the Harvard Graduate School of Education, where he teaches a laboratory practicum course titled Developing Reading in Adults and Older Adolescents. Before joining the NCSALL, he taught adult literacy and ESL for 11 years at the Community Learning Center in Cambridge, Massachusetts. He is now a consultant for World Education in Boston.

CLAUDIA TAMASSIA is an assessment specialist who since 2005 has been working as an independent consultant with various organizations, including UNESCO, the OECD, and the Educational Testing Service. She worked at the OECD in Paris from 1999 to 2004 on the Program for International Student Assessment. Prior to that, she worked at the Ministry of Education in Brazil at the Instituto Nacional de Estudos e Pesquisas Educacionais on implementing their national assessment of basic education.

JACKIE TAYLOR is a professional development specialist at the University of Tennessee Center for Literacy Studies and provides professional development in adult literacy at both state and national levels. Taylor is coauthor of the *Program Administrator's Sourcebook: A Resource on NCSALL's Research for Adult Education Program Administrators* (2005) and is chair of the Association of Adult Literacy Professional Developers. In 2006, she received the NCL Literacy Leadership Award for her extraordinary contributions to improving literacy in the United States through advocacy.